Introduction to Social Administration in Britain

Introduction to Social Administration in Britain

MURIEL BROWN & SARAH PAYNE

Seventh edition

London
UNWIN HYMAN
Boston   Sydney   Wellington

Published by the Academic Division of
Unwin Hyman Ltd
15/17 Broadwick Street, London W1V 1FP, UK

Unwin Hyman Inc.,
8 Winchester Place, Winchester, Mass. 01890, USA

Allen & Unwin (Australia) Ltd,
8 Napier Street, North Sydney, NSW 2060, Australia

Allen & Unwin (New Zealand) Ltd in association with the
Port Nicholson Press Ltd,
Compusales Building, 75 Ghuznee Street, Wellington 1, New Zealand

First published 1969 by Century Hutchinson Ltd.
Seventh edition published by Unwin Hyman 1990

British Library Cataloguing in Publication Data

Brown, Muriel, *1938-*
 Introduction to social administration in Britain.
 1. Great Britain. Social administration
 I. Title   II. Payne, Sarah
361.941

ISBN 0-04-445665-4

Library of Congress Cataloging in Publication Data

Brown, Muriel
 Introduction to social administration in Britain / Muriel Brown
and Sarah Payne. — 7th ed.
    p.   cm.
 Includes bibliographical references.
 ISBN 0-04-445665-4
 1. Social service—Great Britain.   2. Public welfare
administration—Great Britain. 3. Great Britain—Social policy.
I. Payne. Sarah.   II. Title
HV248.B88 1990
361.941—dc20   89-77775
                                                     CIP

Typeset in 10 on 12 point Bembo and printed in Great Britain by
Billing and Sons, London and Worcester

Contents

Preface to the sixth edition

This edition of *Introduction to Social Administration in Britain* appears when the social, political and economic climate is very different from that which prevailed when I wrote the first edition. Many of the social problems of the late 1960s, such as poverty, slum housing, educational inequalities or child neglect are still waiting to be tackled in the 1980s. But new problems of urban deprivation, racial disadvantage and large scale unemployment have become much more urgent. More importantly, the response to social problems in 1984 is a very different one from the responses of the 1960s. Major efforts were being made then to tackle the persistence of poverty and deal with the neglect of deprived groups and reorganize and improve the delivery of social services. The first edition of this book reflected the optimism in social policy of the years in which there were extensive reforms in social security and health and personal services, expansion in higher and nursery education, experiments in community development, participation and educational priority approaches. Criticism and argument abounded, but a basic confidence in welfare, a belief in economic growth and an enthusiasm for social reform was apparent in much of what was written on social policy and administration during those years.

1984 provides a stark contrast. Welfare is on the defensive, attacked both in ideological debates and in a host of practical measures to reduce the role of the state in social provision. The talk is now of Victorian values of self-reliance, of the virtues of inequality, of the fiscal crisis of the welfare state and the limits to welfare. The action involves cuts in public expenditure, the privatization of our health and social services, the suppression of democracy and the increase of poverty and deprivation through measures which penalize the poor. In such a bleak political and economic climate, it is not surprising that dissent, discrimination, even violence, have intruded upon a polarized social scene.

An introductory, but fairly detailed, outline of social problems and social services might appear rather tame in this climate of conflict. But it is important that the facts are known, and set in context and widely discussed if the debate on social policy is to be extended beyond the level of political cliché. This edition, like the first, aims to help some people make a start on understanding the subject of social administration, but it can only be a start and in such a dynamic field students must turn to the growing specialist literature on social policy and social services both for more detailed facts and for more rigorous analysis. It is also important to keep up to date with current developments in practice and in theory. Newspapers and journals help with this, but much information is best derived from government publications, from annual sources such as *Social Trends* and particular reports, consultative documents and White Papers. In this context two non-government publications again deserve mention: the Social Administration Association's quarterly *Journal of Social Policy* (Cambridge University Press) carries, in addition to academic articles, the Social Administration Digest which provides accounts of the recent acts, reports and developments within the main social service fields; and the *Yearbook of Social Policy in Britain* (Routledge & Kegan Paul) which gives more detailed accounts of each year's major policy changes and outcomes.

Muriel Brown
London School of Economics
and Political Science
October 1984

Preface to the seventh edition

The preceding preface, highlighting the contrast between the optimism of the social policy of the late 1960s and the climate of cuts and privatization of the mid-1980s, remains depressingly relevant at the start of the 1990s. Under the guise of radicalism social service provision is still being attacked by a government as dedicated to the enterprise culture as the Victorians were to *laissez faire*. The residual model of welfare is gaining ground while the values of the marketplace intrude upon the public sphere. This edition has been extensively revised and updated in the firm belief that a basic introduction to the social problems and services of Britain can make a contribution to the debate on the goals and methods of social policy that must continue across the next decade.

Muriel Brown
Sarah Payne
University of Bristol
November 1989

Part One

Introduction and basic issues

1
Some definitions
of the subject

Social administration is not an easy field to define. At a superficial level it means a study of the social services. A social service is usually defined as a service provided by the state, whose object is the improvement of the welfare of the individual. To distinguish social services from public services and utilities, this element of individual welfare is always stressed. The provision of roads and motorways is a vital public service that benefits the whole community. The provision of retirement pensions benefits the individual in a highly particular manner: the individual does not share collectively in the benefit but receives it personally for his or her specific use. This concept of collective provision to meet individual need is the hallmark of a social service.

Social administration starts with a definition of social services and a description of them. But as an academic discipline it has proceeded from this starting point to take the definitions deeper and ask fundamental questions about the services: what needs are they trying to meet; why do the needs arise; on what grounds – political, moral, economic – does society base its attempts to meet need; how effective are its policies and, indeed, what are our criteria for effectiveness in this context?

The list of questions is endless and can lead the enquirer into many and diverse fields of interest, but for convenience it is possible to group them into two main areas of study.

First, one can say social administration is concerned with social problems and, second, it is concerned with the ways in which society responds to those problems.

Social problems are problems that affect not just the individuals but the society in which they live. They arise from individual human needs that are common to all members of society. Some needs are obvious, like the need for food, clothing and housing; some are more conceptual and sophisticated, like the need for dignity and status; some are powerful and intangible, like the need for love and affection. These common human needs are largely met by personal and family action: individuals work for their living, find accommodation, establish friendships, and obtain care, security and a sense of purpose within family and social groups. But when the needs are not met, this gives rise to problems that society as a whole increasingly tries to tackle. The basic need to subsist leads to the social problem of poverty if family and individuals are unable to meet the need themselves. The common need for shelter is the basis of the housing problem.

Society does not, of course, always recognize or accept that individual needs give rise to *social* problems. Society can leave the individual and the family to cope with such things as poverty, unemployment and loneliness, or it can see that collective action is taken to deal with them. The scope of social action itself in part determines what we mean by social problems. Poverty and crime are readily accepted as social problems because their effect on society as a whole is so marked that action is taken to deal with them. Loneliness among the aged or child neglect can exist yet not be perceived as social problems if society has neither the will nor the means to tackle them. This is partly because poverty and crime are generally perceived as more threatening to society than loneliness or child neglect and it is important to appreciate that society responds to problems as much out of concern for the maintenance of order as out of altruistic interest in the welfare of the individual.

It is fascinating to probe into why certain social facts become 'social problems' at different times in a society's development, and no one theory of social progress or social control is adequate as an explanation of these changes in perception. However, while there can be no universal agreement on what constitutes or causes a social need or a social problem, it should be possible to agree on what is generally regarded, at a given time, in a given society, as appropriate under such a heading. On this common-sense basis the study of social administration usually proceeds.

Whatever are generally accepted as social problems, together with the concept of human needs that underlies them, must be the first area of study for the social administration student. The second area of study is of the ways in which society organizes itself to meet the needs and copes with the problems. This is a study of social policy and it involves an understanding of the development of social policy, of the legislation that makes it explicit, of the government machinery and administrative procedures concerned with social provision, of the role of voluntary action, of the recruitment and professionalization of staff and of the problems of financing the social services.

Like the area of social problems, the subject matter of social policy is not a fixed territory. As society defines more and more problems, social action is extended into new areas. Moreover, new perspectives on old problems and provisions can reveal that social policy is perhaps more pervasive than was sometimes thought and many economic policies or even foreign policies have social implications that must not be overlooked. An example of this is the growth of interest by students of social policy in the field of taxation. Fiscal policies are not simply a question of money raising but may involve a recognition of, for example, the needs of the family, to such a practical extent that they must be regarded as much as a social policy as an economic intervention. But the focus, or at least the starting point, of the social administration student's concern with social policy will be the social services, which provide the most tangible evidence of social action. Consideration is given to the process of establishing social services; to the numerous factors that determine their development or modify their operation; to the economic and philosophical principles that underlie them; and, increasingly, to attempts to evaluate their performance and measure their effectiveness.

If we define social administration as this twofold concern with social problems and with social response and policy, then clearly it is a subject that must borrow heavily from the basic social sciences. In order to study a problem one must examine it from many different angles, asking questions about size and prevalence, causation and effect. Then one must look at it from sociological, psychological and statistical viewpoints in order to arrive eventually at a reasonable and rounded perception of the whole. Obviously in order to do so one needs to have some understanding of the different disciplines concerned with the study of society.

Let us take one example of a current social problem – old age. How do we know this is a problem? To some extent we know from common sense and observation that many old people are unhappy, that old age can bring a wearisome degree of financial insecurity, a frustrating sense of physical dependency. Most of us have theories or views about the problem of old age – that, for example, the old are neglected by their families, that pensions are not adequate, that there should be more old people's homes, etc. But to take effective action to deal with the problem, to reduce as far as possible the threat of old age, we need to have proper understanding of the situation. To start off with, we need to look at it statistically to find out how many old people there are, how old they are, what proportion of the total population they represent, whether the proportion is rising or falling. Sociology helps us to understand how old people fit into society, what attitudes prevail towards them, how and with whom they live, what their changing role in society is. It is no less important to consider the problem from a psychological viewpoint: what does it *feel* like to be old, how does a person adjust to giving up work, or giving up their home, what are the hopes, the needs, the fears, the compensations of ageing? A study of history can throw further light on the problem: one can find out how the problem has appeared in different times and how and why attitudes and policies have changed. The economics of old age are yet a further important dimension of the problem.

Finally, when we study social policy and social action the response of society to its problems – we need to base our study on some understanding of politics, of public administration, of finance, etc. In order to understand what factors contribute to the formation of social policy we need some grasp of political and economic history, we need to know something of the complexities of the legislative process and of the intricacies of local administration. To turn again to the example of old age, we need to know more than simply what services there are; we need to know how such services, for example sheltered housing or pensions, are administered and financed, how effectively they are run, what is the balance between central departments and local authorities in the making of decisions regarding services, and so on. And we need to examine some of the moral assumptions that underlie our social action and the validity of the social theories on which our policies are based.

Social administration, then, is an eclectic field of study. It takes such facts, methods and ideas from the basic social sciences as are relevant and applies them to the understanding and solution of social problems. The major academic disciplines that underlie this applied knowledge are sociology, economics, statistics, politics, history, public administration, psychology and moral and social philosophy. Other subjects and fields of interest are relevant and in future years might emerge into greater prominence as our understanding of their contribution to social administration deepens; for example, a study of the legal system and the relationship between law and social policy is currently being explored. At the moment, however, the main basic disciplines are those first listed. Obviously students of social administration cannot be experts in all these fields before turning to their final area of study. They will therefore attempt to understand a little of what is relevant from all these diverse and inter-related fields, and will probably gain their most thorough grounding in sociology, politics, public administration and social economics. In many cases, students of social administration have specialized in one particular field and might well regard themselves primarily as historians or sociologists or economists. When they turn to the study of social problems and social action they will approach it from their specialized standpoint. So the economist will deal with problems of old age or housing and the policies we have towards them primarily in economic terms, while the sociologist will take a sociological view. The different views are all valid and all part of our steadily deepening understanding of the subject.

Another way of appreciating the meaning of social administration is to accept that the social services cannot possibly be studied in a vacuum. They can be understood only by reference to the problems they are trying to tackle and in the context of the overall political, economic and social structure of the country. This is so obvious that it is almost overlooked, but in fact even the most avowedly straightforward description of the social services will tend to include references to history, to the economic situation, to political factors, and so on. This is because without such references the description would be not only rather dull but inexplicable. Whether we acknowledge it or not, our social services are based on certain social and economic facts about the distribution of income, the concentrations of population, the kinship patterns in urban communities, etc. It is clear then that in order really to understand the services we must look closely at these facts and try to understand the way in which our society works, the factors that influence the availability of resources and the beliefs and traditions that have shaped our particular response to social problems. So once again we must have recourse to the basic social sciences if we are to appreciate and understand the problems and the policies of our society.

A simple description of the social services of this or any other country would not remain useful for very long, because it would become out of date in a very few years. Social policy is continually developing and the structure and methods of the social services change. This is yet another reason why the term 'social administration' implies so much more than a straightforward picture of the major social services. Once it has been recognized that the social services are an integral part of society and that society itself must be studied in some detail if they are to be understood, it is easily accepted that the services will constantly be changing. Society itself changes all the time. Social needs, the recognition and definition of social problems and the resources available for social policies all change. Social administration by its very approach to the subject acknowledges the dynamic nature of the process. It is essentially concerned with changing needs and developing responses.

Not only does the essential subject matter of social administration change but so too does the academic subject itself. Its early concern was largely to describe the issue of poverty and related social problems. When these were felt to be tackled, as the twentieth century progressed, by social services such as national insurance and public health, the focus became institutional. Services were described and detailed and their structure and administration examined. Social administration was seen as a practical subject providing its students with useful information about the growing mass of provisions made by statutory and voluntary welfare services.

Later the emphasis changed towards explanation rather than description, and studies were concerned to map the origins and growth of particular services. This historical and developmental approach then gave way to a more critical appraisal of the welfare state. Studies looked at the actual effects of services on needs and problems. Crucial questions about who actually benefited from the welfare state were asked and the complacent assumptions of success that underlay many of the developmental studies were strongly challenged. At the same time, interest in theoretical explanations of the rise of social services increased.

More recently there has been a renewed interest in fundamental social problems such as poverty and a search, both on the practical and on the theoretical level, for explanations of the persistence of problems despite the rise of institutional welfare. Related to this is a concern to redefine social policy in order to broaden its scope from the study of the traditional service-based areas to the wider fiscal and economic spheres of governmental activity.

These shifts in the subject matter have taken place alongside a considerable expansion of the study and of the literature of social administration. Much of the early development of social administration was related to the training of social workers, and indeed the subject remains an important part of professional courses. But it is now widely taught in universities as an academic subject in its own right at both undergraduate and postgraduate levels. It is also taught, to some extent, on a variety of related vocational training and in-service courses for people such as doctors, teachers, and civil servants.

Academic social administration has benefited from the growth of interest in social science generally, a growth that has accelerated in recent years. Interest is evident at a variety of levels. A good deal of research and investigation is undertaken by universities, government departments and independent research bodies, both into social problems and into the delivery of social services. From this research stems a bewildering output of books and articles covering many issues of interest to students of social administration. Interest has grown in the comparative aspect of the subject and studies are carried out, reported and debated on the problems and policies of other countries. The mass media have become more responsive to the subject and social services correspondents in the press and documentary programmes on television regularly provide information and discussion about social problems and social services.

All this has stimulated interest in the subject matter of social administration but has not made it any easier to define the field. It should be apparent by now that no definition could ever be entirely satisfactory. What matters is to get the feel of the subject and not worry too much about the precise edges.

I think it would be useful at this point to offer a lengthy quotation that helps to provide a clear focus for much of what has been discussed so far. This is a definition of social administration written in 1966 by Kathleen Jones, Professor of Social Administration at the University of York.[1] It outlines precisely and imaginatively the scope of the subject.

Social Administration is a term which has changed its meaning. Originally, it meant simply teaching about what the social services actually do, mainly for the benefit of intending social workers. The rapid development of the social services since 1948 had led to the emergence of many issues of academic study with much wider implications. The study of housing, for instance, is no longer only a question of re-housing individual families from the slums, but of population distribution and movement, industrial location, physical communications, and systems of regional or local government. The study of the health services is not only a question of how individual sick people are cared for, but of deploying scarce resources in skill, money and accommodation to produce the best results for the health of the whole population. In these and other fields, social administration draws on economics – what can we afford? how can resources best be utilized?; on politics – who makes the decisions? who should make them, and on what grounds?; on philosophy – what do we mean by the good life and the good society?; and on sociology – what is our society like, and how does it function as a whole?

Social administration is problem centred. It starts from the problem end of sociology, which some sociologists call social pathology; but while sociology is concerned only with the identification and description of social problem areas (suicide, crime, poverty and so on) social administration is concerned with action. It proceeds from social pathology to social legislation and social policy, continues to the study of executive action (what is actually done by administrators, and social workers and others – which may not be the same as what is laid on the statute book) and ends in consumer research: how the services affect the ordinary citizen in need.

In the next chapters some of the major social problems and policies in contemporary Britain will be examined. First, we will look at what may be termed the basic social services – those that try to deal with a basic universal need, with a problem in which everyone is to some extent involved. The most obvious problem areas are poverty, sickness, housing, unemployment and the need for education, and we have major services that have developed in response to these, such as income maintenance and the health service. The personal social services are still largely a response to special minority needs, but since they have recently moved towards a position of greater relevance to the needs of the whole community their contribution to social welfare will be examined in the first part along with the other major, functionally organized social services. In the second part of the book a somewhat different approach is taken. We examine the special needs of certain minority groups (deprived children, old people, the disabled and the mentally disordered) and describe the separate provision made to meet these needs, both within and outside of the basic services. Clearly in neither section is the coverage exhaustive. Other basic problems and services could be examined (problems of public transport, for example), and other groups could have their needs and relevant policies and provisions detailed (ethnic minorities or single-parent families, for example). The areas here chosen for examination at an introductory level are simply those generally accepted as the major social services and the most obvious special needs groups. Admittedly arbitrary boundaries have been drawn in order to keep the book to a tolerable length. In the final part of the book some basic administrative and financial issues are examined and some trends and aspects of social policy discussed.

As this is simply a short introduction to the subject of social administration, there will not be space for much detail or depth. However, it is hoped that, in so far as each chapter provides merely a descriptive account of present social problems and services, the reader will realize the shortcomings of this. When the description alone is unsatisfactory the wider objects of social administration can be recalled and the need for deeper analysis and more sophisticated application of the relevant social sciences should become both evident and imperative. Social administration is, in a sense, an approach rather than a subject, and it is this approach that it is hoped will be conveyed through the following chapters. The approach is first to look at social problems, in terms of their causes, dimensions and trends, and then to analyse society's response, through the examination of social action, and to apply to this twofold task the knowledge, skills and theories of the basic, well-established social sciences.

NOTE

1 Taken from *The Compassionate Society* (Seraph Books, SPCK, 1966).

SUGGESTIONS FOR FURTHER READING

Bulmer, M., Lewis, J. and Piachaud, D. (eds) *The Goals of Social Policy* (Unwin Hyman 1989).

Heisler, H. (ed.), *Foundations of Social Administration* (Macmillan, 1977).

Loney, M., Boswell, D. and Clarke, J. (eds), *Social Policy and Social Welfare* (Open University Press, 1983).

Marshall, T. H., *Social Policy* (Hutchinson, 1975).

Titmuss, R. M., *Social Policy: an Introduction* (Allen & Unwin, 1974).

2
Poverty and social security

THE PROBLEM OF POVERTY

Poverty is perhaps the most fundamental social problem because the need to survive and therefore to have the means to survive is universal. Absolute poverty means the condition in which it is not possible to obtain the basic necessities of life. In Britain today mass poverty of this kind does not exist, although it is all too prevalent in many parts of the world. Relative poverty, however, remains a major problem and there is increasing evidence that for some individuals and minority groups absolute poverty is a real threat if not an actual torment.

Relative poverty means basically that some people are poorer than others. It is almost bound to exist unless the whole basis of society and indeed of human nature were to be radically altered, and it is not necessarily a problem. The problem arises when the difference between the richest and the poorest becomes too great. What is meant by 'too great' in this context is very much open to argument, but a simple definition would be that the gap between rich and poor is too great when the poor, while not actually starving or homeless, are nevertheless unable to enjoy many of the goods and services that others take for granted. This, then, depends on what is regarded as the normal standard of living for a particular society. If most people not only have enough to eat and somewhere to live but also have money for entertainments, travel, luxury goods and drinks and fashionable clothing, then the minority who are merely subsisting are justly considered to be, in relative terms, in poverty. And poverty involves much more than lack of money, although that is still a fundamental aspect of it. People who live in slums and have to make use of inadequate, ill-equipped schools and overcrowded, obsolete hospitals are poor even if they have money in their pockets. People whose physical, emotional and intellectual growth has been stunted by poor conditions have been deprived of opportunities for personal fulfilment that no subsequent material comfort can make amends for.

It is obvious that it is very hard to define poverty satis-factorily. The concept of poverty is widely debated and it is regarded as a problem that society ought to tackle, but it is difficult to obtain a consensus of opinion on what actually constitutes poverty in our present-day society. Consequently it is not easy to find out the nature and extent of poverty, although such findings should be the basis of an effective social policy to deal with the problem.

In attempting to define poverty various standards can be used. One of the simplest to grasp, although not necessarily simple to work out in detail, is the physiological standard. Roughly this means that a person is considered to be in poverty if they lack the resources to obtain enough food, clothing, warmth and shelter to maintain a tolerable standard of physical health and efficiency. This standard is a reasonably scientific one in that such things as nutritional requirements can be worked out precisely and data can be collected on the cost and availability of the necessary items, in order to produce figures of what income is required to maintain a person in physical efficiency. A physiological definition of poverty is one that permits relatively easy translation into cash terms. This makes it possible to carry out the measurement of poverty on a large scale. A poverty line is drawn, being the minimum amount of money needed to keep a person out of poverty, and the numbers of people who fall below this line can then be counted. This technique of measuring poverty was first used effectively in Britain around the turn of the century in the pioneering surveys conducted by Booth and Rowntree. At that time the information they collected indicated that, by their rather stringent standards, over one-quarter of the population was living in poverty.

Definitions of poverty in physiological terms can be relatively clear cut and enable precise quantitative assessment of the problem to be made, but they are hardly adequate for a society whose average standard of living is well above mere subsistence level. In any relatively affluent society it is necessary to define poverty by a social standard, that is, to define what society considers is or is not a reasonable minimum standard of living. This standard is reflected in what society is prepared to provide to keep people in a minimal state of health and decency. It will depend on a variety of factors such as the wealth of society, the average standard of living, the numbers in need, the sense of community and prevailing attitudes and ideologies. It is essentially less precise than a basic physical standard but it is rather more relevant in comparatively wealthy societies.

To arrive at a social definition of poverty it is necessary to decide what aspects of a complex pattern of consumption should be regarded as essential. For example, is it essential to have food that is varied and palatable as well as nutritionally adequate? Is it necessary to have clothing that is clean, which means having spare clothing and money for laundry and dry cleaning facilities, or is it enough just to be warmly clothed? Is it necessary to watch television, catch a bus rather than walk, buy newspapers, use cosmetics, stand a round of drinks? At what point does society maintain that a person who lacks resources for these and other goods and services is in poverty? Clearly it is hard to give precise answers to such questions and equally clearly they must be asked. We cannot tackle the problem of poverty until we define it and we must try to do so by reference to the standards of living prevailing in society, by deciding what mode of living is or is not acceptable to society.

A further yardstick of poverty is a subjective one: that is, those people are counted poor who *feel* poor. This personal standard will, of course, vary enormously between individuals according to their expectations and accustomed living patterns. It is not, therefore, much use in calculating a poverty line; nevertheless, the concept of felt poverty must not be ignored.

Recent research has tended to concentrate on whole groups of people whose lifestyles are substantially poorer than those of the rest of society: the old and single-parent families are examples of groups with a high risk of poverty. Yet another approach is to look at geographical areas in which the concentration of poor conditions adds up to a definition of poverty or urban deprivation.

Other ways of defining poverty are possible; the above examples are intended primarily to indicate something of the complexity of the problem. The importance of acceptable definitions is that they allow poverty to be measured, and that is obviously a first step to understanding and dealing with the problem. The most common way of measuring poverty today is to use an income-based 'poverty line' and ascertain the numbers below it. The level of income taken, which is put on a sliding scale according to age, numbers of dependants, etc., is usually enough to raise people above the bare physical subsistence standard with some further allowance for what is vaguely deemed a socially acceptable standard of living. Most commonly the income level taken is related to what is normally referred to as the state's poverty line, that is, the basic level at which the state makes provision for people without alternative resources. In Britain today, as we shall see later in this chapter, that means the income support level. Large variations in requirements and in the cost of basic necessities, particularly housing, or in the distribution of income within the family, make such simple *per capita* or family income surveys of limited use in obtaining a really accurate measure of the numbers experiencing poverty. In addition, poverty may be experienced by individual members within households, where resources are not shared equally, yet this form of poverty is not measured by income surveys that focus on the household as a whole. However, income surveys can be a very important, albeit crude, guide to the level and extent of shortage of resources in society.

Another approach to poverty is to understand something of the causes. In some ways this is more rewarding than seeking precise definitions and measurements of extent, as information on causes has often proved useful to policy makers. Put simply, investigations into the causes of poverty have shown that an enduring major cause is insufficient earnings – either because wage levels are too low or because families are too large in relation to earnings. A further cause of poverty is loss or interruption of earnings due to retirement or inability to work for such reasons as sickness, unemployment, disability and so forth. Of course such explanations of poverty, like simple definitions, beg many further questions: what causes low wages, for example? In the case of a particular individual, the lack of skill, training or opportunity may force him or her to take a low-paid job. Equally, low wages may be explained as the consequence of a general exploitation of labour or as a result of falling productivity. Similarly, while sickness may prevent someone from earning, it need not cause them to fall into poverty if they have adequate financial cover for such contingencies. So, is poverty caused by sickness – or by inadequate social security?

To avoid getting into too much complexity it is useful none the less to talk of immediate 'causes', while remaining aware that these do not provide explanations of poverty. By looking at patterns of immediate causation in this simple sense we can see how the poverty map changes over time. When the first surveys were conducted around the turn of the century the major causes of poverty were found to be low wages and large families. Surveys in the 1930s indicated that unemployment was a major cause of poverty. Recent research has shown that in the 1960s and 1970s old age, chronic disability, large families and single-parent families were all associated with poverty, with low pay still an important factor. In the 1980s dependence on state support rather than earnings remained the principal reason why many people were poor, and the long-term unemployed now figure prominently among those who experience this dependence.

One concept that is useful in understanding poverty is that of the poverty cycle. People tend to experience poverty in childhood, rise above it when they grow up and start earning, fall back into poverty when they marry and start a family, rise above it again when the family grows up and contribute to the household expenses and sink finally into poverty again when the family leave and they enter retirement and old age. This concept is important in showing where help must be concentrated if poverty is to be tackled. It also indicates that many more people experience poverty than the proportion who are found to be poor at the actual time of a survey, and that they tend to experience it at particularly vulnerable points of their lives.

A further important consideration about poverty is the distinction made between primary and secondary poverty. This was first drawn by Rowntree in his original survey (already mentioned), and at that time it could be seen quite clearly: primary poverty was a condition in which a person lacked the resources to maintain himself or herself in physical efficiency, which was the stringent physiological definition of poverty being used. Secondary poverty existed if a person had the resources but used part of them on goods or services, wasteful or useful, that were not strictly contributing to the 'maintenance of physical efficiency', and thereby fell into poverty by that definition. Today, when more generous standards of poverty tend to be used, the distinction is less clear but is still valid. Even though a modern 'poverty line' would be higher than bare subsistence, it would not be likely to include an allowance for such things as cigarettes or dry cleaning charges. So a person who used up part of a very low income or allowance on such things would have to go short of food or fuel or fail to pay the rent, and this would constitute a form of secondary poverty. Some people may manage their finances badly and spend money unwisely and therefore have to go short of essentials even though they appear to have adequate resources. However, poor people, lacking transport, are also less able to make their money go far by buying in bulk, for example, or shopping at cheaper, out-of-town supermarkets. So whilst the idea of secondary poverty is still relevant, it must be used with considerable caution, because it involves a good many value judgements about the way people spend their money and order their lives.

Most attempts to find a working definition of poverty tend to be focused on the cash aspect of being poor. That is, they involve measuring the cash resources an individual or family commands and relating these to a poverty line drawn in monetary terms. This is understandable because, as we have already noted, money is crucial in our society and this approach does facilitate the measurement of poverty. However, more and more attention is being directed to other aspects of deprivation, and attempts are being made to quantify housing standards and the level of amenities enjoyed by different groups of people. It is increasingly accepted that poverty of environment and of education are strongly linked to poverty of monetary resources. A poor background still tends to mean poor prospects for most children – a fact now acknowledged by current concern over the 'cycle of deprivation'.

Further aspects of deprivation that are now considered under the heading of poverty include such things as the relative lack of political power enjoyed by some groups of society, and the poverty of social relationships suffered by some people. But at the same time as the concept of poverty is being steadily broadened out from its earlier preoccupation with cash, the study of this central element of poverty has itself become more penetrating. Measurement of income now tries to take account of all the ways an individual or family ensures, over time, command over the use of resources. This means that income must be seen to comprise not only current cash receipts from wages, salaries, dividends, interest, pensions, benefits and so forth, but also capital assets, occupational benefits and benefits in kind from social services, or from relatives and friends. Only by such a comprehensive approach to income can we begin to determine how far individuals or groups are in any meaningful sense richer or poorer than one another.

POVERTY IN BRITAIN TODAY

It is clear that poverty is not easy to define, measure or explain: how far is it possible then, to provide any facts about poverty in contemporary society? At present, a remarkable amount of information is available about resources and standards of living. This comes from a variety of sources, notably from the government's General Household Survey (GHS) and Family Expenditure Survey (FES), both now regular exercises in finding out how people live and how they spend their money; from information presented to and prepared by the Royal Commission on the Distribution of Income and Wealth (RCDIW), which sat from 1974 to 1979; and from information gathered by government departments and by independent social investigators from surveys of the resources of representative samples of the population or of particular groups. Most prominent among the last category is the information gathered from the massive national survey of household resources and standards of living written up by Peter Townsend as *Poverty in the United Kingdom*. This major research work, published in 1979, is a social document comparable to the pioneering studies of Rowntree and Booth. It provides an enormous quantity of information about the way people live and provides detailed and challenging interpretations of it.

In a sense, then, the difficulty of providing an up-to-date picture of poverty in Britain is that there is almost too much information for easy summary. However, information on levels of income and resources does not necessarily mean information on poverty, since there is still a question of finding an acceptable poverty line. But on the simplest basis – using the level at which means tested benefits are paid as the poverty line – estimates can be made. In 1985, over 2.4 million people were living below the poverty line, a rise of 16 per cent since 1979. A further 7 million people were living on the poverty line, whilst 6 million were living on the margins of poverty – on an income above the level of means tested benefit but less than 40 per cent above it. A total of more than 15 million people (19 per cent of the population) were, therefore, living at what is generally described as 'in or on the margins of poverty'.

These figures, when compared to the figures obtained by Townsend and by the RCDIW researchers, as well as to earlier FES data figures, show that there has been an increase in the number of people living in poverty. This increase reflects a shift in the type of person living around the poverty line. Although it is still the case that many of the people on low incomes are elderly, there are now more families and children among the poor. This is largely the result of the increase in unemployment, but it also reflects the declining relative position of the low paid and the vulnerability of disabled and one-parent families.

Nearly one-third of all children – over 3.5 million in number – are living in families on low incomes, and more than 60 per cent of these are living on or below the poverty line. A number of these children are living in families where at least one parent is earning, but the low paid are more likely than better off workers to be unemployed or to fall sick. Children in large and in single-parent families are particularly likely to be brought up in poverty.

Turning from the question of numbers or the problems of conceptualization for a moment, it is worth remembering that for some people poverty is an experience that is too real to require any definition. Let us consider, very briefly and simply, the effects poverty has on those who experience it. Obviously, absolute poverty can lead to starvation and death, but what effect does living around the present state poverty line have on the families and individuals who are in this situation? Clearly a person who has just enough to live on and no more must be very careful in managing his or her income. With such things as clothes, the family must buy cheaply, make do and mend, and resist the temptation, or the demands of children, to spend money on luxuries or toys. The poor live in constant anxiety, worried that their precarious budget won't work out, that they will be overtaken by debt or eviction. They live in constant humiliation as they observe the cheerful affluence of those around them and have to get by with second-hand goods, with restricted opportunities for a show of generosity or hospitality, with the clamour of children who don't understand why they can't have the things that their friends enjoy. Frequently the poor suffer from malnutrition and even hunger, their actual life expectancy will be lower than average, and their living conditions are likely to be squalid and overcrowded. The response to these ills is often deep despair, an erosion of self-respect, a deterioration of family relationships. In short, poverty means a good deal of physical and mental suffering for those who experience it and it involves the risk of permanent damage to health and well-being and to a person's chances of personal development and happiness.

The effects of poverty on the community as a whole are no less striking and damaging than they are on individuals. Poverty leads to other social problems such as sickness, not necessarily as a direct cause but as an exacerbating factor. The poor are unable to give their children the quality of care they need in terms of such things as safety and play space and this relates to accident and delinquency rates. Poverty leads to slums, which are an eyesore and a health hazard. Poverty breeds unrest and discontent and even violence where it coexists with great affluence and is a growing symptom of grave social injustice. Poverty means a waste of valuable human resources as it stunts the full physical, intellectual and emotional growth of those who suffer it, and that can only be a tragic loss for the whole society.

SOCIAL SECURITY: DIFFERENT APPROACHES

The social policy needed to deal with a problem as complex as poverty must cover a wide front. It must aim to raise the level of real wages, improve general standards of health and education, maintain full employment and raise productivity. It must also cope with the immediate financial needs of the individual and attempt to obtain a just distribution of such things as educational opportunity. The part of the policy that is concerned directly with maintaining income (primarily when people are unable to work), and thereby securing them against falling into poverty in the narrow but important sense of being short of money, is known as the social security system. It is with this aspect of the total response to the problem of poverty that the remainder of this chapter will be chiefly involved. For the social security system, in addition to having a lengthy history, is undoubtedly one of the major social services in Britain and it deserves considerable critical attention.

The most obvious way for a society to deal with straight-forward financial difficulties is to accept responsibility for meeting the needs of any of its members who fall below a certain defined level. If a substantial section of the community lives at bare subsistence level, then the assistance offered by the community must itself be at a very low level and offered to the totally destitute. This is because it is generally accepted that state assistance cannot be so generous, relative to the prevailing living standards, that people are attracted to it from paid work. This is often referred to in Britain as the principle of 'less eligibility' because it was enunciated clearly with the passing of the Poor Law Amendment Act of 1834 in the statement that the condition of the recipient of relief 'shall not be made really or apparently so eligible as the situation of the independent labourer of the lowest class'.[1] It is still considered basically unjust that a person should obtain more money by state assistance than by working for it. Fortunately, once the community lives at a reasonably high standard of living, help for the poor can be offered at a level beneath the general standard but somewhat above bare subsistence. So, less eligibility in the nineteenth century meant the workhouse with its punitive regime and social stigma because it was impossible otherwise to offer relief below the lowest prevailing levels. Today, however, it simply means a definitely meagre existence, which contrasts sharply with the standards of the rest of a fairly affluent consumer society and probably with the previous situation of the people whom misfortune has forced on to assistance. This change reflects the changing interpretation of poverty from the notion of absolute destitution to that of substantial relative deprivation. As we have seen in the discussion of poverty the commonly used definitions assume that living at, or even some way above, the income support level means to be poor.

State assistance to relieve poverty has always tended to carry some stigma, as it is only available on test of need, and the desire to maintain the principle of less eligibility means that it tends to acquire a reputation for the systematic degradation of its recipients. Moreover, it is usually seen as 'charity' in the sense that the better off are taxed to help the poor. It can be the sole source of income for some people or it can be provided to bridge the gap between a person's resources and his or her needs. Assistance can be provided as cash, by regular allowances or occasional lump sums for use as the recipients determine; or as grants for specific purposes, such as clothing; or in kind, as free school meals, for example; or as specific rebates or allowances, as in the rate rebate scheme. But all forms of assistance are selective, that is, they operate through some kind of means test.

An alternative approach to income maintenance is state or national insurance. This is based on mutual aid rather than 'charity', and has been generally regarded as more acceptable than selective assistance as it aims to prevent people becoming destitute rather than to assist them once they are. The insurance idea, put quite simply, is that everybody who is working pays a small amount each week into a fund and then they can claim a weekly benefit in the event of their being unable to work because of sickness, unemployment or any other contingency against which the scheme insures them. Eventually they can claim a retirement pension for which they will have, in a sense, saved during their working life. In an insurance scheme the contributors are protected not only against poverty but also against the humiliation of a means test, as their benefit is their due entitlement regardless of any resources they may have. Insurance means a pooling of risks and a horizontal redistribution of income from those who are well to those who are sick and from those who are working to those who are unemployed as compared to the vertical, rich to poor, redistribution of assistance methods of poverty relief. It also involves a redistribution of income over the individual's life, saving in good times to help out in hard times.

Poverty caused by loss or interruption of normal earnings can be prevented by this method of social security. Investigations into the causes of poverty have shown that loss of income because of inability to work is a major problem. If the main risks of loss of income are determined, then the population can be insured against them. These risks are usually seen as unemployment, sickness and disability and, for women, maternity and widowhood. Retirement is not in the same sense a risk, but it involves a loss of income and can be insured for likewise. If a basic minimum income is assured when a person suffers any of the contingencies that cause loss or interruption of earnings, there should not be any need to have recourse to assistance. Clearly this approach does not help those, such as the congenitally disabled, who never have an income to lose. Nor does it help those whose experience differs from average, anticipated lifestyles, such as the deserted wife. It is essentially an approach geared to the average needs of the normal working population as society interprets these at any given time.

A further method of tackling poverty and maintaining income is to pay, from general taxation, a universal benefit in respect of any of the known common causes of poverty, such as old age – in other words, to pay a pension not just to those old people who lack resources, as in the case of assistance schemes, nor just to those who have paid contributions to entitle themselves to it, but to everyone over a certain age. This method, sometimes referred to as a demogrant, avoids the stigma and disincentive of a means test and the complexity and restrictions of any insurance scheme but it is obviously costly. It can be applied to any category of persons such as the disabled or dependent children.

THE BRITISH SOCIAL SECURITY SYSTEM

The problem of income maintenance can be tackled by any one or any combination of the strategies briefly outlined above: assistance to those who prove their need; insurance against loss of income from a variety of causes; and universal payments to certain categories of persons likely to be in financial need. In present-day Britain the social security system makes use of all three approaches and a variety of methods. It has a National Insurance Scheme to cover the major risks of loss or interruption of earnings, including retirement; a universal Child Benefit scheme to direct extra resources to those responsible for the maintenance of children; and a major assistance scheme, known as Income Support, for those who are not covered adequately, or at all, by the insurance scheme. These schemes were set up more or less in their present form shortly after the Second

World War. They followed recommendations contained in the Beveridge Report, *Social Insurance and Allied Services*, which was published in 1942, although their origins lie much further back in our social history. Basically they indicated that, for most causes of interrupted earnings, the working population would earn its own cover through insurance. For those outside insurance, a safety net of assistance would keep people at basic subsistence levels. There was some redistribution towards dependent children, but not a clear family policy, just a relatively modest allowance towards the cost of second and subsequent children.

Since these basic schemes were established there have been various additions and modifications to the income maintenance service and it has become harder to describe it clearly and to discern any coherence in its principles. After numerous developments in the insurance scheme, legislation in the 1980s dramatically altered the means tested assistance scheme (known previously as Supplementary Benefit) and the role of the state in providing pensions. The means tested element of the state income maintenance system has grown in importance since it was introduced, as more and more people have become dependent on it. As a result, a variety of additional selective assistance measures have been introduced, including support for families, and help in paying rent and rates. However, the most important changes in the assistance scheme came as a result of the 1986 Social Security Act, which followed a review of the existing supplementary benefit system. Essentially, the Act abolished Supplementary Benefit, which was replaced by a system of benefits called Income Support. Income Support is paid as a system of personal allowances, with premiums for different circumstances. The earlier arrangement of payment of allowances for special needs (such as a heating allowance for people with a disability) has been replaced by these premiums, whilst grants formerly paid to claimants who needed exceptional items have been replaced by loans from the Social Fund, which are repayable over time from weekly benefits. There was considerable anxiety over these changes and the effects they would have on claimants. The following sections will describe the present system and then look briefly at some of the problems that have arisen as a result of these changes.

Central administration

The main income maintenance schemes are administered by the Department of Social Security. The Income Support scheme, which in the past (as Supplementary Benefit), was run by a separate, appointed body, the Supplementary Benefits Commission, is now wholly administered by the DSS. A Social Security Advisory Committee advises the government on all social security matters except those relating to industrial pensions. The DSS has overall concern for all levels of administration and has a network of local and regional offices which try to ensure that this highly individual social service does not become too remote from the needs it exists to serve.

National Insurance

The central feature of the present social security system is the National Insurance scheme. This was established in 1946 but has been substantially altered and developed over the years.

The idea of National Insurance is to *prevent* people from falling into poverty when they are unable to earn. The contributions employees pay afford cover against sickness, including chronic invalidity, unemployment, disablement through accident or disease arising from work, and retirement. The scheme assumes that most men will marry and support a family, so their contributions cover benefits for dependent wives and children and cover against their wives' risk of widowhood. Cover also includes orphans' allowances and lump sum payments for maternity and on death. Married women have traditionally been treated as dependent on their husbands, but working women now pay a full rate of insurance and have their own rights to benefits, including a maternity benefit when they interrupt employment to have a child. The scheme is financed partly by regular weekly contributions paid by employees and employers, and partly by the state through taxation. Contributions include a token payment towards the cost of the National Health Service and payment to the Redundancy Fund.

A good deal of discussion of the scheme took place during the 1960s and 1970s. After numerous White Papers and amending acts the system was changed by the Social Security Pension Act of 1975 and the consolidating Social Security Act of 1975. Since then major changes in the system of paying and providing for pensions have been introduced. Since National Insurance is highly complicated and has an alarming number of rules, classifications, categories and conditions, only a bare outline of its main provisions can be given here.

Contributions to the National Insurance scheme are earnings related; that is, both employers and employees pay a percentage of the employee's weekly pay as a contribution. The percentage paid depends primarily on whether or not an employee is a member of an employer's pension scheme. For employees not contracted out, the standard rate of contribution, the Class 1 contribution rate (that is, for average full-time employees) is currently (from October 1989) 2 per cent on earnings up to £43 per week plus 9 per cent of earnings between £43 and £325 per week paid by the employee. The employer pays up to 10.45 per cent of earnings up to an earnings limit of £325 a week. There is a reduced rate for some married women and widows, and workers over retirement age do not pay at all, although the employer must continue to pay the full 10.45 per cent in respect of all employees.

For employees who are contracted out the rates are: 2 per cent of earnings up to a lower earnings limit of £43 a week, and 7 per cent between that and the upper earnings limit of £325 a week, with the employer paying up to 10.45 per cent. People who earn less than £43 a week do not pay any contributions.

Class 2 contributions are payable by the self-employed, currently at a flat rate of £4.75 per week, and the non-employed can pay voluntary Class 3 contributions of £4.65 a week. Class 4 contributions are payable by the self-employed at a rate of 6.3 per cent on all profits or gain between £5,050 a year and £16,900 a year. An individual may have to pay contributions in more than one class if he or she is both working as an employee and has additional income from self-employment.

Contributions entitle people to a wide range of benefits but these mostly depend on contributions record and on class of contributions. Class 1 contributors are eligible for all benefits. Short-term benefits are unemployment and sickness benefit and maternity benefit. They used to have provisions for an earnings-related supplement but these were withdrawn in 1982. Now short-term benefits are payable as a flat-rate weekly sum with additions for dependants.

Various conditions are attached to the payment of each benefit. For example, unemployment benefit is not payable for the first three days off work and is payable only to those who are fit and available for work and for a maximum of one year, after which entitlement ceases. The current rate is £34.70 a week with a dependency addition of £21.40 for an adult dependant. Sickness benefit has now been partially replaced by a new scheme of Statutory Sick Pay under which employers become responsible for paying employees for up to eight weeks of sickness in a tax year, so sickness benefit is not payable so long as any SSP entitlement remains. Maternity allowance is payable to fully insured working women for eighteen weeks beginning the eleventh week before the expected week of confinement. Sickness benefit and maternity allowance are currently £33.20 a week, with £20.55 for an adult dependant. The 1986 Social Security Act replaced the old universal maternity grant of £25 with a means tested maternity payment from the Social Fund.

Long-term or pension benefits are principally retirement pensions, invalidity benefit, industrial disablement benefit and widow's benefit, all generally payable at higher rates than the short-term benefits. Retirement pensions are currently £43.60 per week for a single person, £69.80 for a married couple. Invalidity pension is also £43.60 per week. Invalidity allowances are paid in addition to the pension, depending on the age at onset of the disability and they are continued in retirement. The rates vary from £9.20 where disability began before the age of 40 to £2.90. The rates can be increased by deferring retirement and those who retire but work part time can earn up to £75 before losing entitlement to their full pension. Persons over 80 receive a small age-addition of 25 pence. All old people are now entitled to some pension, even if they were not insurance contributors, but the minority who were never covered receive a smaller pension. People who have retired since April 1979 receive a small additional pension, on top of their basic retirement pension, related to their contributions paid since the 1975 Pension Act came into operation, and some pensioners are entitled to a higher level as a result of former graduated contributions.

The death grant paid on the death of an insured person or close relative of an insured person has been replaced by a means tested payment for funeral expenses from the Social Fund. Widows whose husbands had paid enough contributions are entitled to £1,000 lump sum, and are also eligible for a widowed mother's allowance if they have dependent children. Widows over the age of 55 on the day either when their husband dies or when the widowed mother's allowance ends receive a full widow's pension, whilst widows over 45 on that day receive a reduced rate. Widows without dependent children who are aged less than 45 on the day their husband dies are not entitled to a widow's pension, and receive only the lump sum. Widows' benefits are not payable if the widow remarries or if she is cohabiting with a man as his wife.

Attendance allowances are payable with no contribution conditions to a person who is so severely disabled, physically or mentally, that he or she requires frequent attention or supervision either by day or through the night. Claims for this allowance are decided by the Attendance Allowance Board. Current rates are £23.30 per week, or £34.90 per week for more serious disability involving both day and night attendance or supervision.

Under the Industrial Injuries Scheme, Class 1 contributors can claim when they are injured at work or disabled by a prescribed industrial disease. Injury benefit is not dependent on the number of contributions paid and it applies even to those not paying earnings-related contributions. Injury benefit entitles a person to sickness and/or invalidity benefits plus a disablement benefit, a weekly pension or a lump sum gratuity depending on the degree of disablement. A 100 per cent disablement benefit is £71.20 per week and this can be supplemented by extra benefits such as constant attendance allowance or unemployability supplement where appropriate.

These are the main National Insurance provisions and conditions, but the exact detail of entitlement to different benefits and allowances is very complex. The rates quoted are those payable from October 1989. Benefits are normally revised from April of each year, roughly in line with inflation, although in recent years such increases have tended to be lower than inflation. Details of benefits and contribution conditions and rates are available from the DSS through its local social security offices. An abundance of leaflets is produced to explain people's rights and entitlement to the various benefits. Help is also available from the Citizens' Advice Bureaux and, in some areas, from local authority welfare rights offices.

The scale of insurance is now considerable. Over 23 million people were National Insurance beneficiaries in 1987/8. Nearly 10 million of these were retirement pensioners. The next single largest categories were people receiving invalidity benefit, (995,000), and those receiving unemployment benefit, (845,000), with sickness benefit, industrial disablement, widow's benefits and maternity allowance making up the total. The full cost of insurance is also considerable: in 1987/8 it amounted to over £26,000 million.

Income support

The Beveridge Plan for national insurance was a bold one, particularly in its emphasis on universality – that is, all persons contributing regardless of their income level – and on a comprehensive risk coverage. It was overtaken by economic and social changes and to some extent it failed right from the start to provide the real social security it promised, but nevertheless it remains the basis of our present system.

However effective an insurance scheme is, it can never hope to cover everyone in society but only those who are able to be consistent contributors. Those who are too old when a scheme is introduced, those who outrun their entitlement to benefit or, like deserted wives, lose it, and those who cannot work must all look for help elsewhere. Some scheme of financial assistance is always necessary as a safety net to catch the variety of cases who cannot, for an equal variety of reasons, rely on insurance. In 1948, the National Assistance Act provided this safety net with the setting up of the National Assistance Board. This provided not only a safety net for those outside insurance but increasingly an additional support to National Insurance beneficiaries when they had no resources other than their pensions and allowances. For this reason the NAB changed its name in 1966 to the Supplementary Benefits Commission, and responsibility for insurance and assistance was merged into social security.

Income support is paid as of right and without any contributions to people whose incomes, whether from other benefits or private resources, are below a level of requirements laid down by Parliament. Anyone over 16 who is not in full-time work is entitled to benefit if their resources are less than requirements – although recent changes in legislation on youth training schemes mean that young people without a place on a YTS scheme may be refused benefit. In computing resources certain amounts of income from capital or disability pensions, for example, and up to £15 a week earnings can be disregarded under certain conditions. The income support system of payments consists of personal allowances paid for individuals, couples and dependent children, together with any premiums that the claimant may qualify for. These include premiums for disability, pensioners and lone parents. People who qualify for more than one premium receive only the larger of the premiums. The current rates are £34.90 per week for a single claimant over 25 and £54.80 for a couple, where both are over 18. Lower rates apply for younger claimants. Payments for dependent children vary according to age, currently from £11.75 for a child under 11 to £27.40 for a child aged 18. Payment of income support is normally through order books at the post office and a combined retirement pension and income support book can be obtained. The unemployed claim via the unemployment benefit offices and normally receive their benefit by Giro cheque through the post. People on income support are entitled to exemption from certain other charges – for prescriptions and school meals, for example.

Income Support was only introduced in April 1988 and as yet we do not have figures for numbers of claimants. However, under the old system of supplementary benefit about 5 million people received payments in 1987, and over 8.5 million people depended on them. Government figures for planned income support expenditure for 1988/9 suggest 5 million people will claim income support, and the total cost of income support will be £8,000 million.

Other social security measures

Severe Disablement Allowance (SDA) is a benefit designed to help those unable to perform paid work but whose contributions are insufficient to qualify for sickness and invalidity benefit. It is not means tested, but it is highly complex, having four routes to qualification. It replaced two other benefits in 1984: Non-Contributory Invalidity Pension (NCIP) and Housewive's Non-Contributory Invalidity Pension (HNCIP). This last included a test for married women, who had to prove that, in addition to being incapable of paid work, they were also incapable of housework, before they were eligible to claim. This was held to be unlawful discrimination by the European Court in 1984, at which time NCIP and HNCIP were replaced by SDA, which has no such test. To qualify for SDA, a claimant must be of working age and have been incapable of work for a continuous period of 196 days prior to the first payment. Claimants receive £26.20 per week, plus £15.65 per week for an adult dependant and £8.95 per week for a child.

There are currently two main provisions to help families: child benefit and family credit. The earliest poverty surveys showed what common sense and observation had long suggested – that families, particularly large families, were at risk of poverty. Clearly the costs of dependent children are high and a single wage cannot be stretched indefinitely to cover them, so some redistribution of income towards families is necessary if they are to be kept above the poverty line.

Child benefit is the successor to family allowances, which were first introduced in 1946. Child benefit is payable for all children aged 16 and under, and for those under the age of

19 who are in full-time education. It is payable to all families with dependent children regardless of income level and it is financed out of general taxation. The current weekly rate is £7.25 per child. Child benefit is paid at a higher rate of £12.45 for the first child in a single-parent family. Child benefit was paid to over 12 million recipients in 1987/8.

Child benefit is universally available and is therefore costly to provide and it helps all families whether in need or not. It is not seen as a payment to cover the entire cost of keeping a child, so families with low earnings can still find themselves in poverty. To combat this a selective family benefit called Family Income Supplement (FIS) was introduced in 1971. In 1988 this became Family Credit, payable to families whose normal gross weekly income is less than amounts prescribed by Parliament. The prescribed amounts are based on a figure of £54.80 per week: families with incomes below or equal to this applicable amount receive maximum Family Credit, which is £33.60 for a lone parent or couple, with additions of between £7.30 for children under 10 up to £23.30 for dependent children aged 18. Families earning more than the applicable amount up to a ceiling receive proportionately less in Family Credit. Anyone, including a single person with at least one dependent child, can claim if she or he is in paid employment of more than 24 hours per week. Those who are entitled to Family Credit are automatically entitled to free NHS dental treatment, free prescriptions, etc. However, people receiving Family Credit are no longer entitled to free school meals (as they were under the old system of FIS), as Family Credit payments include a contribution towards the cost of school meals. Those who wish to claim must supply evidence of their earnings and, if eligible, they receive books of weekly orders.

In 1987/8, 210,000 families received Family Income Supplement, under the old system, whilst the government estimates that 470,000 families will receive Family Credit in 1988/9, indicating that a greater proportion of low-earning families will be eligible for this selective measure. However, FIS had a very low take-up rate (50 per cent of those eligible), partly as a result of the complex claims procedure and partly because the amounts received were often small. It remains to be seen whether this higher estimate of number of claimants will be borne out.

The main social security provision is through the DSS, but money is also paid towards income maintenance by the local authorities. Certain education benefits, such as free school meals and clothing allowances, are available on test of need and many of the personal social services, such as home helps, are charged on a sliding scale. But the most important benefit is now housing benefit, which replaced the previous pattern of rate and rent rebates and allowances, together with the housing cost element of supplementary benefit payment.

When a person is entitled to and receiving income support this is now paid *without* any allowance for rent and/or rates. The claimant has to obtain housing benefit, which will normally meet the full cost of rent and up to 80 per cent of the community charge, which is payable to the local authority and which replaces local rates in 1990. Some people who are entitled to income support because they are not working and have low incomes but who are not claiming may be entitled to a housing benefit supplement, which is payable in addition to any housing benefit to cover rent and community charge.

Rent rebates, rent allowances and community charge rebates are paid by the local authority on the basis of actual rents and community charge payable. Rent rebates are available to council tenants, rent allowances to tenants of private landlords and housing associations and rebates on the community charge to anyone paying this, whether they own or rent their home. Housing benefit is calculated on the basis of a level of income fixed by the government, in practice equal to the levels of income support. This is called the 'applicable amount', and for a couple over 18 is £54.80, whilst for a single claimant over 25 it is £34.90. The same premiums as found in income support also apply. Housing benefit is paid in full if the claimant's income is less than or the same as the applicable amount, although it will be paid only up to the level of what is called 'eligible rent', which is determined by market rent rather than actual rent, plus some service charges. If the claimant's income is higher than the applicable amount, he or she may still receive some benefit, based on 65 per cent of the difference between the applicable amount and their weekly income. Payments are made in a variety of ways: either by reduction in the amount of rent or community charge payable, or by books of cheques.

Housing benefit was introduced in 1983 and it has proved a highly controversial measure. It was designed to streamline and simplify assistance with housing costs by replacing the housing payments from supplementary benefits and the local authority rate and rents rebates and allowances by a single scheme. Many people who only needed supplementary benefit to cover their housing costs (because they had other benefits such as retirement pensions for basic needs), would thereby be moved off SB and could claim housing benefit from local councils. This would reduce DHSS (as it was then) staff levels, it was argued, and create savings. Unfortunately the scheme has proved very difficult to administer. Local authorities, particularly at first, proved unable to cope with the staffing requirements, and thousands of claimants were left confused and uncertain of their position, at risk of debt through inflated housing costs and experiencing great hardship.

DIFFICULTIES AND DILEMMAS
IN SOCIAL SECURITY

Social security is highly complicated and costly. Its primary aim is to eradicate poverty but, inevitably, in trying to establish some degree of social justice by redistribution of income it raises more difficult issues. The present system, as the previous sections have indicated, is widely criticized in terms both of its primary aim and of its wider implications. The criticisms are founded on facts as well as on convictions. The substance of the criticisms is, in brief, first, that the present system has failed to keep some people out of primary poverty, and, second, that where people are kept at or above the official poverty line they are kept at mere subsistence level, which is itself regarded in an affluent society as constituting poverty. The first criticism is that the basic aim of a social security system is not being realized. The second is more concerned with issues of social justice than with primary poverty.

Allegations that some people were living in primary poverty – that is, their resources were less than those allowed by the official poverty line (the standard-rate allowance plus actual rent provided by the Supplementary Benefits Commission) – were met with surprise by a nation accustomed to believing that want had been abolished in post-war affluent Britain. Research in 1965, however, revealed that some people, including old people, the chronically sick and members of large families, were actually living below the official basic minimum.[2] The independent research findings were substantiated by two official inquiries.[3]

The survey on retirement pensioners revealed that of the 6.5 million people then claiming retirement pensions about 800,000 were provisionally entitled to assistance but were not receiving it. Of these it was estimated that about 300,000 would have absolutely no resources other than their retirement pensions and would therefore be living in extreme poverty. It was likely that a similar number of non-pensioners also might be in need.

These facts were very disturbing, confirming as they did the suspicions of many social workers and researchers who had noted individual examples of extreme hardship among the old. Action was taken in 1966 by the creation of a Ministry of Social Security and the renaming of assistance as 'supplementary benefit'. These changes were accompanied by a determined campaign to advertise a person's entitlement to a reasonable living standard and to encourage old people to claim their rights. These moves were implemented because the official survey had revealed that the two main reasons why people failed to claim assistance were ignorance of their entitlement and pride, which rejected assistance as charity.

The second survey was on families and it, too, produced disturbing results: that nearly half a million families, containing up to about 1.25 million children, had resources amounting to less than the then current supplementary benefit rates would have afforded. Families were living below the official poverty line because the father was in full-time work and could not be assisted, or because the father was on assistance but subject to the wage stop, which reduced his allowance below his normal earnings. Others at risk included fatherless families and those on insurance benefits but not claiming assistance.

The basic reasons why these families, whether in work or on assistance, were in poverty was the inadequacy of family allowances. These had fallen in value, relatively, and they failed to begin to meet the additional costs of keeping a child. The answer to family poverty seemed at first glance simple – considerable increases in family allowances. But, as allowances were paid to all families, the necessary increases would have proved very costly. As the country was trying to keep down the rising level of public expenditure, this solution was therefore not acceptable and a variety of selective measures was introduced instead.

Since this 'rediscovery' of poverty in the 1960s, anxiety has increased not abated, because despite many additions and modifications to the social security system there is still evidence of disturbing levels of poverty in Britain. As noted in the second section of this chapter, over 9 million people were estimated in 1985 to be living at or below the official poverty line, 2.4 million of them with resources of less than the means tested level of assistance. However, the level of income support is so low in relation to average living standards that to be dependent on it is now generally regarded as to be in quite severe poverty. The former Supplementary Benefits Commission itself recognized this when it said, in evidence presented to the Royal Commission on the Distribution of Income and Wealth in 1977, that 'the supplementary benefits scheme provides, particularly for families with children, incomes that are barely adequate to meet their needs at a level that is consistent with normal participation in the life of the relatively wealthy society in which they live'. Furthermore, the complexity of the social security system is such that many people probably fail to get their full welfare rights from it and, in order to obtain even a part of the help available, a humiliating and bewildering succession of means tests must be undergone. There can certainly be no room for complacency, therefore, in contemplating the detailed operation of the present income maintenance scheme.

In the 1990s, then, there is still considerable anxiety about the continued high level of poverty in Britain today and concern about the working of the social security system. At first glance it might seem that the main problem of social security is that its benefit levels are too low and its discretionary provision is administered too meanly: if more generous amounts of cash were provided for child benefits or old age pensions, etc., then surely the problem of poverty could be solved? Unfortunately the issue is not as simple as that, as the response to the revelations of poverty in the 1960s revealed. Social security currently costs over £46,000 million a year. The raising and distributing of such a large sum of public money is not easy and there is much room for disagreement about how it should be spent. Many people feel that the social security system, particularly the income support system, is too generous rather than too mean, and there is a constant, hostile attack on supposed welfare scroungers. Quite apart from the myths surrounding the topic of abuse, there are undoubtedly real problems of equity in social security, problems of seeing that all parties, contributors as well as beneficiaries, are dealt with fairly. So there is no one simple answer to the social security problem: we have to look at the various areas of difficulty in turn to try to understand them.

Poverty in old age

Looking first at the problem of poverty among old people and the financing of retirement, we can see that this is always likely to be a difficult area because of the sheer size of the group. Old people constitute the largest group of people who depend on the social security system, with nearly 10 million people claiming retirement pensions. The immediate or short-term problem arises from the fact that many old age pensioners have no other source of income apart from their pension, and pension levels are not adequate to live on, so they need to claim assistance to avoid living in severe poverty. The change of name from assistance to supplementary benefit was the response to the official discovery of the plight of old people who would not claim their rights. Since 1966 the position has not changed greatly: it is still difficult to persuade some elderly people to claim supplements. So some old people actually live below income support levels.

Moreover, as we have already noted, even when older people do claim income support they are still having to live on very low incomes. In 1987/8, about one-fifth of all retirement pensioners were claiming a supplementary pension. Under the new income support regulations, pensioners can claim income support and receive the pensioner premium or higher pensioner premium if their income is low; even so, old people on income suppport are relatively badly off, as are those whose income brings them just above the poverty line. People on low incomes are badly hit by inflation, because the smaller a person's income is, the more of it must be devoted to essentials. In recent years the rapid rise of fuel costs has hit older people particularly hard, as heating is crucial for them. Surveys have shown that the very old are vulnerable to hypothermia, potentially fatal loss of body heat, and yet many lack the resources to keep their heating at adequate levels throughout the winter.

There has been considerable debate on the problem of the poverty of the old. In the short term, the answer can only be to raise pension and benefit levels and to protect them against inflation. Pension levels have indeed been raised in recent years, but even so a situation where retirement means a massive drop in income to a flat-rate pension can never be satisfactory. Indeed, the better-off groups in society have long established the idea of earnings-related pensions, which allow them to retire on a proportion of their earnings and maintain a roughly similar lifestyle in retirement to that enjoyed in working life. Most professional groups and many executive-level staff working in industry have developed such good occupational schemes that they have ceased to regard the state scheme as particularly important to them.

Over the past thirty years, and particularly since 1987, there have been substantial modifications to the state pension scheme. The first change came in 1959 with the introduction of a modest graduated pension on top of the basic flat-rate pension. This established the precedent for state wage-related insurance schemes, a precedent that was followed in 1966 by the extension of the wage-related approach to both contributions and benefits for unemployment, sickness and other short-term benefits. The graduated pension schemes also established the idea of partnership between the state and the occupational pension sector, by allowing people with adequate occupational cover to opt out of the earnings-related part of the state scheme.

After this tentative start, various proposals were made, culminating in the 1975 Social Security Pension Act, which provided for a more radical State Earnings Related Pension Scheme (SERPs). Under the 1975 Act the basic universal pension was retained but employees could opt for either occupational cover or SERPs. By basing the earnings-related cover on the best twenty years of earnings, covering women as well as men and guaranteeing pension levels against inflation, it was hoped that everyone would have the chance to earn an adequate pension, and reliance on means tested assistance would be greatly reduced.

These pension provisions became operative from 1978, but further modifications were again made by the 1986 Social Security Act and the 1987 Finance Act (Number Two). SERPs was radically altered and employees were now encouraged not only to opt out of the state scheme for occupational schemes but to take out pension cover in the commercial insurance sector, in the shape of an individually arranged personal pension plan. In addition, there is now the opportunity to pay additional voluntary contributions into either an occupational pension scheme or a personal pension plan, up to certain limits set by the Inland Revenue. Pensions paid to those remaining in SERPs will be lower as a result of changes in the methods of calculation, in particular the move to assessing SERPs over the last twenty years before retirement age, rather than the best twenty years of earnings.

The changes in pension arrangements create a highly complex situation, in which individuals must make difficult choices between alternatives in order to maximize their pension on retirement. They constitute a move away from statutory responsibility for security in retirement and increased reliance on market provision and individual arrangements. Such changes, relying as they do on individual purchasing power to provide pensions, rather than on state guaranteed pensions, will perpetuate inequalities that exist during working lives into retirement age. Whilst the basic state pension remains at a minimal level, as discussed above, the differences between occupational or income groups during working life will be even more marked in old age. In particular, women, whose employment is often interrupted by responsibility for childcare or the care of older relatives, and who earn on average less than men, will continue to be prone to poverty in old age as a result of the low state pension and alternatives that depend on continuous and well-paid employment to provide a reasonable pension.

Towards a family policy?

In addition to the problem of poverty of the old, there is concern over the problem of family poverty, which continues to worsen. Of the 9.4 million people living at or below the official poverty level in 1985, over 2 million were children, an increase of 100 per cent since 1979. This sharp rise in the numbers of families with children at or on the margins of poverty stems from increases in the numbers of families dependent on means tested benefits, as a result of both unemployment and increases in the numbers of single-parent families, and from the increase in the numbers of the low paid.

The rediscovery of family poverty in 1965 led to the foundation of the Child Poverty Action Group. CPAG has now acted as a pressure group in this field for over twenty years, exposing the plight of families, encouraging a welfare rights approach and putting forward proposals to improve the situation. The group has always argued that the root of the problem is the inadequacy of family allowances. Basically the costs of rearing children are high and normal earnings cannot be extended indefinitely to cover them. Where a wife is looking after small children and the family is dependent on a single wage, the risks of poverty are very high. Some redistribution is necessary towards those families currently bearing the costs of rearing children. If family support was really adequate, providing something like the actual cost of a child, then the poorly paid would be lifted over the poverty line and the better off would be helped with their relative poverty.

Moreover, if family or child benefit was really adequate it would mean that working families could be helped to a point where there was no risk of their being better off by not working. Enormous problems are created by the fact that many of the low paid live at or on the margins of the income support scale and, in a sense, might as well not be working. Some could actually improve their financial position by becoming dependent on income support because of the costs (in travel and clothing, for example) of going to work. Few probably do opt for such dependence but fear that they might is one of the major justifications used for keeping benefits low. If family support was adequate, there could be no incentive to depend on income support.

The case for family benefits seems compelling, and support for it comes from comparisons with European provision. However, as noted earlier, in Britain there has been a marked reluctance to support families in a generous way despite the consequent problems of family poverty. Instead of improving universal family benefits, ways have been sought to improve selective help to the low paid. Means tested benefits, such as family credit and housing benefit, have been relied on to help poor families. This selective approach claims to concentrate help on those who need it most, but there is evidence that it fails to do so because of low take up of means tested benefits.

Many of the poorest families are actually those dependent on income support. Here, as noted earlier, the level of benefit, though officially adequate, is depressingly low, especially as regards the often unpredictable cost of child-rearing. We really know very little about the true costs of raising children, but even a modest estimate of the actual costs of minimum requirements of food, clothing, heating, etc., for children of different ages has shown that the present benefit scale rates are quite inadequate. Income support claimants receive a family premium for a dependent child in addition to the weekly rates for children of different ages, but this premium is low.

Poverty amongst families is also exacerbated by the fact that the majority of family benefits – such as income support or family credit – are selective means tested benefits, which have a lower take-up than universal benefits. Take-up is low partly as a result of poor information and practices designed to put people off rather than to encourage them to apply. The fact that more benefits can be obtained when claimants are supported in their claims by welfare rights workers indicates that claimants on their own are often too humiliated or confused to persist in applications.

However, take-up is also low as a result of the stigma that attaches to means tested benefits. This is related to the treatment of claimants in many local social security offices. Unfair and unpleasant treatment is partly the consequence of the heavy workloads of social security offices, which have risen sharply in recent years. In addition, the current government's attitude towards claimants, and in particular the increased emphasis on 'targeting' benefits through the shift to more means tested benefits, and greater resources being put towards the detection of fraud, have fostered a climate in which benefits that are a right are often perceived as charity.

Another harsh rule affecting families is the cohabitation rule, under which a woman on income support loses benefit if she is thought to be living with a man as his wife. The operation of this rule means that women have to reapply for benefit, which will only be paid if they can disprove the relationship. The assumptions underlying this rule – that a man living with a women claimant will be liable for her upkeep and that of any children she may have – are a cause for concern.

The reality of family poverty is now well documented both in terms of the numbers of families with children existing at or on the margins of poverty and in terms of the detailed case studies collected by social workers and the CPAG, which show the struggle and humiliation of actually living in poverty. The problems of dependence on overworked assistance schemes and selective benefits are similarly well documented.

Moreover, families in general have been losing out in recent years because of an increase, relatively and absolutely, in the tax burden borne by families with children. This increase has arisen because of the relative lowering of the tax threshold and the shift from direct taxation on income towards indirect taxation on expenditure, which affects lower-income families disproportionately.

Clearly there is a need for an effective family policy, designed to help all families responsible for bringing up children, but in particular designed to eradicate family and child poverty. How far have we moved towards such a policy?

There has been considerable discussion of family poverty in the past, but remarkably little government action. One of the first serious proposals was that for tax credits, in 1972. A form of income maintenance operated through the taxation system, tax allowances would be replaced by tax credits, which could be set against tax assessed at the standard rate. If the tax assessed exceeded the credit due, a tax would be payable on the amount of the excess. If the tax liability was less than the tax credit, no tax would be payable and instead a payment would be made. The scheme would have covered all in work and all insurance beneficiaries, although it would not have covered those on means tested benefits.

The proposals, though widely discussed, were dropped and a more modest child benefit scheme replaced existing family allowances and child tax allowances in 1975. For a brief time the higher rate of universal tax-free cash benefit was seen as a triumph for the family lobby, but only a few years after its introduction it was failing to maintain its value against inflation. In the last few years increases in child benefit have been extremely low, and the triumph at the introduction of this benefit has indeed been short-lived. It would appear that, despite lip-service paid by politicians to family needs, little will be done to increase their relative position. They have lost tax concessions through the removal of child tax allowances and the reduction of the tax threshold; the value of cash benefits has been eroded; and many of the social services, such as education, on which families rely, are suffering cuts in provision.

Universal improvements in benefits for families are not favoured by the current government, and reliance on means tested benefits continues and increases. One variation on individual selectivity is to consider ways of helping specific groups, and with this in mind the needs of single-parent households were studied by the Finer Committee, which reported in 1974. The committee's report was a comprehensive account of the problems faced by single-parent families, with recommendations for an improvement in their relatively disadvantaged position in society. Although the specific recommendations were not adopted, some help for single-parent families was introduced – including higher rates of child benefit for children in these families. Under income support there is a premium for lone parents, although this is low, and lone parents in employment can claim a dependant's tax allowance. Whilst slight improvements have been made in the provision of childcare and local authority housing, recent cuts in both local social services expenditure and local authority provision of housing have meant that there has been little overall improvement in the situation of this group.

The failure to develop an effective family policy in Britain has resulted in a serious problem of poverty among families. While it is clearly necessary that the poorest are helped, it appears that special programmes to help *only* poor families, or certain groups of families, do not work well. Policies to support *all* families, financially and in other areas of social provision, are more likely to be acceptable and successful.

One of the most depressing consequences of the failure to help all families is the 'poverty trap'. Reliance on selective measures means that poor families who benefit from family credit, free school meals and housing benefit, etc., stand to lose heavily from any increase in their earnings that takes them above their entitlement to benefit. Moreover, many families claiming selective benefits have to pay direct taxes because tax thresholds have not risen in line with inflation. There is now an urgent need to end the poverty trap and provide general family support. The primary aim must still be to provide substantial child benefits related to the actual costs of a child and varying, as do the costs, with the age of the child. Such benefits would clearly end most child poverty and enormously ease the problems of the poverty trap at the margins of income support levels. But despite the immense efforts by organizations such as the CPAG to persuade people of the rightness of such a policy, in a political environment in which targeting and selective measures are paramount such a move seems unlikely.

Unemployment and Social Security

Mention must be made of another specific problem of social security, one that has proved to be increasingly intractable in the 1980s and 1990s – the problem of unemployment. This is related in part to the poverty of families, and of course any improvement in child benefit helps the unemployed family to some extent. But the main income maintenance problem arises from the fact that the long-term unemployed are dependent on income support, which is paid at an inadequate level and which makes the unemployed family among the very worst off. This reliance of the unemployed on means tested benefits rather than insurance-based benefits has grown with the numbers of unemployed, in particular the long-term unemployed who are no longer eligible for unemployment benefit. In fact, the basic problem of means tested benefits such as income support comes precisely from this increase in the numbers dependent on it – in 1985 over 12 per cent of the population were being helped by it, whilst in 1948 means tested assistance was originally seen as offering flexible help to small numbers who were unable to claim insurance-based benefits such as unemployment benefit. Means tested schemes make payments designed to suit particular individual circumstances, but with such large numbers needing help the scheme has come under heavy stress. Accommodation is often inadequate, staff are severely overworked, there are real problems of communication, delays and inaccuracy, and allegations of secrecy, discrimination and bullying.

A review of the scheme in 1978 looked at the problems and considered possibilities for change. It concluded that it was unrealistic to hope for any reduction in the mass role of means tested benefits and therefore suggested ways of streamlining the system to improve its operation. Following this review, the social security legislation of 1980 revised the means tested scheme by replacing discretionary rules with legal rights. This scheme was to be introduced at no extra cost, which essentially meant that most claimants stood to lose money while only a minority gained. A more sweeping review of the social security system, with a similar no-cost brief, was announced in 1985. The Fowler Review, as it was known, proposed the abolition of supplementary benefit and family income support, reductions in housing benefit, the removal of death grants, maternity grants and emergency payments, and the setting up of a cash-limited Social Fund. It also proposed the abolition of child benefit. Despite widespread opposition to the review, the majority of changes proposed – with the exception of the abolition of child benefit, which was saved by vigorous lobbying – were enacted in the 1986 Social Security Act.

Immediately following the implementation of the changes, in April 1988, various assessments were made of the impact of the changes both on existing claimants and on new claimants. It seems that there were both gainers and losers as a result of the changes – and although existing claimants who received less in the new system were protected by a series of transitional payments, such protection merely postponed the loss as payments were frozen until the new rate, with inflation, had caught up with the old one. Overall, there were more losers than gainers; in particular, people with a disability and pensioners were more likely to lose, whilst families with children were, on this occasion, more likely to win.

The changes to the social security system reflect current government thinking on the need for 'targeting' benefits to aid the very poor in a selective way, whilst restraining public sector expenditure. The issues of financing the social security system and the organization of such a system remain both complex and controversial. It is clear that the problem of poverty is highly complex, and it should now be accepted that there is no one simple solution. Any change is difficult because of its costs, the vested interests of long-established schemes, and the range and diversity of the needs it is trying to meet. Above all, change is difficult because of the confusion that abounds over the real aims of social security.

Inevitably when we examine the income maintenance field our primary concern to eradicate absolute poverty must move on to some attempt to tackle relative deprivation and to grapple with the issue of what is meant by social justice. The technological problems of income support are vast, but much more serious in some ways are the ideological issues that divide us. Many people would argue that the state's social security system cannot be operated or examined in isolation from the rest of our social structure: it should not be viewed in isolation from fiscal or occupational welfare measures, or, indeed, from the general distribution of rewards in our society. Poverty in that sense is only one aspect of income distribution. Equally, it is argued that the availability of cash resources is only one aspect of poverty and any effective reforming policy should embrace the concomitant evils of bad housing, lack of education or disadvantages in health.

To sum up, the machinery of social security reflects attitudes and values prevailing in society and can be used to achieve considerable redistribution of income or to underline a callous or patronizing rejection of dependent groups. In attempting to overhaul the social security system, we must therefore look, not only at strategies but at aims. This brings us back to the initial question of what we mean by poverty. In searching for a definition we must, quite properly, raise even more fundamental questions about the whole structure and values of our society, even as simultaneously we struggle to comprehend the economic, administrative and straightforwardly human implications of tedious social security techniques.

NOTES

1   Report of the 1832 Royal Commission on the Poor Law.
2   See Brian Abel-Smith and Peter Townsend, 'The poor and the poorest', *Occasional Papers in Social Administration*, no. 17 (1975).
3   See *Financial and other Circumstances of Retirement Pensions* (Ministry of Pensions and National Insurance, 1966), and *Circumstances of Families* (Ministry of Social Security, 1967), for further details.

SUGGESTIONS FOR FURTHER READING

Ashley, P., *The Money Problems of the Poor* (Heinemann, 1983).

Atkinson, A. B., *Poverty in Britain and the Reform of Social Security* (Cambridge University Press, 1969).

Berthoud, R. and Brown, J., *Poverty and the Development of Anti-Poverty Policy in the United Kingdom* (Heinemann, 1981).

Brown, M. and Madge, N., *Despite the Welfare State* (Heinemann, 1982).

Bull, David (ed.), *Family Poverty* (Duckworth, 1971).

Coates, K. and Silburn, R., *Poverty: the Forgotten Englishman* (Penguin, 1970 and 1981).

Field, Frank, *Inequality in Britain* (Fontana, 1981).

George, V., *Social Security: Beveridge and After* (RKP, 1968).

Holman, B., *Poverty: Explanations of Social Deprivation* (Martin Robertson, 1978).

Kincaid, J. C., *Poverty and Equality in Britain* (Penguin, 1973).

Marsden, D., *Mothers Alone* (Penguin, 1969).

Rodgers, Brian, *The Battle against Poverty* (RKP, 1968).

Townsend, P. (ed.), *The Concept of Poverty* (Heinemann, 1968).

Townsend, P., *Poverty in the United Kingdom* (Penguin, 1979).

Wynn, M., *Family Policy* (Penguin, 1970).

Young, M. (ed.), *Poverty Report 1975* (Temple, 1975).

3

The health services

THE PROBLEM OF SICKNESS

Sickness is a major social problem and a universal one. Humanity is afflicted by numerous diseases – fatal, permanently crippling or merely trivial – which are a constant threat to survival and prosperity. To the individual, sickness is not only a source of immediate suffering in terms of pain, discomfort and dislocation of routine, it is also a source of anxiety, for it can be fatal, and can lead to all the agony of bereavement by premature death; it can also chronically disable, and result in poverty and hardship. It is a problem to the country as a whole, since widespread epidemic and endemic disease can decimate the population and poor standards of physical fitness will lead to low productivity. Moreover, sickness can cause poverty, the break-up of families, the destruction of community life and generally hold up social and economic progress. It is hardly surprising, then, that sickness is widely recognized as a social problem and that efforts are made to combat and prevent it. The preservation of health and the improvement of general standards of fitness are goals common to both individuals and nations.

The problem of sickness and ill-health is many sided. It is in part a biological problem: people have to fight to survive and overcome the diseases that threaten survival by developing medical skill and knowledge. But it is also a sociological problem because many of the factors that promote, encourage and even cause sickness are directly concerned with the way people behave and the environment in which they operate. It is increasingly accepted nowadays that sickness is as much a social as a medical problem, that the conditions in which people live and work influence their health as much as the existence of actual disease organisms, and that emotional and behavioural factors are important in the aetiology of many illnesses. As the more basic threats to life are controlled by medical science, new hazards emerge, which are the consequences of the stresses of complex urban civilizations. So, for example, we can control the spread of fatal epidemic diseases by vaccination programmes but we have to cope with the consequences of increasing numbers of road accidents and a higher incidence of mental illness. Thus the pattern of sickness and ill-health changes, reflecting not only advances in medical science but also the changing habits and conditions of people.

The interrelationship of biological, environmental, behavioural and psychological factors in the causation of sickness is now accepted. It is even more apparent that sociological and biological determinants are interdependent when one looks at the concept of good health rather than sickness. This has been defined by the World Health Organization as a 'state of complete physical, mental and social well-being', which is a strikingly positive concept, involving much more than the absence of sickness, and certainly much more than a mere biological fitness.

One important consequence of the complex nature of sickness is that the policy to deal with it must cover a very wide front. The environment must be made as safe as possible in order to control the incidence and spread of disease and the hazards of contaminated air, noxious industrial processes and the risk of accidents. Diagnostic and treatment facilities must be made readily available so that people who are ill or suffer accidents can receive care and treatment and be cured and rehabilitated. Adequate numbers of doctors, nurses and professional, technical and other ancillary workers, such as pharmacists, laboratory technicians and radiographers, must be recruited, trained and effectively deployed. Health education is necessary so that individuals, organizations and the community at large know how to reduce the risks of contracting diseases, how to ensure maximum resistance to sickness and how to promote health. And efforts must constantly be made to understand the relationships between the biological, environmental, behavioural and psychological factors in sickness in order better to coordinate health and other social policies.

Contemporary Britain is by many standards a 'healthy' society, but this does not reduce the demand for medical and related services; in fact in some ways it has the reverse effect. For example, one way of comparing health standards is to look at mortality rates and at life expectancy in different countries. Britain has reasonably low mortality rates and high life expectancy,[1] but one consequence of this is that there is a high proportion of old people in our society and they need more medical care than those in the middle age groups.

It is difficult to measure or describe concisely the morbidity of a country. Most of the statistics we have relate to the use of medical care facilities, which might only approximate to the actual incidence and prevalence of sickness. National Insurance records can show the reasons for absence from work for certified sickness but this only relates to the working population. Moreover, some people who are sick may not visit their GP or take time off work, particularly if they are not eligible for sick pay. So statistics on morbidity are at best estimates of levels of illness. The Registrar General collects and publishes information on standard mortality rates but not on general morbidity, although some general information is now collected from the government's General Household Survey. Some statistics expose the distribution of sickness by class and region, others by age and sex, but most morbidity studies relate to a particular disease or medical problem, such as lung cancer or venereal disease, and provide detailed information about such specific problems only. Some trends in morbidity are reasonably clear, such as an increase in fatal heart disease and lung cancer and a reduction in infectious diseases like tuberculosis, but it is virtually impossible to generalize about the state of the country's health. The detailed picture is fascinating and also very instructive and it is certainly abundantly clear from what statistics we have that patterns and trends in sickness are strongly and sometimes disturbingly related to environmental and social factors.

The provision of medical care is not, of course, only related to morbidity, although treatment of sickness is always a first necessity. Concern with prevention of disease and the promotion of health has meant that such things as the maternity services, mass screening, vaccination and a full range of medical rehabilitation facilities form an increasingly important part of the health services.

It is clear that a vigorous and comprehensive social policy is required to ensure provision of all the public and personal health services necessary to combat sickness and promote health. As our understanding of sickness develops we modify the structure of our response to it. Once it was accepted that environmental services were fundamental to any effective attack on disease, public health measures were introduced, which were collectively provided and financed. Gradually the role of the state has widened from its initial concern with basic sanitation to involvement in all aspects of treatment and care. The progress of medicine as a science and technology has necessitated the development of large organizations to provide the resources necessary for training and specialization. Such organizations cannot easily be sustained by private entrepreneurial concerns and an extension of the collective approach, already established in public environmental health, has steadily taken place. Moreover, as the connection between environmental conditions and personal health was gradually understood, the importance of linking preventive treatment approaches administratively was recognized.

It is now acknowledged that a high degree of medical skill will not by itself solve the problem of sickness unless it can be backed by supportive services of prevention and care and made readily available when and where it is needed. This necessitates a complex administration and massive public finance. Likewise, high standards of care that reach only a small section of the population will not ensure a healthy nation, so it is necessary to try to spread facilities equitably by class and by area and to organize them on a national basis in order to encourage this.

While sickness remains a personal problem for the individual who is ill and needs appropriate care and treatment, it is now clearly seen as a public problem too, the solution to which must lie in collective action on a wide front. At the same time, the promotion of health, although now a complex technological process involving increasingly specialized and diversified groups of professionals and experts, must ultimately remain the concern and responsibility of individuals. In the next section an attempt will be made to describe in simple terms the complex structure of health provision that has evolved to meet the dynamic and the paradoxical problems that sickness presents to society.

HEALTH SERVICES IN BRITAIN

In Britain the response to the problem of sickness has been the creation of the National Health Service, which has comprehensive concern for all aspects of medical care and public and environmental health. Different aspects of health care had developed in voluntary and statutory hands in a variety of ways, but by the 1946 National Health Service Act they were all brought together into one major social service.

Prior to 1946, primary care through the general practitioner was mostly on a private practice basis, although National Health Insurance gave most workers access to it through the panel system. Hospitals were either provided by local authorities – as poor law infirmaries, public health hospitals or mental hospitals – or they were run on a voluntary basis; in which case they varied from large, well-supported and prestigious teaching hospitals to small specialist clinics and rural cottage hospitals. Finally, local authorities, in addition to running hospitals, had wide responsibilities for environmental and preventive health services and they operated domiciliary maternity, mental health and school health services.

Within these different settings medicine had developed both scientifically and professionally at a great pace. Scientific development meant increasing specialization among doctors and the growth of teaching and research facilities on a large and costly scale. It also meant the growth of numerous professions ancillary to medicine as the scope of medical technology increased. As the potential of medical science had grown, so inevitably had its costs. The state had intervened increasingly in the health sphere, and it had steadily accepted a growing responsibility for the direct financing of health care. But in 1946 the various branches of medical care were in considerable administrative and financial chaos and this was proving detrimental to the quality of treatment offered and especially to the effectiveness of prevention. In many cases two services with two standards of provision were operated, side by side, for public and private use. Medical care was inequitably distributed in two ways: geographically, because some areas (notably the South East), had far higher doctor–patient ratios than others, and also by socio-economic status, because medical care was distributed more according to a person's ability to pay for it than according to his or her clinical need. Moreover, many of the voluntary hospitals were desperately short of funds and had to offer poor-quality care, while the standards of local authority provision varied enormously. So although medicine as a science was maintaining good progress, the financing and administration of health care were badly in need of a coherent rational organization.

The 1946 National Health Service Act aimed to provide this. It created a service that was comprehensive in its scope and universal in its coverage. The aim was to remove all financial and organizational barriers between the doctors and their patients. The Minister of Health was given responsibility 'to provide the establishment in England and Wales of a comprehensive health service designed to secure improvements in the physical and mental health of the people and the prevention, diagnosis and treatment of illness, and for that purpose to provide and secure the effective provision of services'. The state was to finance the health service largely through general taxation so that medical care would be free to the individual at the point of use.

The administrative structure devised was a complicated tripartite one reflecting professional and administrative differences existing prior to 1946. The hospitals were 'nationalized' and they and the specialist services operating from them were administered, under the Minister of Health, by a two-tier structure of regional hospital boards and hospital management committees. Local authorities gave up their hospitals but continued to provide environmental and community health services. The general practitioners continued to operate fairly independently but were under contract to local executive councils. This structure was the outcome of a compromise between competing political and professional interests, and it was far from completely satisfactory. Nevertheless it worked, not without problems, but reasonably effectively for a good twenty years before real efforts were made to amend it. Likewise, the financial basis of the health service remained largely unchanged despite mounting criticism from within and without of gross under-financing. In recent years, however, there have been major administrative changes to the NHS and such radical proposals to alter the financial basis of the service that its very survival has been threatened.

ADMINISTRATIVE REORGANIZATION

The tripartite structure of the British health service was criticized almost from the inception of the NHS in 1946. It was obviously difficult to maintain continuity of care for patients when different authorities were concerned with different aspects of provision. The three branches of the system not only were separate but were administered by different kinds of authority. Hospitals, the most expensive and most visible part of the service, were planned by fifteen large regional bodies with members directly appointed by the Secretary of State. Day-to-day management was in the hands of 330 hospital management committees whose membership was again by appointment. Hospitals were financed directly from the central Department of Health and Social Security. Local authorities on the other hand, with elected members, remained responsible for a wide range of services in the community, including preventive health services and domiciliary maternity services. Money for these services had to come through the local government financial machinery, and the medical officer of health had to compete with other chief officers (from education or social services or housing for example), in bidding for resources. General practitioners remained on

a semi-independent contractual basis separately administered by the 134 local executive councils, with separate
funds.

Clearly this variety and number of responsible bodies was
an obstacle to effective joint management of services. It was
difficult to ensure coordination and flexible use of resources,
and communication and cooperation were particularly difficult between hospital doctors and general practitioners. Some
services such as the geriatric hospitals, and some patient groups
such as the chronically sick, were very badly served. The unfair
and uneven distribution of resources was widely attributed to
the absence of a clearly defined unitary authority for purposes
of planning and the establishment of priorities.

As the necessity for joint planning became more apparent, the pressure for an integrated service intensified. Various proposals for change were made, including some fairly
radical ones from the medical profession itself, notably in
the Porritt Report, *Review of the Medical Services in Great
Britain*, published in 1962. In 1968 the first Green Paper on
*The Administrative Structure of the Medical and Related Services
in England & Wales* was published. After comment and discussion a further Green Paper, *The Future Structure of the
National Health Service*, was published in 1970. This advocated a unified system under the control of about ninety
area health authorities. The detailed proposals were considerably modified after a change of government in 1970 but the
broad principle of integration was retained. A White Paper,
National Health Reorganization: England,[2] appeared in 1972; the
changes became law in 1973 and came into operation on 1
April 1974 at the same time as the reorganization of local
government.[3]

Despite the length of the discussions on reorganization,
and the extensive consultations that took place, there was
widespread dissatisfaction with the new structure of the NHS
after 1974. Proposals to amend it were put forward in the
consultative document *Patients First* in 1980, and implemented
from 1982. Further reorganization followed the NHS Management Inquiry Report of 1983, and both organizational
and financial changes are envisaged in the 1989 White Paper
Working for Patients.

PRESENT STRUCTURE OF THE NHS

Central responsibility lies with the Secretary of State for Social Services and the Department of Health. These are aided by a Health Services Supervisory Board and the NHS Management Board. Extensive advisory machinery is provided in the form of several standing advisory committees covering particular areas such as nursing services, pharmaceutical provision, maternity care, and so forth. Under the reorganization, an advisory service was made available at the different management levels. The object of the extensive advisory provision was twofold: to help members of the health authorities in their decision-making, and to ensure that the various health professionals have some say in the planning and operation of the NHS. But it has meant a further proliferation of committees, and these are notoriously time consuming.

Under the Department of Health the whole range of services that comprise the NHS – hospitals, family practitioner and community services – are administered and managed by a complicated mix of appointed bodies aand professional staff. This complexity arises out of attempts to reconcile the need for centrally coordinated planning of services with the need for effective management by those with professional clinical responsibility for the actual provision of services. The need to allow some consumer say in the running of the health services was also taken into account, and relationships with other social services, particularly in local government, were considered.

Figure 3.1 attempts to summarize the current structure in England. Under the Department of Health there are fourteen regional health authorities (RHA's). Their members are appointed by the Secretary of State and include people with business experience, lawyers and members of the medical profession who are knowledgeable about the needs of the region. They keep close contact with the universities and teaching hospitals of the regions. The RHAs have overall responsibility for planning services in their regions in the light of central government policy and regional needs. They have some powers for directly undertaking major building works and they are responsible for the appointment of senior medical staff. However, their main function is to plan, and

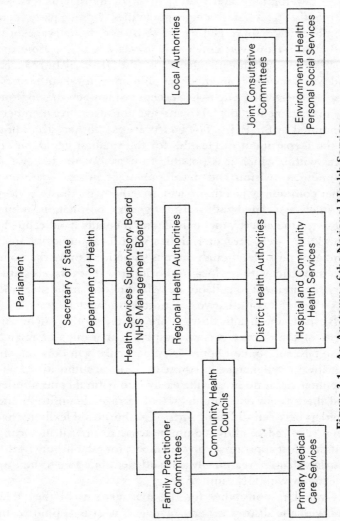

Figure 3.1 An Anatomy of the National Health Service

then allocate resources accordingly to the second-tier bodies, the district health authorities (DHAs).

The district health authorities are responsible for the planning, development and management of the health services within the regional strategic guidelines. In the past, their members were appointed by the RHA and the relevant local authorities. However, under new legislation arising from the 1989 White Paper, the membership of the DHA will be reduced and will not include members appointed by local authorities. Instead, there will be up to five executive members drawn from the management of the DHA and five non-executive members appointed by the RHA. The DHAs are established, according to the Department of Health, 'for the smallest geographical areas within which it is possible to carry out the integrated planning, provision and development of primary care and other community health services, together with those services normally associated with a district general hospital, including those for the elderly, mentally ill and mentally handicapped'. The DHA areas are coterminous with local authority areas wherever possible, though there is sometimes more than one health district within a local authority area. They have a statutory requirement to collaborate with the local authorities and to set up joint consultative committees to facilitate this.

Basically the health districts are related to the catchment areas of the district general hospitals, or groups of related hospitals, and so their boundaries, particularly in London, are not always well matched to those of the local authorities. Metropolitan areas do not divide easily into natural communities and there is always some degree of territorial confusion and overlap between different sorts of authorities. Flexibility has been required to allow common sense to prevail in sorting out the most appropriate arrangements for establishing health districts that are reasonably self-sufficient but able to link up effectively with local authorities.

Overall responsibility for the management of the DHA lies with the district general manager, who is appointed by and responsible to the RHA. The district general manager is supported by the district management team, and is responsible for the overall management of all services in the district. The DHA provides hospital services and a range of community health services, but does not provide the general practitioner services, which are the responsibility of separate family practitioner committees.

Within each district, the day-to-day running of various aspects of the service is organized by units. Units of management consist of the larger single hospitals or the community services for a particular client group and they each have a unit administrator and nursing officer. Health care planning teams are established at district level for different client groups, such as the elderly or mentally ill. Normally led by a clinician, the teams consider the needs of the groups and assess the development of services. These teams do not have a management function but have more of an advisory role and they draw on interested personnel from outside the health service as well as from within. Voluntary bodies and local authority services are represented on the teams, and information and ideas about a wide range of problems and provisions are assembled by them.

At district level there is a system of community health councils (CHCs), which aim to involve the community as the consumer in the provision of health care. The CHCs consist of about thirty members appointed by local government or chosen as representatives of voluntary bodies and universities. They have power to obtain information about health services and they can inspect health premises, including hospitals. They maintain close links with the district management and must be consulted before any major decisions affecting district health services are made, especially any that might involve hospital closures. They publish an annual report that comments on the district health provision from the consumer point of view. CHCs have modest premises and staff, funded by the RHAs, and they aim to promote knowledge about health care generally as well as monitor the provision of their particular districts.

The CHCs aim to involve the consumer positively in the provision of health care. But consumer complaints can also be voiced directly to the Health Services Commissioner. The commissioner, usually referred to as the ombudsman, does not normally investigate complaints until the health authority concerned has investigated and replied to the complainant and only if the complainant then remains dissatisfied, although he can investigate in exceptional cases. This extension of the ombudsman principle is an important acknowledgement of consumer rights in the sensitive area of health care.

The first reorganization of the NHS took place in 1974 and it proved a considerable upheaval. For many people within the service it appeared to be a deliberate disorganization, as existing administrative procedures came to an end and new ones had to be established. In the years following 1974 there was much anxiety and acrimonious discussion about the new structure. The prime objective of the change was to improve the quality of service, especially for the weaker patient groups such as the chronically sick and mentally handicapped. Another important objective was to create a more effective community health service: it was generally agreed that the hospital sector had for too long dominated the health scene and that community-based services lagged behind in development and prestige. This was particularly detrimental to preventive health care, as epidemiological studies had shown the importance of social and environmental factors in much sickness. It was hoped that a unified health service with greater control could bring better management of resources and greater emphasis on preventive and community services.

Criticism of the reorganization continued, however. It was claimed that the new structure was unwieldy and undemocratic and that it was not providing an improved service. The 1974 structure was undoubtedly very complex. It had three tiers of administration: regional, area and district. The area level, roughly coterminous with the local authorities, had been intended as the key operational level, but in practice different patterns of effective administration had emerged, with the district being in many cases the key level. Many critics urged the government to abolish one administrative tier and this was done in 1982. The area health authorities were wound up and the districts, which had previously worked to them, became district health authorities.

Before the effectiveness of this new structure could be assessed, a further inquiry was instituted 'to give advice on the effective use and management of manpower and related resources in the NHS'. The recommendations of the inquiry team led by Griffiths (known generally as the Griffiths Report) were announced late in 1983. They were that there should be a new Health Services Supervisory Board and a full-time Management Board for the NHS. The Supervisory Board would strengthen existing arrangements for the central control and direction of the NHS. The Management Board would ensure that central policy decisions would be carried out.

Griffiths was really more about management style than administrative structure, however. The inquiry team urged the NHS regions to strengthen and extend an accountability review process through all levels of management. At DHA and RHA level each authority had to appoint a general manager 'charged with the general management function and overall responsibility for management's performance in achieving the objectives set by the Authority'. Most of the new appointments were from exisitng NHS staff, with a few from outside the health services. The aim of the changes was seen as an improvement in the management of NHS resources and a reduction in waste and inefficiency. Thus this new style of management replaced the consensus managment of the past. In addition, one of the early tasks of each new general manager was to streamline administration and initiate cost improvement programmes.

The intentions of the Griffiths reorganization were to centralize control and tighten monitoring and budgetary procedures. The concept of expenditure control and output targets was further extended by the introduction of measures to evaluate performance and the reports during the 1980s from the Korner Committee on the statistics that the NHS should be collecting to evaluate and monitor performance.

The most recent, and far reaching, review of the health services, the 1989 White Paper, *Working for Patients*, took this process further still. Proposals include allowing hospitals to opt out of local health authority control becoming self-governing and financing themselves through contracts with health authorities, GP practices with practice budgets, private hospitals and private patients, and possibly other self-governing hospitals.

In addition, the larger GP practices will be able to hold their own budgets, receiving their finance from the regional health authority in relation to the number of patients on their lists. Practices will receive higher amounts for older patients, or if they are situated in poorer locations. In budget-holding practices, GPs will order the treatment needed by one of their patients from whichever service best meets the needs of the patient within the constraints of the budget. The choice can be made from NHS facilities within and outside the region, or from private health care.

Other proposals include greater patient choice, the introduction of a medical audit to monitor services, and tax concessions to people over 60 paying premiums on private health care.

Widespread opposition on the part of the medical profession has challenged the White Paper, due to be implemented in the early 1990s. The overall direction of the changes in the White Paper is seen as an increase in central control and a greater push towards internal markets and privatization. Thus the aims of the White Paper are consistent with previous moves towards privatization, such as the introduction in 1983 of compulsory competitive tendering for health authorities, which were then required to put support services such as laundry and cleaning out to open tender.

FINANCE OF THE NHS

Some people, especially professionals within the health service, argue that the shortcomings of the NHS are not administrative but financial. It is certainly true that, however good an organization is, it cannot function effectively without adequate resources and this is something that it is hard to determine let alone provide for a national health service. There has been a reluctance in Britain to provide enough money for health services partly through fear of insatiable demand, partly because of suspicion over the effectiveness of some costly methods of treatment and partly out of a grudging refusal to accept the urgency of the needs of some of the weaker and less glamorous groups of long-stay patients.

Discussions about finances have for many years centred on arguments about whether or not the health service should be free to the user and financed out of general taxation or whether a private sector should be encouraged. These arguments have been fierce and have detracted attention from more important issues. Health services are labour intensive and extremely vulnerable to the effects of inflation. Costs are, therefore, rising steeply, yet the proportion of GNP spent on health in Britain remains relatively low. There is an urgent need for more money in the health services and relatively little of this comes or is likely to come from the private sector. Those areas of health provision in greatest need of more resources are those least likely to attract private finance, so the bulk of resources must continue to come from the Exchequer. Health services do compete with other services for their resources, so if they are to receive greater priority, especially in times of economic difficulty, then they must justify their use of resources on one method of treatment or care as opposed to another, and match provisions more equitably to needs.

THE HOSPITAL SERVICE

Nearly two-thirds of the NHS costs go on hospital provision. The NHS runs around 1,900 hospitals with nearly half a million beds. The hospital service provides a full range of hospital care, including, for example, psychiatric hospitals, maternity units, convalescent homes and rehabilitation centres, as well as the big general and teaching hospitals. The national ratio of beds is 6.7 per thousand of the population and these are divided between acute, psychiatric, geriatric, chronically sick and maternity specialities. At the hospitals all the appropriate medical, nursing, administrative and ancillary staff are available. There are a vast number of different hospital occupations, from the senior medical staff through laboratory technicians and social workers to domestics. About 44,800 medical personnel work at hospitals and over 400,000 nurses, with 76,000 professional technical staff (such as radiographers) and 170,000 ancillary staff. Patients are mostly referred to hospital by their general practitioners. They may be admitted for treatment or dealt with as outpatients. Consultant specialists are appointed in all branches of an increasingly complex medical field. They head the hierarchy of medical staff that serve the hospitals on the wards and in the clinics, but in many cases they also practise in their consultative capacity outside the hospitals. Both hospital and specialist services are free to the patient, although those who so wish can pay for additional amenities or the full cost of treatment.

The hospital services are large and complicated. As medicine develops it produces more specialists, more techniques and skills, and consequently it requires more space and more ancillary staff. As standards rise, more people can be treated for conditions that once were considered hopeless. Patterns of hospital usage change. For example, there are now fewer TB patients, and acute surgical and psychiatric cases have a more rapid turnover than before the war; on the other hand, more long-stay geriatric beds and more maternity beds are needed. Accordingly, hospitals very easily become both obsolete and overcrowded. This is very striking in Britain where half of the hospitals date from the nineteenth century and lack space for laboratories, elaborate operating theatres, occupational therapy units, etc., as well as being often in poor structural condition with inadequate sanitary and heating arrangements. So there is a need for more and up-to-date hospital accommodation even though overall bed demand has not risen.

A further problem presented by hospital provision has been the uneven distribution of hospital resources. Some areas are well endowed, others grossly neglected, since historical accident determined the location of many of today's large hospitals. This was one of the reasons why the National Health Service was created – so that there could be some overall planning of hospital provision. But in its early years little was spent on hospital building. It was only in 1961 that the Minister of Health asked the regional boards to plan really large-scale expansion of their hospital services. In 1962 the Hospital Plan was published, embodying their programmes for the next decade. In addition to a general acceleration of building plans, attempts were made to reorganize the pattern of hospital provision and provide a rational basis for planning. Accordingly, estimates were made of the number of beds that would be required in any area for the different sorts of cases –

acute surgical, maternity, psychiatric, etc. With these estimates, calculated from the relevant demographic data on population size and age structures, etc., and recommended ratios of bed provision to population for the various categories of patient, it was possible to make more rational plans for provision to meet the likely demand. Moreover, it was possible to think about the organization of hospital facilities in terms of suitable size of units, scope of services, and so on. The plan, therefore, introduced the concept of the district general hospital. Instead of haphazard provision of hospitals, it was decided that for every 100,000–150,000 of population there should be a district general hospital of 600–800 beds. This would be located near the centre of the population that it was designed to service and it would provide, in addition to the ordinary specialities, a full range of diagnostic and treatment facilities for in- and outpatients and would include a maternity unit, a short-stay psychiatric unit, isolation facilities and geriatric care. More specialist facilities such as radio therapy, neurosurgery, etc., would require larger catchment areas and so would only be located at some hospitals. It was anticipated that as the new district general hospitals developed to meet most of the bed-demand, some of the existing smaller hospitals would be closed down or be used as annexes for maternity or geriatric cases only.

Clearly this plan for hospital provision involved massive building projects and considerable reorganization. It was hardly surprising that some parts of it proved highly controversial. Capital expense and, at times, problems of finding appropriate sites for vast new premises slowed down progress. Eventually the idea of concentrating facilities in large hospitals was challenged. It was decided that a continuing place could be found for smaller premises as community hospitals providing care mainly for geriatric and chronically sick patients. By the end of the 1970s a considerable amount of new building and remodelling had been completed, but the situation is still far from satisfactory, with many old, obsolete and inadequate buildings still in use.

Buildings are not, of course, the only or even the most important part of hospital provision. Staff are vital and there are constant problems in obtaining enough medical, nursing and ancillary staff at the required standards. A high proportion of junior hospital posts are filled by doctors from overseas, who will probably return home after finishing training, and there is some anxiety at this high reliance on foreign medical staff. This is especially problematic in the long-stay hospitals. Nursing shortages are no less acute in some sectors of hospital provision. The need to keep demand for staff continuously under review, and to adjust recruitment and training programmes, pay and prospects accordingly, is an urgent one if the hospital service is to maintain and improve its quality.

PRIMARY MEDICAL CARE

For most people the main contact with the NHS is through their general practitioner. About 26,000 GPs, with a further 1,800 assistants and trainees, work for the health service. GPs have frequent contact with patients, often over a considerable period of time, and they have an important preventive as well as diagnostic and curative role to play in medical care. All members of the community are registered with a general practitioner, who is the usual first point of contact for health problems. The GP deals with all minor complaints and chronic conditions and is responsible for referral to hospital and specialist services where necessary. It is therefore important that general practitioners have a high level of diagnostic skill and technique and a considerable degree of rapport with their patients.

The general practitioner's role has changed radically during recent decades, particularly since the creation of the NHS. GPs used to be very much independent entrepreneurs, running their own practices and providing a wide range of medical services for their patients. As medicine has become increasingly scientific and more specialized, the family doctor has of necessity become more dependent on others. They must refer to specialists much more frequently and make use of the services of pathology laboratories and X-ray departments, for example, to aid diagnosis. In many ways the general practitioner feels able to do less than formerly for patients since he or she must often refer them to the hospitals' more specialized care. Many have found this change an unhappy one, and feel dissatisfied with what they consider is a reduced role. But in some ways the range of work of the general practitioner has widened with, for example, the development of modern drugs that makes possible the treatment of quite serious complaints without recourse to hospitalization. The GP's role in social and preventive medicine is also being increasingly recognized.

Some general practitioners have responded well to the change of role and adapted themselves accordingly. Group practices are becoming more common and some groups are able to offer a degree of specialized care – different doctors being predominantly responsible for work with children, old people, mental health problems, etc. Others have experimented with purpose-built premises or health centres, offering accommodation for not only the group of doctors but also some technical, nursing and social work assistance in addition to the usual secretarial help. The advantages of group practices are that they permit the doctors to organize their work better, enabling them to have time off instead of being permanently on call; they offer a more stimulating environment to the doctors; and they make possible the use of relatively expensive equipment and ancillary staff.

Since the establishment of the NHS a central committee, the Medical Practices Committee, has worked with the local executive councils and, since 1974, with the family practitioner committees to ensure an even distribution of primary medical care facilities across the country. The Committee monitors the spread of general practice and has powers to forbid the setting up of new practices in areas it considers to be adequately covered.

Despite these new ideas there continues to be a shortage of good general practitioners, some areas being especially deprived. It has been suggested that the two main reasons for this are the relatively low status of family doctors compared to hospital doctors and the problem of remuneration.

The status problem is largely the consequence of the developments in medicine that have shifted the emphasis in medical care on to the hospital and consultant specialist side. General practitioners have been regarded as non-specialists in a profession tending increasingly to specialization of interest and skill. Recently, however, general practice itself has been regarded as a speciality, with appropriate training provided for doctors who wish to become a GP after their basic training period. This specialist training takes a further three years, with examinations set by the Royal College of General Practice. The training covers extended periods in obstetrics, gynaecology and psychiatry, as well as training in a practice, attached to a GP. After this, the young doctors will become either principals in general practice or hospital specialists. A further suggestion for both improving the status of GPs and making their job more interesting is to involve them in the work of the hospitals, and some experiments are under way on such lines.

The remuneration issue is not divorced from the status problem. Not only high status but potentially high financial rewards are attached to senior hospital posts, whereas the GP is in a job with a fairly steady level of pay but slight career or advancement prospects. Payment of GPs was established on a per capita fee basis, that is, according to the number of patients rather than the amount or quality of work done. This method is regarded as failing to reward the more industrious or ambitious doctor. Attempts have been made to improve this financial position in pay settlements designed to make possible the financial recognition of extra effort and qualification. In 1966 a settlement known as the 'Doctor's Charter' sought to establish a link between remuneration and quality of service. This, together with more opportunity for work in group practices or health centres, encouraged more young doctors to opt for a career in this important branch of medical care.

The general practitioner services are currently provided on an independent contractor basis: the GPs enter into contracts with the family practitioner committee set up by the DHA. After the proposals of the 1989 White Paper have been implemented, some general practices will become budget holders, receiving their finance directly from the regional health authority. However, the FPC will continue to hold the GPs' contracts and monitor expenditure against the budget. Like its predecessor, the executive council, the FPC has thirty members, half of them appointed by the professions involved and the remainder by the DHA and local authority.

The FPC contracts not only with GPs but also with dental practitioners, pharmaceutical services and ophthalmic services. The general dental service aims to provide adequate dental services including all conservative dentistry. Each person can choose his or her own dentist and attend for the necessary treatment. Unlike the GP service, which is entirely free, dental treatment is provided on payment of part of the cost, up to a given maximum payment per course of treatment, with special charges for crowns, dentures, etc. Young people and expectant and nursing mothers are exempted from charges. About 15,000 dentists work as independent contractors and a further 2,000 work in dental hospitals, which are responsible for training dentists as well as developing knowledge and skill in dentistry and tackling the more complex dental problems referred by outside dentists.

The provision of pharmaceutical services in the community is a responsibility of the FPCs, which make the necessary arrangements with local registered pharmacists. Prescriptions are made out by doctors for such drugs, dressings or appliances as are required and these are dispensed by the pharmacist, who then recovers the costs. The patient currently has to pay a charge of £2.80 per item for prescriptions, but children, old people, expectant mothers, certain categories of chronically sick and people on low incomes are exempted from the charge.

There is continued controversy over prescription charges, which are regarded by many as an anomaly in a free health service and by others as a necessary check on abuse. The drug bill is a large and growing one and this causes much anxiety. Prescription charges cover only about one quarter of the actual cost of each item and are not recovered from those categories of people who make most use of drugs. Proposals for a graduated charge related to the cost of the drug were made in 1971 but not implemented owing to administrative difficulties and the unpopularity of the idea, which was felt to reintroduce the financial barrier between patient and doctor that the NHS was designed to remove. Nevertheless, despite the emotion aroused by the 'tax on sickness', charges do appear to restrain the demand for drugs and are therefore likely to remain. A further way to reduce the drug bill would be to reduce the profit of the drug companies and efforts have been made to do this, notably by the introduction of 'listed drugs', a device to limit the range of prescribable drugs to cheaper generic products. Intervention in this sphere causes enormous political controversy however.

Perhaps the most hopeful way of cutting back or restraining the growth of the drug bill would be to reorientate primary medical care more towards prevention than treatment. Both patients and doctors are at times over enthusiastic about drugs, and much education is needed to inculcate more positive attitudes towards health and reduce dependence on drugs. This is particularly important in the case of 'mood–affecting' drugs such as tranquillizers and sedatives, which are now very widely prescribed for conditions of anxiety and insomnia, and that of antibiotics, which again are prescribed with increasing frequency and insufficient discrimination.

Ophthalmic services have, like the dental and pharmaceutical services, a local professional committee that appoints members to the family practitioner committee. The local committees draw up lists of qualified practitioners who can test sight and make up glasses where necessary. Charges are made for lenses and frames approved by the health service or the patient can pay the full costs and enjoy a choice from a wider range of type and style of glasses.

COMMUNITY HEALTH SERVICES

Before reorganization in 1974, public and domiciliary health services were in the hands of the local authorities, which appointed a medical officer of health to be responsible for a wide range of duties under the NHS Act and the Public Health Act. In the reorganized health service, community health became one of the major responsibilities of the new unified organization, with doctors and administrators from hospital and public health working together.

The role of the community physician, the new specialism that was created by reorganization, lies in assessment, evaluation and planning. The community physicians, at both area and district level, study the health needs of the community and plan to meet them. They are particularly concerned with developing preventive health services, so they plan and organize health education and health visiting, screening and vaccination programmes, maternity and child welfare clinics, family planning and school health services. They have a major responsibility for liaison with the local authority, especially over the basic public health duties that remain with local government – the drainage, sewage, refuse disposal and other sanitary services. They also try to cooperate with personal social services departments so that health and social needs can be dealt with together where possible. For many groups of patients, such as the mentally ill and the chronically sick, the need for care is as great as the need for treatment. The local authority has responsibility for care, both residential and in a person's own home, and the importance of cooperation between health and social services cannot be overstated. It is one of the aims of reorganization to achieve better collaboration between health and local government in all these areas.

The scope of community health services is quite considerable. The maternity and child welfare services are well established and comprehensive. Their aim is the reduction of maternal and infant mortality and the improvement of the health of children. Ante-natal, post-natal and infant welfare clinics are established in all districts, run by DHA staff and local general practitioners. At ante-natal clinics mothers can obtain medical checks, attend relaxation classes and receive instruction on labour and the feeding and care of small babies. This service is available for mothers awaiting home confinements; those who expect to have their babies in hospital obtain a similar service there. Post-natal care is offered to all and involves visits by mid-wives, health visitors and, if required, domestic helpers. Mothers are then encouraged to bring their children to infant welfare clinics where routine medical inspection, general advice, regular weighing, etc., are made available and vaccination and immunization programmes carried out. Welfare foods (that is, subsidized milk preparations and vitamin supplies), are on sale at the clinics. Health visitors continue to make such domiciliary visits as are necessary to offer advice on health and hygiene, child rearing and general family problems.

Under section 28 of the National Health Service Act the health authorities have the power to make arrangements for the prevention of illness and for the care and after-care of persons suffering from illness. This covers the provision of a wide range of services, such as sickroom equipment, chiropody, laundry services and physiotherapy classes. The home nursing service is a crucial part of community health provision. The aged are the principal beneficiaries of this traditionally important service, which is a great help to old people seeking to live independently in their own homes.

The school health service is an important part of community health care. Medical inspection and treatment of school children is one of the oldest public health services, pre-dating the NHS by many years. Even today, when all children should be registered with a general practitioner and receive whatever medical care they need, it has an important part to play in preventive medicine. Children are regularly inspected by a school doctor and a nurse, usually a health visitor. Parents are encouraged to attend and discuss with the doctor any health problems the child may have. Action can be taken to remedy any defects. Vaccination and other prophylactic measures can be carried out, and specialist services, such as speech therapy or child guidance, can be brought into play if necessary. Not only do individual children benefit from these regular checks and many who would otherwise be neglected receive some medical attention, but the process of inspection monitors the collective health of school children. Trends in diseases or defects such as malnutrition or hearing problems can be noted and acted upon in the community and important epidemiological information obtained.

Health education is a vital aspect of a community health service, but it has not been well developed in the past. Many personnel, especially the doctors (both in general practice and in clinics), and the health visitors, are actively but informally involved in educating people about their health. But health education, if it is to be successful, can involve the alteration of behaviour patterns in both individuals and the community, which is no easy task. In order to promote better health education a council was set up in 1968. The Health Education Authority has central responsibility for advising DHAs on priorities and helping with the mounting of campaigns, especially through the provision of educational material, and it promotes research in this area. At district level, health education officers are appointed who can concentrate on this work with audio-visual aid staff to assist. They must work closely with social services and education departments, as well as with their health service colleagues. At a time when it can be asserted that more and more disease is self-induced by bad behaviour patterns the importance of health education cannot be overstated and it is to be hoped that it will receive greater priority in the reorganized health service as a vital adjunct to a genuinely community-oriented medicine.

Another aspect of health care that was neglected by the NHS until fairly recently is family planning. Contraception has remained such a controversial subject that the major developments in specialized provision have been through voluntary organizations, especially the Family Planning Association, albeit often working in partnership with local health authorities. In 1974 the NHS took over responsibility for family planning, and health authorities now play a more positive part in this field as recognition of the importance of planned parenthood and population control becomes more widespread.

There has been much hope for the development of a community-oriented health service through the medium of health centres. When the NHS was first established in 1948, local authorities had power to establish health centres that could bring together the work of the family practitioner services and local clinics. Initially, few were established, partly because of lack of resources, partly because of the reluctance of general practitioners to move from established practices. It was thought by some practitioners that really effective health centres could not only serve to bring together doctors, dentists, community nurses and social workers to work in a team situation but act as a focus for health education and truly preventive medicine. Much could be done by way of advice on diet and physical fitness, and the provision of occupational and physical therapy for rehabilitation and prevention, to swing the emphasis away from disease and over to health. In recent years, the number of health centres has grown substantially, and now nearly one-third of all GPs work in one.

ENVIRONMENTAL HEALTH

Outside the new health service, but a crucial support to it, lie the environmental services provided by the local authorities. These include the provision of good water supplies and such services as sewerage, street paving and cleaning and the removal of refuse. A further task is the detection and control of statutory nuisances as defined by the Public Health Act of 1936 and current regulations concerning the control of air pollution. Steps are taken to protect the community from disease through provision for notification of infectious diseases and such measures for isolation and disinfection as are deemed necessary. Special regulations concern seaport and airport health control. Acts regulating the production and sale of food and drugs have to be enforced and control of slaughter houses carried out. The local sanitary authority is also responsible for pest control. Under various Acts local authorities also provide public baths, swimming baths, playing fields and recreation grounds, either directly or by grant aiding voluntary organizations, and all these measures contribute towards the community's health.

The full list of environmental health-care measures is very long. Sanitary inspection and control has a lengthy history and has emphatically proved its fundamental importance in any health programme. The mass of regulations and resultant inspections, reports, licences and registrations provide the unglamorous but vital basis to the nation's health programme. Sadly, the environmental health service is grossly under-staffed and under-funded at present. The water boards are about to be privatized, despite mounting criticism of the quality of water supplies. Neglect of these basic services could gravely undermine the nation's standard of health.

The National Health Service meets the bulk of the nation's demand for medical care and together with the public environmental health services it goes far to prevent and treat sickness and improve the health and physique of the people. The service is comprehensive in scope, although other medical services are available outside the NHS. Doctors may practise privately and numerous clinics and nursing homes are run privately, and for these services patients pay. Industry often

offers limited medical care to its employees and several institutions offer their own medical services, such as the student
health centres, but these services are usually limited in scope
and designed to dovetail into the main NHS provision.

POLICY ISSUES IN HEALTH CARE

Health is a complicated field and it is inevitable that the services
designed to maintain and promote it will have considerable
problems to face, particularly financial and organizational.
Shortage of resources remains a major difficulty in all aspects
of medical care, hence the perennial suggestions for a shift
away from the present system, where care and treatment are
largely free at the point of use, towards provision for more
payments by patients for the services they obtain. The arguments in favour of collective provision and financing of health
care are overwhelming from a medical as well as a social point
of view. The full cost of medical care nowadays is too high
and always too unpredictable for the individual to meet it and
there is no intrinsic reason why expenditure on a collective
basis should not be raised to a point high enough to offer the
required standards of care. Good preventive medicine especially requires that there be early and easy access to medical
facilities for all the population. For all these reasons the *main*
costs of providing health services are likely to continue to be
borne by the community as a whole, but greater efforts will
be made to raise some money from individual users through
higher or extra charges.

Anxiety about costs has sharpened with the larger anxiety
about public expenditure as a whole. Since the mid-1970s,
efforts have been made to check the apparently inexorable
growth in public spending, and cuts in services have followed.
Health services have had to accept cuts despite the claim that
they are already short of funds. The most positive aspect of this
has been the emergence of a real attempt to establish priorities
in health care and allocate scarce resources more equitably.

The DHSS followed the announcement, in the government's 1976 White Paper on public expenditure, of a considerable reduction in the planned rate of growth of health

services with the publication of a consultative document entitled *Priorities for Health and Personal Social Services in England*. This set out guidelines for establishing priorities between different client groups and different forms of provision. In the document it was proposed that priority should be given to services for the elderly, the mentally handicapped, children and the mentally ill. Acute services were to receive a lower priority and maternity services were to be reduced overall in consequence of falling birth rates. The need to redistribute resources geographically in favour of deprived areas and regions was emphasized, and, in provision for all client groups, the need to develop community services was stressed. The crucial roles of primary care and of preventive work were restated and the need to develop joint health and social services planning was pointed out.

Most of the policies set out for different groups were not new: the initiative in the priorities document lay in its setting out and roughly costing a balance of priorities between them. Few people have, in fact, quarrelled with the priorities put forward: the relative neglect of geriatric and psychiatric services, regional inequalities in levels of care, and demographic trends such as increases in the elderly population have long been recognized. The consultative document was followed in 1977 by a further discussion paper called *The Way Forward*. This basically endorsed the broad aims and priorities set out in the consultative document but noted some areas requiring adjustment. For example, a higher priority was suggested for provision to meet the special needs of the chronically sick and disabled. In *The Way Forward*, a broad strategy for achieving the desired priorities was set out and there was further discussion of the practical means and planning techniques involved.

The priorities approach was a worthy response to the acute resource problems produced by the cuts in public expenditure. Indeed, some attempt to ration medical care was long overdue. But in setting out commendable objectives and outlining programme budgets the Department of Health had not really gone very far towards the achievement of a more rationally planned and financed NHS. The consultative documents suffered, perhaps inevitably, from vagueness. There was little guidance on how hard-pressed authorities actually were to operationalize the agreed priorities and, although the Department recommended a cost-conscious, critically evaluative approach, it remained guilty of much woolly rhetoric. For example, tribute was paid to the development of community care, but no attempt was made to assess its true value or consider why such slight progress had been made in this area to date. The need for prevention was stressed, but the practical suggestions for achieving it hardly went beyond drawing attention to the DHSS publication *Prevention and Health – Everybody's Business*. This was worthy, but is no substitute for action to control the behaviour (such as fast driving or heavy drinking), or the environmental problems (such as pollution or congestion), that actually contribute so largely to ill-health. Similarly, the high costs of pharmaceutical services were lamented, but tough action to control them was not discussed. In short, the priorities documents were acceptable statements of good intentions rather than an effective blueprint for reform.

Further priorities guidelines for local health and social services authorities were contained in a publication entitled *Care in Action* which appeared in 1981. The need for prevention was again stressed and the role of the voluntary sector emphasized. The handbook listed useful publications relevant to services for the elderly, the mentally ill and handicapped, the physically disabled, children and maternity care, which were grouped together as needing priority attention. Much was familiar: requests for efficiency; assessment and self-audit, and the maintenance of standards, for example. Joint finance to assist the collaboration of health and local authorities was to be increased and the findings of a departmental study group on community care were summarized. This stressed the importance of self-help and the contributions of both the voluntary sector and the private sector, but suggested that community care needed to be carefully defined and would not necessarily prove a cheap alternative to institutional provision.

The most recent review of community care, the report of the working party chaired by Sir Roy Griffiths, similarly advocated the adoption of a mixed economy of welfare – care provided by both voluntary and private sectors, in addition to the work of the public sector. Griffiths suggested that overall control should be retained by local authorities, whose job it would be to provide some local provision for care in the community, whilst also fostering the development of alternative and competing forms of community care. This report was published in early 1988, but controversy over the proposals delayed its implementation. In mid-1989 the government announced that the central recommendation of local authority responsibility for all community care would be acted upon, but doubt remains about the level of funding.

On a similar note to the priorities documents, the report of the Joint NHS/DHSS Resources Allocation Working Party (RAWP) was published in 1976. The RAWP report contained clear proposals for reallocation of resources within the health service between areas rather than groups. The working party recommended that the criteria for allocating the money available for health care should be clearly set out as follows: the size of given area populations and their demographic structure; other health indicators such as local mortality and fertility rates; gaps in existing provision; and contributions made to medical and dental provision. Proposals for allocating resources on such criteria appeared sound enough and, as with the priorities proposals, it could be argued that they were long overdue in a National Health Service that had failed to achieve an equitable distribution of resources. But the detailed working out of the implications of the RAWP proposals caused considerable controversy, especially in the metropolitan areas. Some regions and areas stood to gain by reallocation, but inevitably some were faced with massive cuts in future resources and consequent redundancies and closures. It has not proved easy to shift resources of buildings and staff without arousing a passionate defence of jobs and of traditional provision. The tragedy is that the RAWP report appeared when projected cuts in public expenditure were already threatening existing levels of provision in all areas, so there was a minimum flexibility in the use of resources and maximum resistance to change.

Although the RAWP approach proved to be a useful, albeit crude, formula with which to redress balance in the distribution of health care, the 1989 White Paper, *Working for Patients*, dropped the RAWP formula from future resource allocation calculations. It is to be replaced by a capitation basis which reflects not only the health and age distribution of the population of different health regions, but also the relative costs of providing services. In the White Paper it was argued that regional differences had largely been eradicated in the years of using the RAWP formula, despite the fact that a number of health regions remained under target at the time of the review. Under the new system, the London health regions will receive higher levels of funding than under RAWP, despite the fact that these regions were those that were most above their target, and it seems no further attempts to rectify geographical inequalities in the funding of services are planned.

In the same year as the RAWP report was published, a Royal Commission was appointed as a result of growing discontent over the provision and funding of health care in Britain. The Merrison Report in 1979 was a comprehensive consideration of health services, and also health issues beyond the NHS. Proposals for changes included encouragement for primary health care and preventive health, greater provision for community care and public participation in decision-making in the NHS. The newly elected Conservative government responded with a consultative document, *Patients First*, which adopted one proposal from the Merrison Report, that of abolishing the area health authorities and thereby one level of management in the tiered system, with the aim of simplifiying the NHS structure. Since then the administration of the NHS and the question of resource allocation are issues that have dominated the debate over health care.

Linked to the resource issue and provoking intense political controversy is the question of the relationship between private practice and the NHS. At the creation of the NHS in 1948 the question of the work by NHS medical staff in private practice was resolved by allowing senior medical staff to retain private consulting rooms and private 'pay beds' within NHS hospitals. This caused great acrimony, with those against arguing that it allowed queue jumping for those who could afford it while the full economic costs of treatment were subsidized by the NHS. The health service unions and the Labour Party were both against pay beds in NHS hospitals, and in the mid-1970s the Labour Party made a commitment to phase out a quarter of these beds.

The issue of private health care has more recently focused on private health insurance and the recent growth of American-style private hospitals, which provide treatment on a fee-for-service basis. Private health insurance has grown rapidly in the past decade, with 9 per cent of the population now covered, a large majority of them through their employment. The 1989 White Paper, *Working for Patients*, further boosted private health care, both through the tax subsidies offered to people over retirement age who take out private health insurance, and through the creation of an internal market within the NHS. Thus budget-holding GPs and NHS hospitals can buy health care from the private sector if the terms offered are favourable, and self-governing NHS hospitals can sell treatment in NHS hospitals to both private health insurance companies and private hospitals direct.

The focus of the current government on the structure of the NHS was reinforced with the 1983 Griffiths Report on management, which further modified the system with the introduction of a new function of management at every level down to district. The emphasis on accountability and budgetary control that this new structure brought in reflects the firm commitment of the Conservative government to public expenditure control. This commitment has been expressed in an increasing focus on the management structure of the NHS and a level of funding generally seen to be below the level necessary to maintain standards of health care into the 1990s. In calculating health service funding requirements, account must be taken of the changing population and of growth in medical technology. The proportion of the population who are over retirement age, and particularly the very old, has grown tremendously in the past few years, whilst people with a disability are now living longer also, and these demographic changes mean more money must be spent on the NHS just to maintain the level of service as it is. In addition, new demands on the health services are made by newly discovered diseases, such as AIDS, and developments in medical knowledge and technology that require extra funds to support new methods of treatment. In fact, increases in funding in the NHS in the 1980s did not match these new demands, and in the late 1980s we witnessed unprecedented industrial action and outcry by medical professionals concerned at this under-funding of the health services.

Sadly, the government's answer to the funding crisis has been to attempt to increase efficiency by adopting market mechanisms within the NHS, and to encourage those who can to buy private health care. The question remains whether efficiency in health care can be measured in the same way as efficiency in non-service industries, and whether qualitative judgements, such as the need for care and making treatment accessible, can be involved. The greatest fear is that these are the first moves towards privatizing large parts of the NHS, leaving a residual service for those who cannot afford private health care. The American model is often cited by advisers on the right as an example of the private health care market in operation, but when we consider the large gaps in provision, and the differences in quality of care between rich and poor in that country, the desirability of moving towards such a system in Britain must be questioned.

The survival of a universal, free and comprehensive National Health Service in which the people of Britain can take pride is clearly no longer something that can be taken for granted. The NHS will have to be fought for, politically, by those who use it and by those who work in it, if it is to be maintained as the cornerstone of the welfare state.

NOTES

1 Life expectancy at birth in 1986 was 71.7 years for males and 77.5 years for females.
2 Cmnd 5055. Proposals for health care in Scotland, Wales and Northern Ireland were made separately, but on the same principles.
3 Local government reorganization is described in Chapter 12.

SUGGESTIONS FOR FURTHER READING

Abel-Smith, B., *Value for Money in Health Services* (Heinemann, 1976).
Blaxter, M., *The Health of the Children* (Heinemann, 1981).
Brown, R. G. S., *The Changing National Health Service* (RKP, 1978).

Cartwright, A., *Human Relations and Hospital Care* (RKP, 1964).

Cartwright, A., *Patients and their Doctors* (RKP, 1967).

Cochrane, A. L., *Effectiveness and Efficiency: Random Reflections on the Health Service* (Nuffield, 1972).

Dalzell-Ward, A. J., *Textbook of Health Education* (Tavistock, 1975).

Doyal, L. with Pennell, I., *The Political Economy of Health* (Pluto Press, 1979).

Forsyth, G., *Doctors and State Medicine* (Pitman Medical, 1960).

Ham, C., *Health Policy in Britain* (Macmillan, 1985).

Illych, I., *Medical Nemesis* (Calder & Boyars, 1974).

Jaques, Elliot (ed.), *Health Services* (Heinemann, 1978).

Levitt, R., *The Reorganised National Health Service* (Croom Helm, 1979).

Lindsey, A., *Socialized Medicine in England and Wales* (Oxford University Press, 1962).

McLachlan, G. (ed.), *Problems and Progress in Medical Care*, Series 1–7, 1964–72, *Challenges for Change* (Nuffield, 1971).

Robinson, D., *Patients, Practitioners and Medical Care* (Heinemann, 1978).

Rowbottom, R., *Hospital Organization* (Heinemann, 1973).

Townsend, P., Davidson, N. and Whitehead, M., *Inequalities in Health: The Black Report and the Health Divide* (Penguin, 1988).

4
Education

THE PROBLEM

The formal education system exists to meet the need of individuals to obtain the information and skills necessary to live full, satisfying and capable lives and also the need of society to have a responsible and productive population. When society is a modern, industrialized democracy, as Britain is today, these basic needs are considerably sharpened. A democratic society needs a people who are literate, reasonably well informed about domestic and foreign affairs, and able to exercise their democratic rights in a responsible manner and to participate at a variety of levels in the process of government. An industrialized society demands a skilled population and the scientists, technologists, technicians and business administrators necessary to keep industrial development moving and to compete effectively with foreign competition. As we have become more generally civilized, humane and cultured, we have increased the need for more doctors, social workers, teachers, artists, etc. In other words, the more complex and advanced the social, political and economic organization of the country becomes, the greater is the need for a well-educated people. And as this complexity, and the resultant specialization and differentiation of role, continue, the need for a more advanced education becomes increasingly important to individuals if they are really to use their capacities to the full and find their place in modern society.

Education is the key to success in most walks of life today. Without basic literacy and general knowledge people don't know their way around, they don't know their rights or duties, cannot obtain jobs or command recognition or respect. Without training they cannot so easily advance in their careers or obtain good positions, or earn money and status. Without education people are unable to make full use of the growing amount of leisure that higher productivity brings nor can they benefit from cultural opportunities or develop their personalities and interests widely. Lack of education can result in problems of sickness and mental health and inadequate methods of child care, thus leading to much personal unhappiness and frustration, which might be perpetuated through generations.

Education is clearly vital, and more education both at higher levels and on a more broad and socially relevant basis is increasingly necessary as society progresses. A good deal of education is, of course, an informal process. People learn about life, about themselves, all their lives. Children learn from parents, from older children and from their own observation and experience. But formal education in literacy, in skills, in appreciation of culture and in use of leisure is obviously necessary if learning is to be rapid and integrated, and this has long been recognized. Formal education used to be a voluntary and private concern, but now, although both of these elements are still present, it is primarily a statutory service.

When the state first entered the educational scene during the early nineteenth century it was concerned with elementary education – that is, with reading, writing and arithmetic, together with religious instruction. This was because the need for a literate population became urgent with the advent of democracy, industry and urbanization. By the end of the century, as industry grew more competitive, the need for skilled workers increased and there was a corresponding development of vocational training in technical colleges and central technical schools. Secondary education and higher education were at that time the preserve of a privileged minority consisting of the wealthy who could finance their own education and the exceptionally bright who won scholarships. But gradually the statutory provision widened to bring secondary and higher education within the reach of more and more individuals as the need to make use of the potential talent and capacity throughout the population became more apparent. Today the statutory system is concerned with the whole range of educational facilities, as it acknowledges both the need for more and better-educated people and the right of people to education.

An effective education system should be constantly adapting to the social and economic changes within society. It should be highly sensitive to these changes and able quickly to reflect them by developing the training most suitable for individuals and the output of skills most needed by the country at any given time. Education is, of course, itself a powerful instrument of social change, which can do a great deal to advance or retard developments in the pattern of life and work of any society. So there is also much room for discussion on the philosophy of education as well as on its more practical aims and the effectiveness of its methods.

Unfortunately the education system tends to lag behind many changes of emphasis in the organization and structure of society. For example, it was slow to reflect in its curricula and the extent of provision an increasing emphasis upon science and technology in industry, politics, war, etc. Consequently many individuals have finished their formal education lacking the necessary skills and information for success in a technological age, while the country has experienced a grave shortage of certain kinds of scientists, technologists and technicians. Similarly, higher productivity has resulted in greatly increased leisure for all classes, but there has not been a rapid enough development of education for leisure so that far too many people constantly and passively require entertaining, instead of being able to use some of their free time in a creative and satisfying way. Even more subtly, changes in Britain's social structure and international role have not been reflected adequately in her education system. We still tend to have an elitist system, concentrating on the production of a handful of top people rather than on maximizing the potential of the bulk of the population. We still tend to emphasize qualities more suitable for imperial control than for competitive business management. That the system lags behind the very changes it should be in the van of is partly because education very easily acquires powerful traditions that can frustrate changes in its aims and organization. These are reinforced by the natural reluctance of the current adult population – among them Her Majesty's Inspectors (HMIs), the education officers, teachers, and so on, who are now responsible for the system – to admit that there is anything wrong with a system that was a vital formative influence on them: to do so would be tantamount to criticizing themselves as products of the system. But clearly there are no absolutes in education, no right or wrong systems. The aim should be a system capable of changing with society and sometimes itself capable of contributing to change. So it should essentially be flexible and dynamic. One of the major problems of the British system is the pervasion of a heavy nostalgia for the old ways, which precludes a more objective assessment of contemporary educational needs.

THE PRESENT SYSTEM

The education system is largely administered by central and local government. At central government level the Department of Education and Science, working for the Secretary of State for Education, is responsible for national educational policy. It is concerned with the whole range of educational provision from nursery schools to higher education. Two central Advisory Councils for Education, one for England and one for Wales, advise the Department on educational policy. They have been responsible for the production of several important reports, such as the Newsom Report of 1963, entitled *Half our Future*, which was concerned with the secondary education of children of average and below-average ability. There is also a central inspectorate, which is nominally an independent service under the Crown rather than a ministerial body, in the hope that this will ensure standards are maintained without undue political control of education. HMIs aim to advise and encourage schools and ensure some

uniformity of standards throughout the country. They visit
and report on schools and colleges but see their role more
as one of positive advice and support-giving than one of rigid
investigation.

At local level the local authorities have considerable responsibility for education. They are the actual providers of the
services: they build the schools, employ the teachers and
carry out all the duties laid down by the 1944 Education Act.
Following local government reorganization there were 104
local education authorities (LEAs), comprising the thirty-nine
counties of England and eight of Wales, the metropolitan
district authorities, the outer London Boroughs and the Inner
London Education Authority (ILEA). Since the Education
Reform Act of 1988 dismantled ILEA, all the London Boroughs, inner and outer, are now LEAs.

The 1944 Education Act, often referred to as the Butler Act
since it was under Lord Butler's presidency of the then Board
of Education that it was passed, is the legislative basis of the
present state system of education. It provides for three stages
of education: primary, secondary and further. Primary and
secondary education are available free and are compulsory
between the ages of 5 and 16. The majority of schools are
provided and run directly by the local education authorities, but voluntary bodies (mostly religious) also provide
premises as assisted schools at which running costs (mostly
teachers' salaries), are met by the local authority. Private
or independent schools, often confusingly known as public
schools, are financed largely by fees charged for attendance,
and they remain outside the state system except that some
are registered as efficient by the central department.

Nursery education

LEAs can provide education for children from the age of 2
but have provided it only for a small minority to date. The
importance of nursery education has long been recognized
but it has never been given much priority. Educationally the
pre-primary school years are very important. This is when
children can get used to the idea of school gradually. They
have the opportunity to meet and mix with other children

and so enhance their social and emotional development. Their intellectual ability, especially in language and creativity, is also stimulated and their physical development aided. Nursery education prepares a child for primary education and is particularly valuable for children from homes where, for a variety of reasons, they may receive little effective encouragement or preparation for schooling. It is also of considerable benefit to mothers if their young children can attend nursery schools, as it releases them for part of the day either for work or for giving more attention to younger children.

For all these reasons an extension of nursery schooling has been urged for many years, but the number of places remained small until the late 1960s. As part of the urban aid programme, local authorities were then encouraged to provide more nursery schools, especially for children in deprived areas, and some development took place. In 1972 a White Paper, *Education: A Framework for Expansion*, outlined the government's proposal to make, over a ten-year period, nursery schooling available without charge to all children aged 3 and 4 whose parents wished them to benefit from it. As a result of this, a start was begun on the expansion of nursery education, which meant that the proportion of children aged 3 and 4 who benefited from a nursery place more than doubled, from just over 20 per cent in 1971 to nearly 48 per cent in 1983. Most of this growth, however, was through the development of nursery classes attached to primary schools. Such classes are primarily for the older child who is 'rising 5' and many of them only take the children part time. There has been little or no growth in nursery schools as such.

This expansion was long overdue and the scale of it should not be exaggerated: the proportional increase was as much due to a fall in the numbers of children in the age range as to an increase in places. With the present trend of an increase in the birth rate there needs to be further expansion of places if the proportion is not to decline again. The benefits of nursery education, for the parents as well as for the children, have been well documented. They are particularly relevant for children who suffer the multiple deprivations of life in the decaying areas of large cities and for children from ethnic minorities who have language difficulties and who may experience racial harassment and discrimination.

The comparative neglect of this area of provision by the education authorities has led to considerable development of private and voluntary activity. The most important and dramatic example of this has been the growth of the pre-school playgroup movement. Playgroups exist to provide the social benefits and often the educational benefits of nursery education in an informal setting. Many groups began on a neighbourhood basis, mostly using the mothers of the children concerned to staff the groups on a part-time rota and using a variety of make-shift premises. In 1961 the Pre-school Playgroups Association was formed to aid and encourage the spread of groups, most of which can now obtain grants for equipment and accommodation from the local authority. The development of these groups is now vital in view of cuts in local authority nursery education. Playgroups have been criticized for their predominantly middle-class character, but they have played a vital part in developing awareness of the needs, both of children and of their mothers, and in showing what can be done by involving people in the organization and running of the services they need and want.

Primary education

Primary schooling is currently provided for children in two stages: infants from 5 to 7, years and juniors aged 7 to 11. All children receive a primary education, many beginning before the age of 5. The emphasis throughout primary education is on development, activity and experience rather than on the acquisition of facts. There is a real attempt to involve the children in the learning process rather than to dictate to them. Primary schools are fairly small, the majority of the present number (something under 25,000 schools), catering for around 100–200 children. Numerous experiments in educational method are under way, especially in new methods of learning to read and in the 'new maths'. At their best Britain's primary schools are very fine, stimulating, flexible and humane, offering an excellent opportunity for children to develop confidence and capacities and awaken interest in learning. But the best is not always available. Far too often the aims of primary schooling are frustrated by inadequate premises, lack of suitable equipment and a shortage of teachers, which lead to over-large classes and high staff turnover.

In 1967 the Central Advisory Council for Education (England) produced a report on primary schools, having been invited in 1963 'to consider primary education in all its aspects, and the transition to secondary education'. This report, the Plowden Report, made some very important recommendations and gave a detailed analysis of the existing situation. It pointed clearly to the fact that some schools were falling well below acceptable standards both in material and in educational terms. Among its suggestions were some for improving relationships between schools and parents and the development of schools that were more integrated with the communities they served. Most importantly, it recommended a national policy of 'positive discrimination'. This involved the designation of educational priority areas (EPAs): areas where general social conditions were poor. The Plowden analysis of existing schools had shown to some extent that poor areas had 'poor schools'. The new policy was to bring the schools of poor areas up to the level of the best, in part to compensate the children for their social deprivation. To this end they were to be given extra books and equipment, priority in building and improvement plans, and encouragement to attract and retain good teachers by offering an additional payment at EPA schools. Numbers in classes were to be limited and teachers' aides recruited to provide more adult contact with the children.

The Plowden policy was a new departure, insisting that equality of opportunity in education could only be achieved if there was positive discrimination in favour of the most under-privileged. Some efforts were made to implement its recommendations. The expansion of nursery education, with priority for deprived areas, was tentatively begun. Educational priority schools received some extra help for new building, and a substantial programme for the replacement of unsatisfactory premises, initiated in 1972–3, further emphasized the need to shift educational building resources towards the primary schools. Teacher training and recruitment were reviewed and attempts made to improve links between schools and colleges of education, while generally a good deal of interest and discussion were focused on primary education.

Arising out of the Plowden Report a small programme of action research began in 1968 to experiment in ways in which an educational priority policy could best be implemented and to evaluate its results. The research team, led by A. H. Halsey, were concerned to link their study of the practical difficulties and methods of compensatory schooling with the broader aims of education and more especially the place of educational policy in the context of wider social and economic problems. Their findings were published in 1972 as *Educational Priority: EPA Problems and Policies*. As with the Plowden Report, it is difficult to summarize the report's findings because the issues involved are so complex. But at a simple level the Halsey Report endorsed the validity of an educational priority area approach, emphasized the value of a pre-school education, and claimed that it was possible to improve the links between home, school and work towards the creation of community schools.

Secondary education

Secondary education is provided for children of 11–19 years. After the 1944 Education Act, a tripartite system prevailed in secondary education: that is, children were sorted out, usually by the now-notorious 11+ examination, for grammar, technical or modern schools. This system was partly the natural outcome of the historical development of secondary education, which at first was available only to the minority of very able or relatively well-to-do children. In part, also, it was the consequence of the belief that different children required different kinds of education reflecting their wide variation in aptitude and ability. Not all children, it was felt, would want or benefit from the traditional grammar school education and an alternative, but not necessarily inferior, pattern should be developed in the new 'modern' secondary schools.

In the event, roughly 25 per cent of children received an 'academic education', mostly in grammar schools, after the

1944 Act. This in practice tended to mean an emphasis on book learning and training for the examinations that give access to higher education, currently the General Certificate of Secondary Education and the advanced General Certificate of Education. A wide range of subjects were taught and as many pupils as possible encouraged to obtain some GCE qualifications and stay on for specialized sixth-form work well beyond the minimum school-leaving age. For some children, technical schools offered a less academic and more vocationally oriented education, still with some emphasis on study for examination.

For the remaining 75 per cent, secondary modern schools aimed to provide a good general education, usually up to school-leaving age, with little or no interest in examinations, until the Certificate of Secondary Education was introduced in 1965 to give secondary modern school children some chance of leaving with formal assessment. These schools varied enormously in character and quality. At best some real attempts were made to provide a rich educational experience for the child of average and below-average ability. Courses were made as stimulating and as socially relevant as possible. But some schools, especially those in inadequate premises, tended to become little more than minding places where children waited apathetically or sullenly for release to the adult world of work. Increasingly it was realized that much of secondary modern education failed to develop the capacities and potential of many pupils and the whole concept of the tripartite selective system of secondary education was powerfully attacked and partially replaced by comprehensive schooling.

The tripartite selective system was criticized on several grounds, some of them educational and others social. Over the years doubts arose about the accuracy and fairness of the actual selection, since it proved very difficult to measure innate rather than acquired ability. Clearly a child's background, particularly as regards parental attitudes towards education, and the quality of primary schooling, were influencing the selection. Surveys tended to show that the selection of pupils for grammar schools was biased in favour of the middle-class child of a small family from a good area.

Moreover, the percentage of places available to children for grammar schooling varied widely over the country, so that geography rather than ability could determine a child's type of schooling. The concept of the late-developer became generally accepted: the idea that some children would not demonstrate their full potential at the age of 11, however fair the test. On social grounds, it was argued that the division of children into different kinds of schools exacerbated class differences. On psychological grounds, it was claimed that the failure of children at the age of 11 to reach the grammar school entrance standard could thwart their further intellectual development and encourage anti-social attitudes. Undoubtedly, the fair concept of different schools for different types of children had been turned, by many people, into a strong division between good schools for the clever and successful, and dumping grounds for the failures and rejects. Despite the actual quality of the education offered, many secondary modern schools were perceived as inferior to grammar schools and many pupils, and their parents, therefore sensed failure rather than sensible selection when allocated to them. But the main and overwhelming argument put forward was that the existing system, because of the discouraging effect it had on many children and the inferior academic opportunity it offered them, failed to make good use of the nation's resources of ability, and the country could not afford this wastage. Far too many children were leaving school at the minimum school-leaving age or well before they had reached the level of education their ability warranted, and most, though not all, of this wastage was from the secondary modern schools.

There were strong arguments on the other side, however, defending the existing tripartite system. Many people felt that the alternative system of comprehensives would produce schools that would be too large and impersonal, that the brightest children would be held back and the dullest make no greater progress. It was held that, if teaching was to be possible at all, streaming would be necessary and this would be as socially and psychologically damaging as selection for different schools. Much of the opposition was inevitably based on prejudice rather than facts about comprehensive schooling, since experience of it was limited. But a telling and practical argument undoubtedly lay in the vast expense that would be involved in reorganization, particularly when other education priorities, such as the raising of the school-leaving age, were being canvassed. Also, in many areas the sheer physical difficulties of utilizing the existing pattern of school building along different lines were very daunting. But the main argument against reorganization was focused on the folly of destroying what was good in the existing system for the sake of a rather intangible idea of educational equality. To many people, the prospect of the end of the separate identity of the grammar schools, some of them with centuries of tradition and high academic standards, seemed one of wanton destructiveness. Others felt that the best of the modern schools would be sacrificed in comprehensives dominated by grammar school practices and aspirations.

The debate over comprehensive or selective education became a party political issue and different governments urged different solutions on the local education authorities. For several years there were experiments with different systems, but in 1965 all LEAs were asked to submit schemes to the Department of Education and Science for the reorganization of their secondary education on comprehensive lines. Most authorities did so and non-selective education became the norm for secondary as well as primary education. Over the next decade the percentage of secondary pupils in maintained schools attending comprehensives rose from around 8 per cent to just over 75 per cent. Several LEAs were reluctant, however, to comply with the 1965 circular and many managed to retain a degree of selectivity and some grammar school education. They were rewarded for their determination when the government changed and in 1970 revoked the offending circular. A further change of government brought a reissue of the circular in 1974 and, when this still failed to produce plans for comprehensive reorganization from a small number of LEAs, an Education Act was passed in 1976 to enforce this. Despite the legislation, however, it remains difficult to force a policy for non-selective education on local authorities that are profoundly opposed to it, and a certain amount of selectivity seems likely to remain.

The great tragedy of this battle over secondary school reorganization is that so much of it has been fought out on political, emotional or financial grounds while the real educational issues have been neglected. The organization of a secondary school system is important, but more important is the content and quality of the education provided within it. And there have been grave reservations about this, in particular about its suitability, at academic and at general levels, for children of the present technological, leisured and rapidly changing age. Two important reports have been issued by the Central Advisory Council for Education (England) relevant to this issue. The first, the Crowther Report, published in 1959, was concerned with the education of children aged 15 to 18. It recommended the raising of the school-leaving age, more technological education, proper courses for modern school pupils leading to an external examination and the creation of county colleges for sixth-form pupils. It also canvassed the concept of 'minority time', for the grammar school children in particular, to ensure the literacy of scientists and the numeracy of arts specialists, urged the development of a strong youth service, and made suggestions for the improvement of technical education.

The Crowther Report contained a wealth of material about background changes in population structure, social and economic needs, etc., as well as much information and advice on how to make the education system more relevant to the society and age group it was designed to serve. Unfortunately not all its recommendations have been taken up, at least with the necessary vigour.

A rather similar fate awaited the Newsom Report, *Half our Future*, which pointed out that the children concerned would in time constitute half the country's citizens, workers, parents, etc., and they deserved, accordingly, rather more attention than the existing system gave them. Apart from many detailed recommendations, the Newsom Report was important in stating authoritatively that 'there is much unrealized talent, especially among boys and girls whose potential is masked by inadequate powers of speech and the limitations of home background. Unsuitable programmes and teaching methods may aggravate their difficulties . . . the country cannot afford this wastage, humanly or economically speaking'.

Among its many suggestions for improving the situation were, once again, the raising of the school-leaving age, research into teaching techniques to help backward children, particularly those with linguistic handicaps, development of audio-visual aids and improved curricula to make subjects more relevant and interesting to the pupils.

In 1972 the school-leaving age was raised to 16. As indicated, this had been advocated for many years and strongly recommended by the reports of the Central Advisory Council, but it has not been an unequivocal success. By the time it was implemented many secondary schools had been dominated by the selective/comprehensive battle for several years and far too little attention had been paid to the development of curricula suitable for non-academic adolescents. Many of the new comprehensive schools are very large and impersonal; others are still coping with unsuitable collections of old buildings. Most importantly, too many schools lack staff who understand the objectives of a comprehensive approach. Many teachers are baffled and threatened by reluctant school children who can see little gain from prolonging their education, and many would prefer to concentrate attention on the more academic. As a result, secondary education in general and comprehensive schools in particular have been having a difficult time in recent years. Some improvements have been made to teaching methods and curricula and some schools have attempted to provide a broad and relevant education for their pupils. But many are still dominated by outmoded concepts, values and regulations and as a result truancy levels are high, especially among the older children, and discipline problems loom large within the schools. There is clearly a need for much experiment and thought about the meaning of secondary education and some renewal of faith in its importance and value for all children.

Public anxiety and political concern about education, particularly embattled secondary education, led to the initiation of a series of meetings and regional conferences, which became known as the Great Debate on Education. These were initiated by a speech by the Prime Minister in 1976 and culminated in the publication of a Green Paper, *Education in Schools*, in June 1977. Ministers and departmental officials, representatives of LEAs, teachers, employers, trade unions, parents and pupils were all involved in the Great Debate which concerned itself with the school curriculum, assessment of standards, teacher training and school and working life. Many views were aired and the whole exercise was an enjoyable experiment in collective discussion, but the end result was uncontentious and disappointing. Few clear suggestions for change emerged and real dilemmas – for example, deciding between the need to concentrate more on basic skills, lest standards in these should be falling, and the competing need to diversify the curriculum to teach more on topics like careers, sex education and the problem of a multi-racial society – were not faced up to squarely.

The Great Debate was supposedly embarked on because the organizational issue was settled, but clearly the issues of educational structure and success are not so easily separated. It could be argued that some of the continuing problems of education are directly linked to the controversy over selection. Certainly much of the public anxiety about schooling was fuelled by publications such as those known as the Black Papers on education, which appeared from 1968 to 1977, and strongly challenged the egalitarian principles of comprehensive schooling and linked their criticisms of attainment and standards to this challenge. The view that comprehensive schools must lead to lower standards of educational attainment is widely held and canvassed, although there are no convincing facts to support it. Sadly the Great Debate did little to clarify the factual questions over standards and ended with little more than familiar, vague hopes for 'good' schools.

More recently, concern has focused on the issue of public examinations in secondary schools, particularly on the relationship between GCE and CSE examinations. In 1984 proposals to introduce an integrated system of examinations were announced by the Secretary of State for Education. From 1986 the new intake at secondary schools embarked on a curriculum leading to the General Certificate of Secondary Education, and the first GCSE exams were taken in the spring of 1988.

The Education Reform Act of 1988 further changed what is taught in schools with the introduction of a National Curriculum – a basic set of core and foundation subjects that all maintained schools must provide. Whilst the Act does not lay down the timetable to be followed, or the teaching methods or textbooks to be used, it allows the Secretary of State for Education to determine assessment arrangements. The National Curriculum specifies subjects all children will study and sets attainment targets that are to be tested at the end of four key stages of education – at the ages 7, 11, 14 and 16. The Act also introduces a requirement for schools to have collective worship of a broadly Christian character. Parents who wish their child to be excused from this must apply for permission to the school.

Private education

Private education plays a part in all aspects of education but is perhaps most obviously seen as an alternative to state secondary provision. As anxiety about educational standards and disillusion with the state system have increased, especially among the middle classes who greatly mourned the loss of grammar schools, support for the private sector has grown. In addition to private schooling, the direct grant schools provided a much sought after grammar alternative to comprehensives in many areas.

Both private schooling, especially that provided by the prestigious public schools, and direct grant schooling have been heavily attacked for their role in perpetuating an educational elite. The persistence of segregated schools alongside comprehensives tends to cream off some of the more able and academically motivated children. This has made it difficult for the comprehensive school to compete effectively, in terms of proving academic standards, with the segregated system it has only partially replaced. The hold of the public schools in particular over recruitment to key positions in the country's social, political and economic institutions is an extremely tenacious and disquieting one. The public schools accentuate the unequal distribution of rewards and privileges in our society and to many people appear incompatible with democracy.

In 1965 a Public Schools Commission was set up to consider ways in which the public schools could be integrated with the state system. The first report of the commission in 1968 recommended the creation of a Boarding School Corporation to supervise this integration. The second report in 1970 recommended an end to direct grant status and fee-paying schools. Both reports have aroused much controversy but nothing has as yet been done radically to alter the position of independent schools.

An end to direct grants to certain selective schools was announced in 1975. This provoked considerable opposition both from those who wished to save the schools as fine, traditional grammar schools, and from those who feared that such action would result in a strengthening of the independent sector in secondary schooling rather than a reinforcement of the comprehensive ideal. The outcome has indeed been that many former direct grant schools became independent schools rather than allow themselves to be merged with the comprehensives. There does not appear to be any shortage of parents willing and able to pay the fees for this schooling, but several of the long-established schools were genuinely sorry to have to take only those children whose parents could afford private education for them. Traditionally the schools selected pupils on grounds of ability; as independent schools, they lost the talented, but poorer children. Moreover, the schools genuinely believed that the disciplined academic education they offered provided invaluable opportunities for clever children.

This belief, that the very bright child deserves a special chance, is quite widely held, along with the conviction that the comprehensive system must somehow fail such a child. This led in 1980 to the passing of an Education Act that provided for a number of means tested assisted places in independent schools for clever children. The scheme is, naturally, strongly opposed by those who object to the elitist tradition of the independent sector and by those who fear that state comprehensives will be further weakened by a creaming-off process financed from public funds.

Participation

As we have seen in discussing the battle over comprehensive education and the Great Debate on educational standards, potential dissatisfaction with state secondary schooling has been quite marked in recent years. One outcome of this has been the strengthening of the independent sector, but another has been the development of interest in parental rights, particularly rights over choice of school.

Schools differ markedly in terms of their organization, of their success and certainly of their reputation. Recent research has confirmed the strong belief that in terms of both attainment and behaviour it matters which school a child attends, and this has intensified the concern of parents to keep the right to choose their child's school. Unfortunately parental choice is usually exercised by parents wishing to support reputedly good schools often to the neglect and detriment of schools with a poor reputation. All too often the parents' freedom to choose is in conflict with an authority's attempt to keep standards even and help the poorer schools achieve a fairer intake of pupils.

Related to the parental choice issue is the whole question of parental interest in the running of schools. The key question here is to what extent should parents, and for that matter children, share with the state and the teaching profession the responsibility for educating children? A report on this subject was issued in 1977, entitled *A New Partnership for Our Schools*. The Taylor Report, as it came to be known, concerned the composition of the governing bodies of individual schools. It recommended a degree of power-sharing on these bodies between representatives of the LEA, of parents, of teachers and of the local community, and there was much discussion of how representatives could be chosen and of the exact functioning of governing bodies. In the event it seems that, although more parents have been asked to perform more duties on these governing bodies, there is no real shift in the balance of power and no substantial extension of parental rights has actually taken place.

Opting out

The 1988 Education Reform Act also introduced the possibility for schools to 'opt out' of local authority control, by obtaining grant-maintained status. Such schools will receive a maintenance grant from the Secretary of State, rather than local authorities, whilst the property rights and liabilities of the grant-maintained school are transferred from the local authority to the governing body, which then has control over all expenditure on behalf of the school. Pupils will be able to apply to attend schools of their choice within local areas. Whilst the employment of teachers in grant-maintained schools is subject to the same statutory provisions as apply to teachers employed by the local authority, grant-maintained schools will also be able to appoint teachers without qualified status.

The decision as to whether a school should apply for grant-maintained status is taken by a ballot of the parents, which can be instituted either by the school governors or by a minimum number of parents approaching the school governors with a request for a ballot on 'opting out'.

Further education

Turning now to further education (FE), the third arm of the statutory LEA system, this term covers an extraordinarily wide field – from the big technical colleges to the local evening institute. 'Education' here is broadly interpreted to cover the vocational, cultural, social and recreational needs of everyone over school-leaving age who is not in full-time secondary or higher education.

The main concern of further education, in terms of resources devoted to it, is vocational training, mostly of a technical nature. The main fields of study are: technology – in engineering, building, etc.; commerce and social studies; art and design; service trades, such as catering; and GCE overlap courses. These studies are catered for in a variety of technical colleges, art colleges, colleges of commerce, etc.

A programme of expansion and reorganization from 1957 to 1962 graded colleges according to the level of courses offered and the type of qualification that could be obtained by students, and began the deliberate process of concentrating higher-level studies in fewer colleges serving wider areas. Colleges were accordingly designated local technical colleges, area colleges and regional colleges. At the top of the pyramid were a few colleges of advanced technology but these were soon given independent university status.

The next step of reorganization was to convert the regional centres into polytechnics, which offer advanced courses in a variety of fields, often as a result of combining colleges of technology, commerce and art into single polytechnics. This policy of concentration was made explicit in a White Paper, *A Plan for Polytechnics and other Colleges*, published in 1966, which provided for higher education in the further education system. Henceforth, as an alternative to a much greater expansion of the universities, polytechnics have offered degree-level work and opportunities for research while maintaining to some extent their technological bias and links with industry, commerce and the professions. This development, offering as it does an alternative opportunity for higher education outside the universities, resulted in there now being a binary system in higher education, a situation that many educationalists find disturbing. However, it has indubitably led to a concentration of resources on polytechnics and rapid growth in buildings, staff and student numbers and scope of courses.

Most recently, and in line with the current government's emphasis on privatization, polytechnics have been separated off from local authority control. Since April 1989 they have had independent status as self-governing institutions financed directly by central government through the Polytechnics and Colleges Funding Council. Their governing bodies have strengthened the links with industry.

The courses provided at local technical colleges and area colleges are mostly on a part-time basis, taking students on day release or evenings or, nowadays, on block release from employment. Many of the courses are expected to dovetail into the practical training provided by industry in order to provide fully trained craftsmen, technicians and skilled workers.

On the industrial side, the 1964 Industrial Training Act was designed to improve the training offered by the traditional apprenticeship system and put it on a more equitable and uniform basis. Industrial training boards now operate for most industries to bring together the employers and the education authorities and ensure that adequate training is provided.

On the technical college side, the courses offered lead to a bewildering variety of qualifications, such as the City and Guilds Craft Examinations and the Ordinary and Higher National Certificates. For degree-level work the Council for National Academic Awards was created, but this work is now concentrated in the polytechnics. The Haslegrave Report of the Committee on Technicians' Courses and Examinations, issued in 1969, made recommendations that have led to the establishment of Councils for Technician and Business Education which aim to keep the courses and examinations relevant to the vocational needs they serve. These include a variety of careers in industry and commerce, so the range of work done, in terms of both subject matter and level attained, is astonishingly large. Technical education contributes enormously both to the nation's demand for skilled personnel and the individual's need to obtain education and training to the level he wants and desires. However, much development could still take place to ensure that more young people, especially girls, have the opportunity to benefit from further education.

On the cultural and recreational side of further education, LEAs provide a wide range of classes under the general heading of adult education. Classes are run at adult education institutes or centres, often situated in local schools or FE colleges, mostly on a once-a-week basis, although some LEAs run adult education colleges offering short-term residential courses. Adult education is run in cooperation with voluntary bodies, notably the Workers Education Association and with the extra-mural departments of the universities. Domestic subjects, physical activities, arts and crafts, music and drama, foreign languages and practical skills account for the bulk of adult education, with a limited input of more academic courses.

Adult education was the subject of a searching review, which resulted in a report, *Adult Education: A Plan for Development*, published in 1973. The Russell Report endorsed the need for adult education and recommended the establishment of national and local development councils to encourage and guide the expansion of the service. The report indicated that existing adult education was not sufficiently directed towards the disadvantaged and the educationally deprived. An Advisory Council for Adult and Continuing Education was established by the Secretary of State for Education and Science in 1977. The Council exists to advise generally on all matters relevant to the education of adults 'with full regard to the concept of education as a process continuing throughout life'. An Adult Basic Education Committee was established because the Council's first task was to report on a strategy for the basic education of adults. This followed an adult literacy campaign in the mid-1970s that had demonstrated the scale of educational deprivation among the adult population. The need to provide basic education for adults, including literacy and numeracy and the teaching of English as a second language, is now recognized alongside the traditional cultural and recreational provision.

Further education is also responsible for the statutory youth service. Most LEAs have a youth officer and provide a network of clubs, outdoor pursuits centres and the like. In 1960 the Albemarle Report on the Youth Service was published, which recommended that the youth service, as part of education, be considerably expanded and developed. The Youth Service Development Council was established to foster discussion and monitor progress and considerable experimentation took place in the following decade. Particular efforts have been made to reach the young people who were not interested in the traditional clubs and formal youth organizations. Detached youth workers have been appointed in many areas and informal coffee bars and centres opened. Much of the experimental work has been undertaken by voluntary organizations, encouraged and grant-aided by the LEAs.

The Development Council examined the future of the youth service in a report published in 1969. Entitled *Youth and Community Work in the Seventies*, the report recommended that the youth service become increasingly community oriented. For the older age group, especially, it was felt that the work should be flexible and involve young people themselves more directly in running their own organizations and projects. More contact should be made with local agencies, firms and trade unions and more use made of existing facilities, especially educational ones. The hope was that youth workers could help young people to take a more involved and participating part in the development of their society. No formal action has been taken on the report and the council itself was wound up, but the trend throughout the country has been for youth workers to move out into the community wherever possible.

Special education

A further important responsibility of the LEAs under the 1944 Education Act is the provision of special education. This is provided for children who are handicapped and may be in special residential or day schools or in special classes within existing schools. Some schooling is also provided in hospitals for school-age children there and a peripatetic service is available for children bedridden in their own homes. Special education has to be provided for the following groups: children who are blind, partially sighted, deaf, partially hearing, epileptic, physically handicapped, delicate, emotionally maladjusted, educationally sub-normal, have speech defects and, since 1971, who are mentally handicapped. Many of the special schools, particularly the residential schools, are in fact provided by voluntary organizations and the LEAs pay to send their children to them.

By far the largest category of pupils requiring special education are the educationally sub-normal. For these children and for the maladjusted children there is difficulty in finding enough places in the schools. The relative newness of responsibility for the mentally handicapped, who were previously looked after by local health departments in junior training centres, means that there is a need for development of schools for this group. For other groups the provision appears to be adequate.

However, there has been growing controversy over the manner in which provision is made. Some educationalists argue that all children should, where possible, be brought up in the same schools and that to segregate the handicapped child is to add social difficulties to the sensory or emotional ones he or she already possesses. Moreover, many children suffer from having to go to boarding schools, as it is usually uneconomical to provide day schools for small numbers and there is a limit to the amount of daily travelling children can be expected to cope with. If they can attend their local schools they can remain in their own homes. There has, therefore, been some movement towards making this kind of provision available but, at the same time, some tendency to provide even more specialized schooling for different groups. For example, schools are being provided for spastics or for spina bifida children. And within certain categories, e.g. blind children, special provision has been made for the brighter children capable of benefiting from a more academic education. Most of these specialized schools are provided by voluntary organizations, which argue that the very particular needs of the groups they cater for demand completely specialized provision.

In 1978 the Warnock Committee produced its report, *Special Education Needs*. This set out a whole new framework for special education with the emphasis being on the children's needs rather than on their categories of handicap. An Education Act was passed in 1981 to implement the main recommendations. It proposed to extend the local authorities' duties to make suitable educational provision for children under and over compulsory school age; to introduce new procedures for the identification of children with special needs; and to provide for a new definition.

On the question of integration, the Warnock Committee had endorsed the provisional ruling of the 1976 Education Act, which requested local authorities to arrange for children with special needs to be educated in ordinary schools wherever possible. The new legislation replaced this and hence emphasized that integration was to be the norm except where it would be quite impracticable or incompatible with efficiency. It is to be hoped that authorities will continue to be reasonably flexible in making their provision, as there cannot be a hard and fast ruling in every case on what is or is not practicable or efficient. What undoubtedly is needed is more provision of specialized teacher-training courses, so that staff are available with additional qualifications to teach the handicapped child. Courses are provided, especially for teachers of the blind, the deaf and the maladjusted child, but the output is not nearly great enough. More attention should also be given to the questions of vocational training and the transition from school to work, which present particular problems for the handicapped school leaver. Handicapped pupils remain at school at least until the minimum age of 16, but of course much of their time is taken up with overcoming their disabilities rather than on general learning, so many need even more time before they can benefit from vocational courses. Although some colleges offering pre-vocational courses are now available, more needs to be done in this field. On the placement side, the links with the careers service are being improved, but the need here is for continuous assessment during the school career rather than a final discussion at school-leaving age. For some severely handicapped pupils the possibility of liaison with social services departments providing occupational and social welfare services for the handicapped is to be encouraged.

Other local authority responsibilities

A careers service is provided by LEAs to offer vocational guidance to young people when they are at schools or colleges, and to help them find employment when they leave. It is particularly important for the majority of young people who do not proceed to higher education. The service should help ease the transition from school to work, and ensure that young people are aware of the full range of job and training opportunities open to them. It is especially valuable now when unemployment is high and youth unemployment a very serious problem.

The careers officers have access to reports on the young people's ability and progress at school and on their health and general character. They should also have detailed knowledge of the availability of local employment and training. They discuss each young person's future career with them and with parents, taking account of ability and interests, and make available both advice on careers and information about actual jobs.

The careers service was reorganized under the Employment and Training Act 1973, which provided for major changes in the provision of employment services. Under this Act, the independent Manpower Services Commission was established to take over training from the Department of Employment. For the careers service, the LEAs remained responsible directly to the Secretary of State for Employment. Under the MSC there were three main divisions, concerned with employment services, training services and special programmes.

One such special scheme was the Youth Opportunities Programme, which aimed to provide short courses to prepare young people for work and to offer a variety of work experience. The scheme was widened in 1981 following a White Paper on training, and under the Youth Training Scheme (YTS) young people were able to obtain some basic work experience whilst receiving a modest weekly allowance. Although the scheme can help young people learn more about industry, and their own aptitudes and interests, it can easily be abused as cheap labour. In the past, take-up has been low, although recent changes to social security legislation that prevent young people not on a YTS scheme from claiming income support are designed to increase take-up by removing alternatives to participation in the scheme.

In 1988 the MSC became the Training Commission, and many of the former responsibilities of the MSC – such as help to the unemployed in finding paid work and responsibility for sheltered employment – were passed to the Department of Employment. The Training Commission – or Training Agency as it became in September 1988 – retained responsibility for YTS and in addition founded a new scheme, Employment Training. ET is aimed primarily at 18–24 year olds who have been unemployed for six months or more, and is a mixture of directed and practical training leading to a qualification. Like YTS, ET has been criticized as being disguised unemployment. Most importantly, schemes such as YTS and ET, however well meant, cannot in the long run help young people to find jobs that simply do not exist.

Schools, especially primary schools, have had a long tradition of concern over the health and welfare of children. Before health care was more generally available, the school health service provided medical and dental examination for all school children. After 1948, the service was operated by the local health authorities, although it retained a separate administrative identity. It is now one of the responsibilities of the health authorities to ensure that schools are provided with facilities for examination and health education. Regular check-ups can play an important part in preventive medicine, especially if adequate treatment facilities are made available and parents are kept closely informed of their children's medical and dental state.

Some education authorities run child guidance clinics for the special treatment of emotionally disturbed children. In other areas, this facility is provided by the health authority. Child guidance clinics operate on a team basis, with help offered by psychiatrists, social workers, psychologists and therapists to both parents and children in the handling of problems of maladjustment. The school psychological service provides facilities for assessment of children with learning difficulties. Speech therapy clinics are also available to help children with speech defects.

The provision of such special facilities varies considerably in different authorities. In large cities there tends to be a greater range of specialist services for children with problems than exists in rural areas. For some problems, such as dyslexia, provision of help is very slight and uneven and can often depend on whether individual teachers, psychologists or parents have taken an interest and urged action.

Some general welfare facilities may be provided by schools such as school meals, milk in infant schools, and special transport facilities. Despite rising standards of living, it is still the case that a significant number of children cannot make the best use of such education as is offered to them because of family poverty. To alleviate this a small amount of help is available – for example, free school meals, clothing grants and maintenance grants for helping with the costs of keeping children on at school beyond the minimum school-leaving age. Unfortunately, such selective benefits are not as well used as they should be, partly because of the complexity of means tests and partly because of the stigma that is attached to receipt of such services as free meals. Even where these services are made use of, there are many activities at schools – outings, holidays, extra lessons and such like – that increasingly form part of the total education provision, for which money is needed that poorer families can ill afford. This is certainly an area where positive discrimination could well be applied to ensure that all children in schools can make the fullest use of the facilities available.

Investigation of cases of need is one of the tasks of the education welfare service. Education welfare officers visit schools and families checking on cases of truanting and non-attendance, assessing families for grants, and working with families where there are problems of child neglect or juvenile delinquency. Some workers are school based and do counselling work with children who have difficulties.

Following the creation of unified social services departments in 1970, there was considerable discussion about the future of education welfare officers. It was suggested that social services should provide social workers for the schools, but this was resisted by many educationalists who felt that there was some advantage in an education-based welfare service. In recent years local authorities have been allowed to experiment with different patterns of organization, and the administrative issue is still unclear. But whichever department operates the services it is clear that the social needs of children can often be recognized at school and there is a great need for social workers to help make the link between home and school as effective as possible.

HIGHER EDUCATION

The universities are not strictly a part of the statutory education system as they are independent, self-governing institutions. A large part of their income, however, now comes from the Exchequer. The Universities Funding Council, which apportions this income, links the central government department with the separate universities and attempts to define a national policy for higher education. Moreover, LEAs play their part in providing grants for the payment of fees and for maintenance of students from their areas who enter on courses at colleges and universities.

A committee was appointed in 1961 by the Prime Minister under the chairmanship of Lord Robbins 'to review the pattern of full-time higher education in Great Britain and in the light of national needs and resources to advise HM Government on what principles its long term development should be based . . .' The Robbins Report, published in 1963, contained a detailed analysis of patterns of higher education in universities, colleges of education and colleges of further education. It recommended dramatic expansion of the numbers in higher education from the figure of 8 per cent of the age group that obtained at the time of the report to one of 17 per cent of the age group by 1980/1. The increase in places was to be achieved by the foundation of some new universities and by the expansion of technological education through the creation of technological universities and special institutions for scientific and technological education and research. Some of Robbins' recommendations – for example, for the setting up of a Council for National Academic Awards degrees for work in regional and area colleges and for the introduction of degree courses for suitable teacher-training candidates – have been implemented. Expansion has certainly taken place both in the older established universities and in some new foundations. The number of students admitted and taking degrees more than doubled in the decade after Robbins. By 1986/87 there were 350,000 UK students taking degrees at universities, together with a further 57,000 students from overseas.

In addition to expansion of numbers of university students, there was also dramatic growth in opportunities for higher education in the new polytechnics, as was mentioned in the section on further education. It was envisaged that expansion of higher education within further education would continue until it took up roughly half the demand. The opportunities for education offered by universities and polytechnics would continue to include degrees in a wide range of subjects, postgraduate work of a specialist nature, and a variety of vocationally oriented courses. A new shorter two-year course was made available in both sectors of higher education leading to a Diploma in Higher Education.

An important part of higher education, and one that is in some ways a more readily acceptable investment because of its vocational purpose, is teacher training. Most teachers are trained at colleges of education, run either by local authorities or voluntary bodies, but some receive training at universities after graduation. The split between graduate and college-trained teachers has always caused friction and the aim now is ultimately to have an all-graduate teaching profession. Thus the college of education courses are becoming more of a general education with some training and practical experience added.

An inquiry was held into the whole issue of teacher training and the *Report of the Committee on Teacher Education and Training* (the James Report) was published in 1972. Not all its recommendations were taken up, but those concerning expansion of in-service training were accepted and its suggestion of a Diploma in Higher Education was adopted for a wider purpose. The content and standards of teacher-training courses are determined by a balance of the main interests involved – the Department of Education and Science, the LEAs, the universities and the voluntary colleges – with advice from the major professional bodies concerned. Notable among these are the National Union of Teachers, the National Association of Head Teachers, the Association of Teachers of Technical Institutions and the Headmasters' Conference.

It was hoped that by the 1980s the Robbins targets for higher education would have been exceeded and a considerable proportion of the relevant age group would have the opportunity of going on to university or college. But the expansion of higher education was always controversial and it is now a clear target for public spending cuts. Higher education is certainly an expensive service and it has been criticized on the grounds of costs and also in terms of its lack of relevance to the employment situation. Cuts in public spending are now seriously threatening higher education. Measures to force overseas students to pay higher fees were accompanied by financial penalties to those institutions reluctant to discriminate. Severe cuts in grants have followed, necessitating the closure of university departments and threatening staff redundancies. The attack on higher education is to be deplored because it severely reduces opportunities for young people to complete their education and damages the independence and academic standards of the institutions.

It can be seen from this brief survey that the present education system is highly complicated, and evaluations cannot easily be made. At a very simple level the need is for education, which the service provides, compulsorily and free of charge for all children between 5 and 16 and more selectively for young people and adults thereafter. However, one must ask if the education system does meet the needs of the state and of the individual fully – not just does it start to attack basic ignorance, but does it provide the right sort of education on the right levels to satisfy the interests both of the state and the individual?

This sort of question, as the foregoing outline of the system will have shown, is not easily answered. It is easy to say that everyone should have the 'right' sort of education to the right level, but how do we determine, for example, how many years of compulsory education we should have, or how special-ized higher education should become? In addition, there is the question of how achievement is measured, and how we decide what should be taught. There is increasing concern over the need to recognize within education different cultural backgrounds, not only in terms of the curriculum but also in terms of how standards of attainment are assessed. However, this important debate within educational circles has been cur-tailed by the introduction of both the National Curriculum and standards of assessment on the new curriculum, and the compulsory collective worship, which is broadly Christian in nature despite the needs of children from different ethnic and cultural backgrounds.

Moreover, one must ask not only if the education system meets the needs of society, as far as we can determine them, but if it does so in the most just, efficient and economical manner possible. This raises questions about the meaning of equality and the definitions of efficiency in an educational context. Much emphasis has been laid in the past on the education system providing equality of opportunity for everyone to make the most of their lives. More recently it has been seen that, even with educational priority approaches and comprehen-sives, the school can only partly compensate for fundamental deprivations within the family and the community. We are now sharply aware that education alone cannot make amends for poverty, but it still has a major part to play in shaping our society. Constant efforts must be made to understand and assess the education system, to see whether it is appropriate and relevant to the current social and economic structure, whether it does deal fairly with different sections of society, whether it is carried out in an efficient manner.

It is fair to say of the present British system that, while it contains many features of which we may be proud, it has many weaknesses that urgently require remedy. Some of these are relatively practical, like the shortage of good teachers, outmoded premises, shortage of nursery school places, etc. Others are more concerned with the content of courses: whether these are too academic, whether they fail to encourage a lively, critical approach to society, whether they ignore much of what is most relevant in life in failing to teach their students enough about the implications of science, the meaning of aggression, problems of race, conflict and emotion, etc. Education ought to be a reasonably controversial field and most certainly a rapidly changing one, and it ought to be debated against the background of wider moral, philosophical and social issues. It is undoubtedly one of the most fascinating topics of study in the field of social administration.

SUGGESTIONS FOR FURTHER READING

Benn, C. and Simon, B., *Halfway There* (Penguin, 1972).

Blackstone, T., *Fair Start* (Allen Lane, 1971).

Dent, H. C., *The Education System of England and Wales* (University of London, 1963).

Douglas, J. B. W., *The Home and the School* (MacGibbon & Kee, 1964).

Douglas, J. B. W., *All Our Future* (Peter Davies, 1968).

Jackson, B. and Marsden, D., *Education and the Working Class* (Penguin, 1962).

Pedley, R., *The Comprehensive School* (Penguin, 1963).

Reports of the Central Advisory Council for Education (England):
Crowther Report, *15–18* (HMSO 1959).
Newsom Report, *Half Our Future* (HMSO 1963).
Plowden Report, *Children and their Primary Schools* (HMSO 1967).
Swann Report, *Education for All: The Report of the Committee of Inquiry into the Education of Children from Ethnic Minority Groups* (HMSO 1985).

Robinson, E., *The New Polytechnics* (Penguin, 1968).

Rogers, R., *Crowther to Warnock* (Heinemann, 1980).

Rubinstein, D., *The Evolution of the Comprehensive School* (RKP, 1969).

Rutter, M., Maughan, B., Mortimore, P. and Ouston, J., *Fifteen Thousand Hours* (Open Books, 1979).

Troyna, B. and Williams, J., *Racism, Education and the State* (National Youth Bureau, 1986).

5
The housing problem

HOUSING NEED: THE GENERAL PROBLEM

Housing is a very important and very complex issue. The basic need is for all people to have shelter, a roof over their heads. However, this is overlaid with more sophisticated needs for a suitable house, that is, one of the size, price, position, etc., to suit each household's particular requirements. Merely having enough dwellings for the number of households that claim to want one would not remove the housing problem: the question of standards, location, security of tenure and so on would remain. Further, the quality and price of available housing itself influences demand, so the number of households requiring a separate dwelling cannot be calculated without reference to the prevailing standards. Housing need is hard to define and the social policy that is the response to the need is a complex one. There is no one clear social service to cope with such a universal need, and individual and commercial as well as public housing efforts must all be considered in looking at society's total response to the problem.

Apart from the simple need for shelter, many factors contribute to the formation of housing need. Size of dwelling is clearly important: it must be related to the size of a family and its particular way of life; and the type of dwelling – flat or house for example – must also be considered. Location is extremely important: the dwellings must be available in a part of the country that offers suitable employment opportunities and in the immediate locality of shops, schools, transport facilities, and so on. The amenities of the house – standard amenities such as running water, bathrooms, indoor lavatories, and more luxurious amenities such as garages, gardens, etc. – are also important considerations. The condition of a house is vital – whether it is in good structural order, weather-proof and not too damp. Personal tastes interfere in housing need – whether a house is in a socially acceptable area, whether it has charm, seclusion, architectural merit and so on. Finally two major factors are those of price and security: housing must be available at prices, including rents, that people can afford, and rented property must offer reasonable security of tenure.

So, for housing need to be met and a satisfactory housing situation achieved, there would have to be a surplus of dwellings over known households, and a good variety of type and size of dwellings in all parts of the country situated conveniently for access to work, shops, etc. Moreover, these dwellings would have to be in good order, possessing accepted amenities and available at suitable prices and on secure terms. But it is very difficult to ensure a satisfactory situation. One reason for this is the difficulty of forecasting demand. Demand increases, obviously, as the population grows, but it also increases according to the number of potentially separate households that are formed within the total population. The numbers of separate households have tended to increase more rapidly than the overall population because people marry younger, live alone, live longer, etc. New homes must be built to meet this increasing demand. At the same time, existing houses are becoming obsolete or even totally unfit for human habitation, partly because they grow old and decay and partly because standards and accepted amenities change and good housing of a hundred years ago lacks facilities adequate for modern living. Old houses have to be replaced and many houses, while not necessarily in poor condition, are in areas needed for road widening, urban redevelopment, etc. This raises the problem of where to put the new houses. Cities are congested, suburbia sprawls and towns encroach on the countryside, so it is not easy to find room for more and more new homes.

At times the housing problem seems to constitute a crisis that demands a more urgent solution than the steady flow of building targets, planning regulations and so on that are the main lines of housing policy. This is when the supply in terms of numbers and quality of dwellings falls far short of the existing demand. An actual shortage of dwellings results in a variety of social evils. Prices tend to become exorbitant, especially in areas of highest demand. This means the poorest suffer, especially families with several children, as they cannot afford the accommodation they require. Multi-occupation of property occurs, with consequent lowering of standards of privacy and amenity. Overcrowding of small dwellings results in difficulties such as young children lacking space for play and older ones a quiet place to study. Sharing houses with relatives or living in one- or two-roomed flats imposes intolerable strains on marital relationships. High rents lead to arrears of payment and consequent anxiety. If accommodation is not available, or is overcrowded or too expensive, some families literally find themselves homeless and confronted with all the consequent indignity, insecurity and disruption of life. Local authorities have an ultimate responsibility for providing temporary accommodation for the homeless but rarely can this be done without severe damage to the unity and morale of the family. The personal suffering that stems from this situation is so great that one must conclude that the housing position that permits it to occur (except in rare and virtually unforeseen events, such as floods), is seriously unsatisfactory.

The existence of bad standards of housing is as grave as an actual shortage. Where houses are unfit for human habitation there is a clear risk to the health of the occupants. Slum dwellings are frequently damp, verminous, insanitary and structurally unsafe. But slums are equally bad for the morale of their occupants. It is easy to give up caring about personal standards of cleanliness if decoration is rendered futile by damp, and cleaning is arduous because of lack of hot water and corroded or crumbling surfaces. There is a constant, but losing, battle against disease, high infant mortality rates, and general child neglect. Despair at the squalor and a sense of inadequacy in the face of such dreariness can lead to recrimination and argument and become one factor contributing to the misery that leads to broken homes.

The individual house, its price and condition, is very important to the people who live in it, but so also is the environment in which it is situated. Lack of amenities may be tolerable in a country cottage but in urban areas there are no compensations such as fresh air and space around. Where poor-quality housing is massed together, the whole area becomes unfit, as there is a general lack of light, clean air, greenery and open space. Refuse tends to accumulate and noise levels are appallingly high. Moreover, if individual houses are cramped and unattractive their occupants will spend more time outside, children will play on dangerous streets or among refuse and old cars on vacant lots. Older children will stay out late and, lacking facilities on which to expend their energies and test their powers, will the more easily turn to anti-social activities and delinquent behaviour. There is evidence that children from slum areas fail to take enough advantage of educational opportunities and are generally restricted in their development as a result of their environment. Apart from obvious problems such as child neglect and delinquency which are associated with such areas, there is an incalculable loss, hard to estimate or assess but very real, to the people who live in slums in their lack of opportunity to enjoy space and beauty and attractive surroundings and to take pride in their homes and gardens.

Slum clearance is clearly desirable but though it solves many problems it can also create them. The break-up of extended family and neighbourhood ties can put a strain on welfare services, and rehousing on overspill estates can bring its own difficulties. Long journeys to work can tire as well as prove expensive and new estates often lack a sense of friendliness and real community. Loneliness can become a real problem and over-competition in the decoration and embellishment of new homes can lead to severe financial strain. It takes longer to build new communities than it does simply to put up the houses, shops, schools and factories that form their physical structure.

THE HOUSING PROBLEM IN BRITAIN TODAY

The list of damaging personal and social consequences of an unsatisfactory housing situation is a long one. Having looked at the situation in general terms let us now look at the actual situation in Britain today.

Currently there are approximately 21.3 million separate dwellings in Great Britain. Since the 1960s there has been a growing overall excess of dwellings to households and every region can now claim some surplus accommodation. But the extent of the surplus varies considerably, so that some localities still experience actual shortages, and the quality of accommodation available varies so much that there is no room for complacency on the overall figures. The total housing stock increases each year, although new building is offset by losses through clearance and redevelopment. In 1987 there was a total net gain of some 201,000 dwellings, over 11,000 dwellings having been demolished or closed that year.

According to the 1986 English House Condition Survey, fewer than 1 million of the 18 million houses in England were considered unfit for human habitation, 0.5 million lacked basic amenities and 2.4 million were in poor repair. The total number of dwellings with one or more of the three types of deficiency was nearly 3 million in 1986, which was about 15 per cent of the total housing stock. Since that survey took place, more slums have been cleared and more dwellings repaired and improved, but likewise more will have decayed and declined.

The statistics on quantity and basic quality can be regarded as reassuring: there is no longer an acute overall shortage, levels of overcrowding have declined, the outright slums are steadily disappearing and there is a general rise in standards and amenities. But neither the bare statistics, nor the simple historical perspectives demonstrating growth and improvement, fully reveal the complex reality of the housing situation. Housing in Britain remains a highly problematic area and it is necessary to look more closely at certain aspects of it to understand this. One aspect is the remarkable persistence of inferior housing, even of actually unfit housing, despite the overall rise in standards; a second is the arrival of new problems such as high-rise living and depressed estates; and a third issue concerns the widening inequality between tenure groups and its social consequences.

The basic fact remains that, while most people enjoy higher standards of housing than ever before, a minority of the population is condemned to live in grossly inadequate dwellings in unsuitable surroundings. The fact that actual slum conditions continue to exist at all is an indictment of the housing situation. And all too often it is the most vulnerable groups in society – the elderly, families with young children and the disabled – who have to put up with the worst housing conditions.

To understand the persistence of slums it is necessary to consider not just the age and quality of the housing stock but also the tenure pattern, as this is linked to the question of standards. The tenure pattern in British housing is changing. Of the total housing stock, around 59 per cent of separate dwellings are now owner-occupied, about 29 per cent are local authority owned and the remaining 12 per cent are privately rented from landlords or housing associations or held as tied accommodation. The proportions of owner-occupied and council dwellings have been increasing in recent years, while the private rented sector has been declining. While each sector has some good and some bad accommodation, there are striking overall variations in the housing conditions enjoyed by different tenure groups. On the whole, the owner-occupiers have good amenities, as do the tenants in the public sector, while the privately renting tenants tend to be worst off in terms of what they pay and what they get. The major part of privately rented property is old stock and therefore more likely to fall below acceptable levels of fitness. In some cases owners cannot afford improvements, while in others they lack the will or the financial incentives to make them. This sector of housing is shrinking as councils clear slums and owners seek to sell off their unprofitable property, and, apart from some luxury flats in fashionable locations, little property is now built privately for renting.

Unfortunately the groups of people who rely on it for accommodation are not shrinking. Large numbers of people who lack the capital or credit to become owner-occupiers or the qualifications to get council housing or who, like students, are young and mobile, need to rent from private landlords. So, as the sector shrinks, the demand increases, even for sub-standard accommodation. Conditions deteriorate, aggravated by fears of compulsory purchase and clearance, and multi-occupation is common. Prices are high and are accompanied by all the evils of shortage – overcrowding, extortion, eviction and even outright homelessness.

The existence of outright homelessness is perhaps the most severe indictment of the present housing situation. A substantial and increasing number of families and single people find themselves literally without a home at all. They have to seek help from their local councils, accepting temporary accommodation in hostels, bed and breakfast hotels or sub-standard properties. In extreme cases, families are broken up and children even taken into care because of homelessness. And many of these families never knew more than the claustrophobic squalor of a one-roomed flat in a damp, multi-occupied, terraced slum when they were technically housed.

So the familiar evils of multi-occupation, slum living and homelessness remain part of the present housing scene. Meanwhile other problems have arisen, sometimes as the direct consequence of policies designed to deal with the basic problems of unfit housing. In trying to tackle the problems of slum clearance and deal with long waiting lists by building new homes local authorities ran up against the fundamental difficulty of where to put all the houses. In many cases building took place on city perimeters, far from tenants' places of work and old contacts. Frequently it involved the use of very high blocks of flats. Both the fringe estate and high-rise living have led to considerable problems for tenants. Flats have been consistently unpopular and they certainly create difficulties for families with young children. Large estates all too often provide a dismal environment for families. They tend to lack adequate amenities such as shops and play space, they are poorly landscaped, lack trees and mature gardens, and they may be poorly serviced by public transport so that tenants become isolated. More intangible problems arise from stigma and reputation. Certain estates become labelled as undesirable, initially because of environmental difficulties or just bad architecture, and they then become prey to vandalism. A vicious circle of deterioration, stigma, avoidance, allocation of vulnerable groups, poverty and further deterioration can set in, until the estate becomes a totally unattractive and undesirable place on which to live.

Linked to the problem of where to put all the new homes and whether to build high or not is the larger issue of town and country planning. There are many aspects to this. It has long been recognized that efforts should be made to preserve the countryside and to limit the growth of cities which, if unrestricted, tend to coalesce into bigger and bigger conurbations. This is partly to ensure that city dwellers have some access to green fields and country air and partly to control the costs of urban sprawl. Britain is predominantly an urban country with over 80 per cent of the population clustered in cities and urban areas, and the problems of city life, such as traffic congestion, are very severe in terms of economic as well as social costs. But despite long-standing awareness of the damaging social consequences of the trend, the growth of conurbations continues.

In recent years concern has shifted from the problems of urban sprawl and encroachment on the countryside back to the problem of the inner-city areas. The physical decay and overcrowding that characterized traditional slums have been seen to be associated with overall economic decline and poor living standards. This widening of the old concept of slums to the interrelated problems of inner areas has been prompted by several developments. One is the propensity for new immigrant groups to settle perforce in the areas of poorest housing and to add the new dimension of racial disadvantage to the scene. The other is the so-called gentrification process in certain areas – the acquisition of inner city housing by middle-class owner-occupiers and its subsequent improvement. This development, by sharpening the contrast between the decaying multi-occupied rented housing and the rehabilitated or gentrified housing, has tended to emphasize the social and physical problems of the neglected areas.

In many inner-city areas some of the worst housing and dreariest surroundings occur on old council estates. Although, as indicated, old housing in the privately rented sector still causes most concern, much of the worst housing is now being either cleared or sold and improved. But the public rented sector in the cities also contains much old stock, arguably with less potential for improvement than the Victorian terraces it once replaced. The grim and unattractive older council estates with ugly blocks of cramped flats, outside staircases and bare asphalted yards are often made worse by vandalism and neglect. In environmental terms, they offer a very desolate and depriving experience to those families who have little or no choice in obtaining housing. And as with the large estates on the city boundaries, the environmental deprivation suffered by the tenants is often compounded by problems of social stigma.

The deterioration of the public sector housing stock is likely to be exacerbated by the sale of council housing, as most sales are of the newer and better properties and of houses rather than flats. It is linked to another problem in housing: the increasing polarization that is occurring between the tenure groups. While there are some poor people in all tenure groups, just as there is some poor housing in each sector, current trends indicate an increasing concentration of poor housing and people with low incomes in the public sector. In one sense this means that public housing is reaching those most in need, but unfortunately it tends to do so by allocating poorer people to poorer housing and creating dismal ghettoes on the worst estates. Moreover, the housing experience of most people is a cumulative and reinforcing process: the poorest get labelled and pushed into poor accommodation from which it becomes almost impossible to move, while the better-off invest in housing and consolidate their position with capital gains and inheritance. There is no real situation of choice in housing: access to different tenures is controlled and limited. This blatant differentiation of life chances is a deeply entrenched part of the housing scene and it must be understood if the more basic problems of slums and homelessness are to be tackled.

THE ADMINISTRATION OF HOUSING

Housing is a problem that to some extent affects everybody. All people need to find accommodation to suit their particular requirements, and whether or not they succeed is determined by the total prevailing housing situation even if they are not actually caught up in the more dramatic and problematic aspects of it such as homelessness or slum dwelling. Similarly, housing policy concerns all aspects of the housing situation and not simply those areas in which the state makes direct provision. The government is concerned with the condition, price and distribution of housing generally, in addition to the actual provision of council housing. So although fewer than one in three households live in local authority homes, all households, including the majority looking for houses to buy or rent in the private market, will be affected by the national housing policy. For example, local government clearly determines the price of council housing when it fixes rents, arranges rebate schemes, etc. But the price of private accommodation is influenced by the availability of mortgage facilities, tax relief, rent regulation, the rent element of income support and so on, which are determined or influenced by government action.

Inevitably housing policy and administration are confused because they concern so many issues. There is a great deal of legislation relating to housing and town planning, rent control and so forth, some of it dealing broadly with the powers and duties of local housing authorities, some of it concerning particular and detailed aspects of the housing scene such as the prevention of eviction.

The government's concern in the housing situation dates back to the nineteenth century. At the start it was a public health concern that led to the introduction of legislation empowering local authorities to clear slums and make by-laws to improve building standards. This was because the unfettered jerry building of the early nineteenth century had led to major problems of sanitation and consequent ill-health. Housing was shoddily constructed and massed together in appalling densities and the rapidly increasing population of the new urban areas were forced into it under grossly overcrowded conditions.

It was really only after the First World War that the government took a more positive role. Local authorities were urged not only to clear slums, but to build houses to meet general housing need and to let them at rents the needy could afford. It was realized that only by such direct provision could there be any chance of a real improvement in the housing conditions of the bulk of the working class. Moreover, the central government itself made subsidies available to help the local building effort. Henceforth the local authority concern for clearance and standards was matched by efforts to provide homes 'fit for heroes' to live in. Meanwhile, restriction had been placed on private rent levels during the early war years and government concern for control in this sector continued to some extent. Gradually the area of state intervention widened and its policy grew more positive and comprehensive. Concern was shown for town planning, and the distribution of housing generally, and attempts made to relate housing need and provision to economic development, the growth of industry and transport facilities, etc.

Central government responsibilities

It might be helpful to summarize the current administrative position in this complex field. The three main sectors of housing are owner-occupied, private rented and local authority rented. The central department, the Department of the Environment, is responsible for the formulation of policy and the provision of some information and advisory services. The principal providers of new homes to buy or rent, however, are the local housing authorities, private builders and landlords. The department attempts to secure the cooperation of the local authorities in carrying out its policy with regard to slum clearance, for example. It attempts, too, to influence the amount of new building by its discussions with the building industry, building societies, and so on. It also tries to control the quality, price, security and availability of accommodation in the private rented sector. While its influence may be pervasive, the department's power remains limited and many of the current trends and problems in housing are barely understood let alone directed and controlled as part of a clear housing policy.

The department has no overriding statutory responsibility for ensuring the execution of a national policy, but it attempts to formulate one. It has powers of various kinds over the activities of the local authorities, which in turn derive their powers direct from housing legislation. For example, the central department controls the subsidies that are a vital part of the local housing departments' revenues and it must confirm local clearance orders or compulsory purchase orders. It uses these powers to persuade local housing authorities to conform to a national policy, though they not only play the major active role in housing but retain some scope from their statutory powers to determine their own lines of action.

From 1957 to 1975 the department was advised by a Central Housing Advisory Committee, which advised on policy, conducted investigations into specific problems and produced some useful reports. In recent years six regional offices situated at Manchester, Newcastle upon Tyne, Birmingham, Leeds, Bristol and Nottingham have been opened. Regional studies of housing need and planning policy have been prepared that attempt to consider housing in the context of industrial development, migration patterns, transport facilities, and so on. Central government policy is formulated as a result of the information gathered from its advisory bodies and regional studies, together with the statistical material collected centrally and the results of research. It is announced largely by the publication, prior to legislation, of White Papers, which set out the main lines of policy, establish targets and priorities and tentatively attempt some forward planning.

An example of these is the paper of 1965 entitled *The Housing Programme 1965–1970*. This purported to be 'the first stage in the formulation of a national housing plan'. It set out the objectives of housing policy and discussed methods of achieving them – setting, for example, a target of building half a million new homes a year. This was to meet the existing needs by clearing slums and eliminating overcrowding and to keep pace with new demands arising from population growth, household formation and urban redevelopment. The paper discussed the question of who should build these houses – private enterprise or local authority – and considered the need for private building to let as well as for owner-occupation. It discussed the building industry's capacity, the problem of land allocation and acquisition, standards, finance, building methods, tenancy and rent policy, and improvement of existing housing stock.

This demonstrates the department's overall concern with the many aspects of housing policy despite its lack of statutory powers of control. The department has numerous divisions and directorates to develop policy in different areas such as the Housing Directorate and the Inner Cities Directorate. It has links with various building research groups to encourage the development of standardized and industrialized techniques for the contruction industry and to disseminate information on the best modern practices. It was also responsible for the establishment of machinery for the setting of rents in the private sector and for initiating the establishment of the New Towns.

Local government responsibilities

The role of local authorities in housing is an active and varied one. They have a general responsibility for meeting the housing need of their areas. There are a great many local housing authorities, as the London Boroughs, the county districts of England and Wales and new towns are all involved in this field. The administration of housing at local level varies considerably, not all authorities having a clear-cut housing committee, department and manager. Some authorities divide their housing responsibilities between different departments. This often reflects the varying priorities given to housing by the different local authorities. Clearly it is of the utmost importance in a large city and less so in a sparsely populated rural area, and administrative arrangements reflect this. However, the central department has recommended that housing management should be the responsibility of a major committee and the job of trained staff.

The first statutory concern for housing gave the local authorities responsibilities first for the clearance of individual unfit premises and then of whole areas, and for the making of by-laws to prevent further building of potential slums and to ensure some minimum standards. Most authorities acted slowly on their new powers, since clearance and rehousing were such costly and difficult enterprises. But after the First World War, aided by government subsidies, they embarked on a vigorous and positive house-building programme. Since then they have been prominent in the housing field not only for the enforcement of standards but also for their direct provision of accommodation. And today a major part of their task is the building, managing and letting of council houses and flats to meet the general housing need.

Since council building has been taking place for many years the present housing is quite varied. Some accommodation built early this century has become old and obsolete, while some is dramatically modern. Initially it was provided to rehouse people from the slums, then it became more widely available. Immediately following the Second World War there was an acute housing shortage and local authorities were encouraged to build as many houses as possible as quickly as possible, to meet the general need. Local authorities rather than private builders were relied on to ensure a rapid increase in the depleted housing stock. From the mid-1950s a change in policy led to an increased emphasis on private building and the public housing authorities were encouraged to concentrate their efforts on slum clearance and redevelopment rehousing. More recently they have been urged to make more provision of small dwellings, especially those suitable for older people. These changes in national policy are effected at local level partly by the operation of subsidies, which can be paid to local authorities in respect of schemes that gain departmental approval.

The provision of local authority housing is always problematic. Because of subsidies from the central government and from the rates, and to some extent because of the relative economy of building on a large scale, council houses are available at comparatively low rents for the quality of accommodation they provide. They are therefore highly desirable for large numbers of people, especially those whose incomes and family commitments make the prospect of buying a house extremely remote. This results in long waiting lists of people seeking council houses, and local authorities have to decide to whom they should give priority – those who have waited longest or those who live in the worst conditions. Moreover, the concentration on slum clearance often means that there is very little accommodation available for people on the waiting lists as most new building is taken up by rehousing clearance families.

This in itself is always a difficult operation. All too often rehousing is offered on estates on the perimeters of cities and this means a loss of contact with familiar areas, long and expensive journeys to work, and adjustment to living in new, often rather characterless, areas that lack the neighbourliness of the old urban communities. Attempts to redevelop the cleared city centre areas usually involve the use of high blocks of flats in order to achieve high densities with some open space. 'Living high' itself imposes new problems and the flats are disliked by many tenants.

Then there are questions of who should pay for the housing, how far it should be subsidized, whether tenants should pay according to their income and so on. A continuing area of controversy concerns whether council housing should be offered for sale to its tenants.

It is very difficult to keep everyone happy, and the role of local authorities in housing has never been clearly defined. Are they definitely operating a welfare service, providing housing for those who cannot provide it for themselves and, therefore, clearly giving priority to those in greatest need, or are they managing, on a fair and reasonable basis, decent property at moderate rents for respectable tenants? If the latter is the case, they can argue that it is sensible to exclude the more difficult and unreliable families despite their genuine need. This is still very much an open question.

The local housing authority builds, manages and lets housing and this is one of its major functions. But it is also concerned with standards and conditions of privately owned and rented property. It makes by-laws to ensure the maintenance of good standards in new property, and it has a variety of powers and responsibilities as regards existing property. The most obvious of these powers is that of the demolition and clearance of housing that is deemed unfit for human habitation. Local authorities have to ascertain the numbers of slums in their areas and plan to clear them and rehouse their occupants. They can then redevelop the cleared areas as they see fit. In recent years they have also shown increased concern for property that is not up to present-day standards but is not yet included within a scheduled clearance programme. Some authorities have adopted a policy of 'deferred demolition'. They buy areas of old property that still has some future and put it into reasonable repair. It is then added to the stock of accommodation available to be rented. This ensures that the worst neglect is remedied and the tenants have a landlord, the council, who will keep the property in basic habitable condition. Local authorities have also had power since 1949 to make grants to the owners of old property for its improvement and repair. Following the publication of a White Paper in 1968, *Old Houses into New Homes* (Cmnd 3602), local authorities have had powers to deal with whole areas of unsatisfactory housing by systematic improvement.

Housing authorities also have wide powers and duties relating to rent regulation and rent allowance. Rent Acts have brought more and more privately rented property under controls that affect both the rents asked and the security of tenure. Since the Housing Finance Act of 1972 they have had some responsibility for the operation of rent allowance schemes and since 1983 for the housing benefit scheme. And finally, since 1974 they have had, as housing authorities, responsibility for housing the homeless on a temporary basis as well as a continuing and fundamental responsibility for providing for long-term housing need.

HOUSING POLICY

In discussing central and local authorities and their organization and functions much has already been said about housing policy. The housing problem, with its present symptoms of homelessness, slums, land shortages and soaring costs, remains a major concern of governments and numerous statements are made about policies and priorities. The amount of legislation in the housing field is formidable, but despite statements of intent and increasingly complex machinery for control the actual housing situation remains intractably difficult. This is due partly to the fact that housing policies are politically controversial and subject to sudden changes of direction when successive governments replace one another.

The broad and generally agreed goal of British housing policy is to provide a separate home at a decent standard for every household that needs one. The controversy begins when means of achieving this goal are considered. A major aspect of housing policy is basic supply of new dwellings. In this area there is less disagreement about how many homes are needed than about who should provide them. Targets for house-building have been set as high as 500,000 dwellings a year, but this level has never in fact been attained. The highest number of houses built was reached in 1968 when 425,000 houses were completed in the United Kingdom. The level of housing starts has been dropping ever since, and the 1987 figure stood at 195,000 dwellings.

The job of building new homes is shared by local authorities and private enterprise and policies have differed over which should play the greater part. In the decade following the last war the local authorities built roughly three-quarters of all new homes. During the next decade private building was encouraged and public building restricted mainly to clearance replacement. As a result the private sector overtook the public in building new homes. Private enterprise maintained a substantial lead throughout the 1980s. In 1982, only 56,000 houses were started by the local authorities, new town corporations and housing associations, while 145,200 were started by private builders.

Local authority building has been open to much criticism on the grounds of its standards, amenities and location. Standards of building tended to decline for reasons of economy and in 1961 the Central Housing Advisory Committee produced the Parker Morris Report, *Homes for Today and Tomorrow*, to give authorities acceptable standards of space, heating and other amenities to conform to. A further report in 1967, entitled *The Needs of New Communities*, suggested ways of improving life on new estates, and there has been some development of tenants' associations to encourage tenant involvement and improve social facilities in areas of new housing. Clearly the major priority is building homes, but it is necessary to maintain standards both for individual dwellings and for whole areas of development. Some examples of imaginative and satisfying municipal housing schemes do exist, but the general picture of local authority building is a depressing one, with unimaginative layouts and poky dwellings being all too common. Private enterprise, it must be added, does not often do much better by way of developing attractive and viable communities and there is clearly much still to be learned about effective town planning and development.

Part of the problem of new building has always been that of finding adequate sites. Brief mention must be made here of the new towns policy, the most bold and imaginative solution adopted so far. New towns are designed to provide homes for people alongside opportunities for work and leisure, education and welfare, shopping and transport, etc., in accessible, community-conscious groupings. Following the New Towns Act of 1946, fourteen new towns were designated by 1950, eight of them situated around London to cater, in part, for metropolitan overspill. After a gap during the 1950s in which only one town was designated, the 1960s saw a steady addition, and there are currently twenty-nine new towns.

Another solution to the problems of congestion and overspill is provided under the Town Development legislation. This facilitates the transfer of population from overcrowded urban areas to small towns wishing to expand. Both the exporting authority and the receiving authority can gain by this procedure, which is less radical than that of founding actual new towns.

The success of these policies, however, hinges on whether industry and hence employment can be attracted to the new centres of population. Without work opportunities new houses are useless to the people who need them and in this area of housing policy the interdependence of industrial development and social policy is sharply drawn. Some interesting growth has resulted from new towns policy, but the experiment is still on a fairly small scale compared to the haphazard growth of new development in and around existing towns and cities.

A good many of the new homes built by local authorities are used to replace those lost by clearance and redevelopment. Slum clearance has been an important part of housing policy since government intervention in housing began. The work of clearing slums was halted during and after the Second World War, but local authorities returned to it during the 1950s. In 1956, the general needs subsidy, which encouraged building to house people from the waiting lists, was abolished. Thereafter councils concentrated their housing efforts on clearance and redevelopment. After a decade of clearance, enthusiasm for wholesale redevelopment began to wane. There was mounting concern at the slowness of clearance programmes and the consequent blight on areas awaiting redevelopment. Following an inquiry into slums by the Central Housing Advisory Committee and the publication in 1966 of its report, *Our Older Homes: A Call for Action*, the government adopted a policy favouring rehabilitation rather than clearance. This was set out in the 1968 White Paper, *Old Houses into New Homes*, and endorsed by the 1969 Housing Act.

Improvement of existing homes has long been recognized as an important way of husbanding the housing stock. Since 1949 grants have been made available to owners of older property at the discretion of the local authority for the improvement of houses up to certain defined standards. The policy was hesitant at first and grants tended to be hedged around by conditions that put off a great many owners. Since 1959 authorities have been bound to pay grants to owners installing the basic amenities – baths and water supplies, etc. – in their houses and have had wider discretion to pay towards general improvement.

In 1964 the concept of the improvement area was introduced. This gave councils certain powers to compel improvements in designated areas. The 1969 Act built on existing improvement provisions but reduced the conditions around grants and extended their limits. It also made provision for the declaration of general improvement areas, where improvements to the environment as well as to individual homes could be encouraged. After 1969 the level of grants, previously running at a very modest rate, rose sharply. In 1967, when the first National House Condition Survey was carried out, nearly 4 million dwellings lacked basic amenities. A further survey in 1971 showed that this number was substantially reduced. The survey also showed, however, that the incidence of bad conditions was variable between different parts of the country and between different tenure groups. Only 4 per cent of owner-occupied houses were found unfit as against 23 per cent of privately rented houses. As a result, a higher grant rate for improvement was introduced in 1971 for development and intermediate areas in which the largest concentrations of poor housing were found.

In 1973 the White Paper *Better Homes: The Next Priorities* introduced the concept of housing action areas to help local authorities give priority to the remaining areas of worst housing. The criteria for declaring an area a housing action area include: numbers of households living in overcrowded conditions, numbers of furnished tenancies and shared accommodation, houses lacking standard amenities, and the incidence of elderly people and large families in the neighbourhood. Housing action areas are fairly small, typically containing about 500 dwellings. The local authority works directly on improvement and encourages existing landlords to cooperate. Housing associations are encouraged to acquire and manage accommodation so that it can be improved and rented. Preferential rates of grant are available for housing action areas.

As a result of these developments improvement became a substantial element of housing policy. The change of emphasis from clearance to improvement did not, however, go unchallenged. Many houses are now in better condition and many areas have been improved without wholesale destruction of older property and community life. But there were criticisms over the effectiveness of improvement schemes, partly on the grounds that they did not help the worst housed, and partly because they encouraged the postponement of necessary clearance and new building.

In the outline of the present housing situation it was noted that the private rented sector was shrinking. The greatest loss has been of cheap rented accommodation, since there has been some development on the luxury apartment front. The loss is felt most seriously in urban areas, especially in London where it has been the biggest single factor in the rise in the numbers of homeless families in recent years. It is due primarily to slum clearance, which mostly affects cheap, rented property, and the fact that it has not been profitable to build or convert property to let. This last factor is influenced in part by the cost of land and building but also by the effect of rent control.

Rents were controlled by government intervention during the First World War and, since control implied not only fixed rents but also security of tenure, it proved extremely hard to end without great hardship being caused. Undoubtedly, frozen rents have at times been unfair on landlords, who have received only nominal incomes from their property and consequently had little interest in maintaining it in good repair. The 1957 Rent Act brought a considerable measure of decontrol, both directly by the immediate decontrol of property above certain rateable values and indirectly as a result of a clause that allowed decontrol on change of tenancy. The rate of this indirect 'creeping' decontrol proved to be much faster than anticipated and many families suffered severe hardship as a consequence. Little if any new property came into the private rented sector as a result of the 1957 Act because rent control was not the only reason why investors were reluctant to build or buy property to let. Indeed, a good deal of property promptly left the sector as decontrol enabled many landlords to sell their property for owner-occupation.

As house prices rose, the rush to sell property led to an acceleration of unscrupulous practices on the part of landlords to gain vacant possession. The Prevention of Eviction Act was passed in 1964, followed by the Rent Acts of 1965 and 1968. These Acts gave greater security of tenure and some protection of tenants from harassment or unfair eviction. The Rent Act of 1965 also introduced the concept of rent regulation to the unfurnished sector. Rents were to be set by rent officers at a 'fair' level, having regard to current prices but discounting scarcity. Landlords and tenants both had a right of appeal to a Rent Assessment Committee if they disagreed with the rent officer.

The system of rent regulation was reviewed in 1971 by a Committee on the Rent Acts. The report of this committee, the Francis Report, claimed that by and large the system was working well and the principle of fair rents was later extended.

The protection of tenants afforded by the Rent Acts is that they can only be evicted for certain offences, not merely because the landlord wants possession. This applied only to unfurnished tenancies at first but the Rent Act of 1974 extended protection to furnished tenancies where the landlord is non-resident. Where the landlord is resident the tenant can get up to six months' security from the rent tribunal. Security of tenure is vital to protect tenants from being forced out of their homes because landlords seek to sell or change the nature of the accommodation. Lack of security of tenure was a reason for many families becoming homeless. Unfortunately, tightening up on security helps existing tenants but it does nothing to help those seeking homes to rent. The supply of accommodation to rent continues to drop and landlords become reluctant to let property when they feel the balance of advantage lies with the tenant.

Whatever the effect of the Rent Acts, homelessness continues and in London especially has been increasing sharply in recent years. Clearly when the housing situation is bad in terms of availability of accommodation and security of tenure, some families will find it impossible to obtain a satisfactory home. The most vulnerable groups in society – the poor, large families, immigrants and single-parent families – tend to suffer most in the housing shortage and most often find themselves homeless. But when the shortage of rented accommodation is acute, as it is in London, then even small, stable families in well-paid employment find it impossible to obtain homes.

Homelessness in London has several times been investigated and reported on and yet solutions appear impossible to find. For most homeless families, council accommodation seemed the only solution as the private rented sector shrank and was competed for by larger groups, especially of the young and single. But although councils have housed many families from temporary accommodation there seemed no end to the problem. The responsibility for providing temporary accommodation, originally a welfare or social services department function, was transferred to housing authorities in 1974. But many authorities cannot cope and the homeless are increasingly relegated to bed and breakfast hotels, which provide accommodation but not a home.

The Housing (Homeless Persons) Act, 1977, attempted to improve the situation by making the responsibilities of local authorities clearer and defining homelessness in a more realistic manner. The Act made it quite clear that homelessness was to be regarded as an aspect of housing need, and that the homeless therefore require housing rather than welfare or social work provision, but then it attempted to identify 'priority need' groups in terms of the personal characteristics of applicants. Basically it identified vulnerable families with dependent children, including single-parent families, as having high priority, and childless couples and single homeless persons as having relatively low priority. The Act clarified some administrative issues but by no means solved the real problems of homelessness.

The long-term solution can only liie in making more accommodation available generally and in reducing the power of London and the South East to attract so many people. Powerful and coordinated policies that extend beyond the province of local authorities are needed to achieve this.

In the short-term, councils cope by increasing use of short-life properties and some have asked for more power to take over empty property for use in this way. Meanwhile, illegal occupation of empty property has increased, especially among young people, as the homeless have taken to direct action. Squatting is not, however, usually much help as a solution to the ordinary family's needs, as it can only be a short-term proposition in most cases. The work of housing associations is more helpful here in buying up old property for cooperative management and use. Housing associations have been actively encouraged since 1961 by government loans. In 1964 the

Housing Corporation was set up to stimulate activity in this field.

Housing finance

A crucial aspect of housing policy is finance. The cost of housing is affected by many factors, including building costs, land prices and the cost of borrowing money. Local authority building is subsidized both from the rates and from central funds. The provision of private house-building is encouraged by help to owner-occupiers through tax concessions on mortgage payments and help to the building societies. Rent levels in the private sector have long been subject to control and regulation.

Housing finance is both complex and controversial, and government intervention at times appears contradictory and incompetent. House prices have risen sharply in recent years and so has the cost of borrowing money. Fortunes have been made out of property speculation, while for most ordinary people housing of all kinds has proved more difficult and costly to obtain. Governments have been urged to make money available at low rates of interest for housing purposes to encourage building and help stabilize costs. The nearest approach to such a policy in Britain was the Housing Subsidies Act of 1967, which made it possible for the government to subsidize local authorities by making up the difference between the cost of borrowing at 4 per cent and the actual cost. But there has been much dispute over the issue of equity between the different tenure groups and the whole subsidy system was changed by the controversial Housing Finance Act of 1972.

This important Act set out to change the approach to housing finance and it was indeed a very radical departure from existing policies. In the White Paper *Fair Deal for Housing* (Cmnd 4728), which preceded it, it was asserted that subsidies to the public sector were inequitable because they were largely used to keep rents low rather than finance more building, while in the private sector rent control was acting unfairly to favour tenants at the expense of landlords. Help to owner-occupiers was noted but its extent was not criticized. The solution to the problem of housing finance was therefore seen to reside in an extension of the fair rent principle, coupled with rebate and allowance schemes to help the poorer tenants, and the concentration of Exchequer help on those local authorities with the worst housing problems.

The main provisions of the Housing Finance Act were threefold: the extension of the 'fair rent' formula, introduced by the Rent Act of 1965 for private rented unfurnished accommodation, to the public sector; the reform of the subsidy system for local authorities; and the introduction of a national rent rebate scheme for all council tenants and rent allowances for the private tenants of unfurnished dwellings. Under the fair rent extensions, rent officers were to fix the fair rents of all council properties and rents would rise to these levels over a limited period.

The Housing Finance Act was implemented despite unprecedented opposition from some councils. It did allow some generous rebates to be paid, but it was generally viewed as an attack on local authorities and their tenants. Local authorities lost their freedom to set rents and manage their accounts and council tenants were faced with steady increases in their housing costs, with subsidies to poor tenants (both private and public) being paid for by the better-off tenants.

The Housing Rents and Subsidies Bill, introduced in 1974 following a change of government, restored local authorities' powers to set rents at 'reasonable levels' and created new subsidies to enable them to cope with housing shortage. Evidence from housing research at this time showed up both the inequalities of the subsidies to different tenure groups in the housing market, and also a disturbing trend towards a long-term intergenerational polarization of housing standards between tenures. This polarization is a trend extended by the actions of the Conservative government since 1979, in particular in relation to new legislation affecting local authority housing.

Whilst local authorities have long been able to sell to tenants, the 1980 Housing Act extended this right to buy by replacing local authority discretion with a statutory right, and extending this to virtually all council properties and virtually all secure tenants with more than three years' tenancy. In addition, discounts on the price of the property were offered to buyers, up to a maximum of 50 per cent. The legislation encouraged council tenants to buy their homes, and the numbers doing so rose rapidly in the early 1980s. Further amendments in legislation enacted in 1984 and 1985 gave yet more tenants the 'right to buy', whilst the 1986 Housing and Planning Act increased discounts, particularly in respect of council flats, which had, until that point, proved less easy to sell to tenants.

These changes in legislation have greatly reduced the number of council properties on local authorities lists, and, as there has been very little new building by local authorities because of public expenditure control, council house waiting lists have lengthened greatly over the past few years. In addition, the local authority housing that has proved easiest to sell are the older dwellings, mostly houses, mostly in good repair and on good estates, whilst the tenants who have bought are mostly white, in employment and older than average. The effect of this has been to increasingly marginalize the local authority sector, with the property remaining being of the poorest quality, in poor repair, with a high proportion of flats and houses being on the poorer estates. Similarly, tenants in the local authority sector are poorer, with a higher proportion of unemployed, single parents and black families than prior to the increased sales. This polarization of the housing market has an important effect of increasing the stigma that attaches to the residual local authority sector, whilst the type of property that is available to those who do eventually get to the top of the council waiting list is clearly more limited than before.

The 1986 Act also increased the power of local authorities to dispose of council properties by allowing them to sell council property to private sector landlords, even where there were tenants in residence. This move towards drawing increasing resources from the private sector into local authority housing was reinforced with the 1988 Housing Act, following on from the White Paper, *Housing: The Government's Proposals*, which set up Housing Action Trusts. These trusts take over local authority housing in predetermined areas, with the objective of improving run down housing before passing it on to new forms of ownership and management, which may or may not be local authority.

These moves reflect the current government's policy of promoting home ownership whilst reducing the role of the local authority in providing housing. In promoting the private ownership of local authority housing, by both individuals and private landlords, the government is clearly committed to a marginalization of the role of the state in the housing sector, preferring a housing market based even more firmly on market forces than the present one. However, inequities in the system of housing finance continue to exist, with home-owners receiving subsidies from the government through tax relief on the interest on their mortgages (under the MIRAS system), at a time of rising council rents, deregulated rents in the private sector and cuts in local authority expenditure on new housing. Rates of homelessness have risen dramatically in the past decade, and the health costs of 'temporary' bed and breakfast accommodation for those without permanent homes are increasingly apparent.

Housing need is complex, and the housing market in Britain has shifted substantially in the 1980s. From the discussion above it can be seen that to meet housing need an informed, vigorous, comprehensive and equitable housing policy is needed. In Britain we do not currently have such a policy. Policy endorses and promotes the trend to owner-occupation, at a cost of decreasing the role of state provision to a minimal, low-standard and stigmatized service. So, despite an overall improvement in housing standards, numerous problems remain and, for some, are becoming increasingly entrenched. Housing raises basic issues of the role of government in society, of the causes and consequences of deprivation and of the nature of inequality, which are not easily settled. It is an important area of study within social administration and one that will always prove controversial and demanding.

SUGGESTIONS FOR FURTHER READING

Berry, F., *Housing: the Great British Failure* (Charles Knight, 1974).
Burke, G., *Housing and Social Justice* (Longman, 1981).

Cullingworth, B., *Housing Needs and Planning Policy* (RKP, 1960).

Cullingworth, B., *Housing and Local Government* (RKP, 1966).

Department of the Environment, *Housing Policy: A Consultative Document*, Cmnd 6851 (HMSO, 1977).

Donnison, D. V. and Soto, P., *The Good City* (Heinemann, 1980).

Donnison, D. V. and Ungerson, C., *Housing Policy* (Penguin, 1982).

Forrest, R. and Murie, A., *Selling the Welfare State: The Privatisation of Public Housing* (RKP, 1988).

Greve, J., Page, D. and Greve, S., *Homelessness in London* (Scottish Academic Press, 1971).

Lansley, S., *Housing and Public Policy* (Croom Helm, 1979).

Muchnick, D. M., *Urban Renewal in Liverpool* (Bell, 1970).

Murie, A., *Housing, Deprivation and Inequality* (Heinemann, 1982).

Reports of the Central Housing Advisory Committee:

Cullingworth Report, *Council Housing: Purposes, Procedures and Priorities* (HMSO, 1969).

Dennington Report, *Our Older Homes: A Call for Action* (HMSO, 1966).

Parker Morris Report, *Homes for Today and Tomorrow* (HMSO, 1961).

Ungerson, C., *Moving Home* (Bell, 1971).

Watson, S. and Austerberry, H., *Housing and Homelessness* (RKP, 1986).

6
Unemployment

THE NATURE OF THE PROBLEM

Getting and keeping a decent job is clearly a fundamental prerequisite of welfare. A job provides income, not only during work but in many cases, through pension schemes, for retirement as well. It may provide many other practical benefits, such as subsidized meals, housing, health, social and sporting facilities, cars and travel allowances. It also provides important intangible benefits such as status, personal satisfaction and fulfilment, companionship, friendship and credit.

The rewards of work vary quite dramatically from job to job. Some jobs carry high rewards in terms of both financial gain and satisfaction, while others are both low paid and unpleasant. The job a person holds can to a considerable extent determine not only their income and standard of living, but their access to a range of life chances in terms of health, housing and education. The job of a head of a household tends to determine the overall socio-economic position of all members of the household, and hence their various life chances.

All those who are in work (that is, employees or the self-employed), and those who, though unemployed, are looking for work make up the total labour force or the economically active population of a country. In Great Britain in 1987 there were 27 million people in the labour force, the majority of them men. A growing number of women, including married women, have joined the labour force in recent decades. By

1987, 50 per cent of all women over 16 were economically active, compared with 73 per cent of all men. Early retirement has contributed to a decline in the overall activity rate for men; but 94 per cent of men aged 25–44 are active in the labour force. Of the total labour force in 1988, 5 million employees were in manufacturing jobs, 1 million were in construction, and over 15 million were in service jobs. A third of a million were in agriculture, nearly half a million were in energy and water supply industries, whilst nearly 3 million were self-employed. Around 3 million were unemployed, of whom 2.7 million were registered unemployed claimants.

Unemployment rates vary considerably between different regions. In 1987 the unemployment rate – that is, the numbers of registered unemployed as a percentage of the total labour force – was 10.2 per cent for the United Kingdom as a whole, but it was over 13 per cent for Wales, and nearly 18 per cent for Northern Ireland, and there were considerable regional variations within England. There is marked stability in this regional variation: regions that are currently suffering the highest rates did so in the pre-war depression too.

Unemployment has increased very sharply in recent years. In 1961, the overall rate was 1.3 per cent of the labour force, which meant fewer than 300,000 people out of work. By 1971 it had increased to over 3 per cent and 750,000 people. By the 1980s it was over 10 per cent and climbed steadily to over 13 per cent in 1984. The official number stood at 2.7 million in 1988, but this is claimed by many people to underestimate the true number seeking work. It is suggested that, as it excludes students who want temporary work, married women who do not bother to register and those who have retired early or are on special schemes rather than in proper jobs, the real numbers could be much higher. Some commentators would also count those workers who were on short time or denied overtime as suffering the effects of unemployment. On the other hand, it is argued that the numbers could be reduced if school leavers, those temporarily out of work and a category they call unemployable were omitted. Whatever the exact figure, however, it is quite clear that it is uncomfortably high and is now a serious problem affecting a substantial number of people. A very worrying aspect of high unemployment rates is the increase in long-term unemployment. A disturbingly high proportion of the total registered unemployed have been out of work for over a year.

Unemployment is experienced by all kinds of people – men and women, young and old, professional and unskilled – but it is concentrated among certain social groups: young people who lack qualifications and experience, older workers, people with a disability such as a physical handicap and members of ethnic minorities are most likely to suffer unemployment. It is also quite heavily concentrated among the lower-paid unskilled workers.

Unemployment has a displacement effect in that people with skills, qualifications and experience will tend, when there are few opportunities for work, to accept jobs that may well be paid less or have a lower status than they would have hoped to get in better times, thereby pushing out those with more modest skills. Clearly the most vulnerable groups – those with no qualifications or skills to offer or with a physical or social handicap to overcome – are pushed out of work altogether. The unskilled and low paid are both more likely to have repeated experience of unemployment and to suffer from long-term unemployment.

THE SOCIAL MEANING OF UNEMPLOYMENT

Not all jobs are satisfactory – many are low paid, others are dangerous or unpleasant, some carry health risks and a great many are repetitive and tedious. Sadly the fact remains that inequalities at work are consistent: the most unpleasant and boring jobs tend to have the lowest pay and the greatest insecurity, while the higher-paid ones are often the more fulfilling and attractive. Nevertheless, any job is to some extent better than no job at all; the penalties of having no job are even more severe than those of the poorer, least desirable work situations. Work provides a range of satisfactions and a crucial sense of role. To be out of work in a work-oriented society is a major deprivation and one that has many aspects.

The most obvious consequence of having no job is having no wage. Nowadays, social security provides some basic income for unemployed individuals and their dependants but, as we shall see when we look in more detail at the social policy response, it is a very basic provision. So, for most people, unemployment means a major drop in income. Living standards fall, often quite drastically, hire purchase commitments cannot be honoured, promises for presents or holidays, etc., cannot be kept, debts easily accumulate. The unemployed and their families face poverty and, in many cases, being on the dole (as benefits for the unemployed are usually called), is a long-term prospect. A study of the dole that compared standards of support in 1980 with those available in the 1930s (Piachaud, 1981) showed that, while benefits had risen in value by about 27 per cent, average material standards of those in work had doubled. The relative poverty of the unemployed is real. Piachaud's study concluded that 'the level of material living available to unemployed people is basic and bleak'. Several other surveys of the financial situation of the unemployed and their families have endorsed this conclusion. Benefits replace on average only about half of the income available in work. Since the low paid are most likely to suffer prolonged unemployment, the persistence and severity of poverty for some families is indisputable.

Poverty is linked to other deprivations such as poor housing. The link between unemployment and ill-health is a complex and controversial one. There is growing evidence that loss of a job can lead to depression, alcoholism and even suicide for the individual, but the overall impact on the nation's health is harder to assess. According to the work of Brenner there is a statistical association between certain indicators of social welfare, such as mortality rates, mental hospital admissions, etc., and economic indicators such as per capita income, inflation rate and levels of unemployment. The changing employment rate, according to Brenner's hypothesis, is the most significant indicator: high levels of unemployment are followed, after a time lag, by increased mortality rates.

Brenner's work is controversial because it is difficult to sort out the relationships between mortality and unemployment and mortality and other factors (such as changes in behaviour and developments in medical technology), in any precise or conclusive way. But his general argument is disturbing because it is in line with much of the evidence from studies such as the Black Report on *Inequalities in Health*. These stress the overall importance of socio-economic factors in the causation of ill-health and of high mortality rates. One researcher concluded a study of the impact of unemployment on morbidity and mortality with the observation that high unemployment merely accentuates the general consequences of low income, so it is as much the poverty of the unemployed as the stress of their situation that damages health.

Whatever the long-term effects on the health of the whole population, it is quite clear that unemployment brings considerable physical and psychological stress to individuals. Despair, apathy and chronic depression are widely reported and are associated with vulnerability to minor ailments. An increase in addictive habits such as smoking and drinking alcohol has been noted among the unemployed. These are bad for health directly and, since they are costly, they can exacerbate poverty and lead to poor nutrition. The health effects of unemployment extend to the families of the unemployed. A growing number of children now grow up in families with unemployed parents and there is evidence that they are at risk of material, physical, educational and emotional stress. The poverty that is one immediate consequence of unemployment is bad for health. So, too, is living with chronically depressed adults. Children can suffer stress from the stigma of unemployment and their educational performance can suffer.

Young people who experience unemployment on leaving school have their own difficulties to cope with. They are effectively prevented from taking on adult roles as wage-earners and heads of households and are inhibited from becoming husbands or wives or parents. The dependency of youth is extended for an apparently limitless period and this can intensify identity crises and erode precarious self-esteem. Young people who have never had a job are excluded from a key area of experience in our society and they may become severely depressed and apathetic or angry and defiant, while relationships with family and friends deteriorate.

The impact of unemployment on the living standards, health and happiness of individuals is a harsh one. The impact on communities is no less severe. Whole towns, neighbourhoods or regions that experience chronically high levels of unemployment show all the signs of impoverishment and depression. Physically the environment suffers from the neglect of closed factories and abandoned yards. Housing tends to reflect the prevailing poverty, becoming shabby and unkempt, while public services and facilities often share the general dreariness. Shops close and commerce moves out of areas where people are short of money, leaving gaps and vacancies on high streets. Vandalism increases and litter and graffiti add to the general air of decay. The morale of unemployed communities can fall to low levels because of the collectively low self-esteem and lack of resources. Occasionally angry despair can turn to violence: unemployment has been implicated in the street violence of several inner-city areas and it can exacerbate racial and sectarian tensions.

High levels of unemployment, particularly persistent unemployment, are damaging to the economic and social life of the country as a whole as well as to individuals and communities. The possible consequences for the health of the country have already been noted, and the poverty of whole areas and regions with high rates of unemployment is clearly damaging to the overall prosperity of the nation. It is fundamentally unsound from the economic point of view to have a substantial part of the labour force standing idle – it is a tragic waste of valuable human resources. The closure of factories and workshops or mines and shipyards that could be productive is also a waste of resources. Some shedding of surplus labour or closure of obsolete plant is inevitable in times of rapid development of technology and changing patterns of production, but the enforced closure of sound industrial premises and consequent redundancy of skilled and experienced workers are a terrible waste and a clear sign of an unhealthy economy.

WHAT CAUSES UNEMPLOYMENT?

Much thought has been given to the whole question of the causes of unemployment. Not surprisingly, there are no simple answers to questions about why unemployment persists, or why it increases at some times and decreases at others. Sadly, many theorists have tried to put the blame for unemployment on the unemployed themselves. They have argued that the unemployed are not actively seeking work, that they lack the skills necessary for work, that they will not move to areas where work is available, that they are in some finite, tautological sense 'unemployable'. While it is true that a person with energy, skills and mobility will usually have a better chance of getting a job than a person in poor health, with no skills and with close ties to a particular area, this does not and cannot explain unemployment. Large numbers of people with qualifications and skills who are ready and willing to move are out of work when unemployment is pervasive and running at a persistently high level. The vast majority of the unemployed are out of work because there are no jobs. To look for explanations of unemployment in terms of individual shortcomings is both insulting and unproductive.

Why, then, are there currently no jobs for over 10 per cent of the labour force? In order to answer this question, it is clearly necessary to break down the large numbers and look at different kinds of unemployment and the different reasons why each has increased or decreased. Early this century economists and social scientists seeking to understand the phenomenon of unemployment argued for a breakdown into three main categories: the frictional and seasonal unemployment that follows from small fluctuations in demand for particular goods or services; the enduring unemployment that comes from structural changes in the economy, whether brought about by new technology or shifting patterns of world consumption; the unemployment caused by baffling variations in the overall demand for goods, the upward or downward swings of the international trade cycle. They further considered that some people labelled unemployed were too disabled, physically or mentally, to hold down steady jobs.

All these categories of unemployment are currently being experienced in Britain. There is still a good deal of localized seasonal work, and variations in fashion affect the viability of many small firms. Technological development has changed established patterns of production and service and made large numbers of workers, with various skills, redundant. Most recently, the microelectronic revolution has hit many industries and encouraged talk of a new age of leisure and a permanent reduction in the amount of work to be done in our society. And the world recession, coupled with the impact of the energy crisis, has had a severe and enduring effect on the British economy, dependent as it is on international trade.

An alternative theoretical approach is to break down explanations in terms of either the supply side of the labour market (the levels of skills, etc., of individuals competing in the market), or the demand side (the overall structure of the labour market). Explanations on the supply side will tend to consider levels of training and skill in different population groups. Those on the demand side will consider changing patterns in the balance of industries.

At these broad theoretical levels there is a considerable consensus about the range of causes of unemployment. But more precise explanations of the unemployment of the 1980s become both more technical and more contentious. Industrial problems, particularly labour problems, high wage levels, inflation, the increased entry of married women to the labour force, the movement of capital abroad, the growth of the service sector, the decline of the work ethic, the attack on public expenditure – all these and more are implicated by some observers in the causation of the current problem of unemployment. Economists are no more in agreement than politicians about causes, trends, outcomes or appropriate responses to unemployment in Britain today.

THE RESPONSE TO UNEMPLOYMENT

Disagreement and confusion about the causes of high and chronic unemployment do not help the development of an effective response to it. Because unemployment is so damaging to individuals and to communities the main policy thrust should be in creating more work and ensuring that more of the labour force are fully employed. However, there is no real agreement on how this should be done. Some economists argue, along the lines suggested by Keynes, that governments should manage the economy by increasing public investment in works such as hospital building programmes or road schemes when private investment in industry slackens, thereby evening out the demand for labour. Others argue that high public expenditure is damaging to the economy and must be cut back, even if it increases unemployment, in order to allow industry to recover and become more competitive internationally. Some theorists would argue for more protection for British industry and goods, while opposing theorists urge a more ruthless exposure to foreign competition and the slimming of excess labour and capacity to increase productivity and viability.

Basically there is no real agreement either about whether unemployment could or should be tackled, or about how it should be. Economic policy is ultimately a question of political belief and it sharply polarizes the whole political scene at times of high unemployment. Different economic strategies are advocated and pursued by different governments in the hope of stimulating the economy. Policies to stimulate economic development in the depressed regions, enterprise zones and some other inner-city initiatives have an element of job creation about them, but larger monetary policies concerning inflation or public expenditure probably have more impact on the economy. These policies may or may not have as a central aim the reduction of unemployment. Clearly economic policies are critical to welfare, especially in the realm of employment, but although their relationship to social policies, especially those concerned with poverty and income maintenance, is widely recognized, they do not necessarily have coinciding aims.

In the absence of any clear and agreed response to the basic economic and political problem of the lack of work, social policy tends to be concentrated on attempts to relieve the *consequences* of unemployment. It does this in two main ways: by providing basic income maintenance for the unemployed and their families, and by helping people to find what work there is through the provision of training and retraining schemes to give them the required skills and of Job Centres to put them in touch with employment opportunities. These two areas of provision will now be described.

Income maintenance for the unemployed

All members of the labour force participate to some extent in the National Insurance scheme and this provides an entitlement for the employed worker (*not* the self-employed) to claim unemployment benefit when out of work. To get unemployment benefit a claimant must be capable of and available for work and have paid or been credited with enough NI contributions. The contribution conditions are quite complicated as they are calculated on a person's contribution record in a given tax year related to a given benefit year. If an unemployed person is entitled to benefit, that will be for them, plus extra benefit for any dependent children and for a dependent wife or husband. Unemployment benefit is currently payable at the rate of £34.70 per week to a single person, with £21.40 for an adult dependant, making £56.10 for a couple.

To claim unemployment benefit a person who is out of work has to go to the local unemployment benefit office at regular intervals. Those over 18 no longer have to register for work at the local Job Centre. Unemployment benefit is not payable for the first three days of a period of unemployment and benefit is now payable only after two weeks off work, as it is paid fortnightly in arrears. Once payable, benefit is available for up to a year in any period of 'interruption of earnings'. After receiving benefit for the maximum period, an unemployed person cannot claim benefit again until he or she has been employed for at least thirteen weeks.

The payment of benefit as of right in return for contributions goes back, in Britain, to the Employment Insurance Act of 1911, which first introduced the insurance idea. The scope of unemployment insurance was expanded after the First World War, but the scheme ran into difficulties with the high levels of unemployment of the depression years of the 1920s and 1930s. A restricted insurance scheme was retained and means tested employment assistance was introduced for those who had exhausted their right to benefit. In the comprehensive insurance scheme devised by Beveridge during the Second World War, unemployment became one of the risks covered by comprehensive National Insurance (see Chapter 2), and unemployment assistance was expanded to become the general safety net of National Assistance.

The principle, therefore, seems to be well established that insurance cover can only be provided for a defined period of time. Beyond that the unemployed have to rely on means tested assistance (now income support). However, flat-rate insurance does not really provide adequate income, so even those on benefit may have to apply for extra help. Thus, unemployment benefit is too low, it is hedged around with conditions, and it does not last. The majority of the long-term unemployed and their families are dependent upon income support and housing benefit. This does not really provide an adequate standard of living, particularly for families. The current income support rates, excluding housing costs, provide between £20.80 and £34.90 for a single person and between £27.40 and £54.80 for a couple, depending on age, together with a variable amount for dependent children, according to their age.

An additional problem for many unemployed families, particularly among the unskilled, is that the family income would normally be made up of wages earned by the wife as well as by the husband. When a man is unemployed and his wife is working, his entitlement to insurance benefit is affected only in relation to extra benefit for a dependent wife. If a wife is earning more than the adult dependant benefit, no extra benefit will be payable for her. An unemployed claimant can also earn up to £2 a day and not lose benefit provided that he or she remains available for full-time work. Once entitlement to unemployment benefit is exhausted and income support is necessary, the income of the wife is taken into account in calculating entitlement to benefit. Very little of any extra earnings can be disregarded while a family is dependent on income support, so there is almost no chance of the families of the long-term unemployed improving their position financially.

Indeed, in the last few years changes in unemployment benefit legislation have had the effect of increasing the extent of this dependency on income support. The 1988 Social Security Act increased the period over which a claimant needed to pay contributions in order to be eligible for unemployment benefit from one year to two years. In addition, the period of disqualification from unemployment benefit, for those seen as 'voluntarily' unemployed, was increased from thirteen weeks to twenty-six weeks, whilst the level of income support available to claimants during the period of disqualification was reduced. Also, claimants over 55 who are in receipt of an occupational pension of £35 or more per week cannot claim unemployment benefit. Such changes, in particular those that have increased the reliance of the unemployed on income support, mean that unemployment is more than ever associated with poverty.

The relative poverty of the unemployed, and the indignity of their being forced to rely on means tested benefits for long periods, mean that financial provision for unemployment is far from satisfactory. There is clear evidence of hardship among the families of the unemployed, a hardship that is likely to worsen as the period of unemployment lengthens. Constant financial anxiety, debts and disconnections of fuel supplies are a further cause for depression and stress among the unemployed.

There is certainly no real sense of social security for the unemployed in Britain. Despite this, there is a peculiarly unfair and demoralizing tendency among those in work to blame the unemployed themselves for their situation and even to accuse them of deliberately choosing not to work in order to live on the dole. Talk of welfare scroungers and glib assumptions that people are better off on social security payments are very prevalent. This remains the case even when there are such large numbers out of work. The popular press tends to support unsympathetic attitudes to the unemployed, running stories about people leading a 'life of luxury on the dole'.

The facts of the situation are that there is remarkably little abuse of the benefit system. Some people undoubtedly do defraud the system − by not declaring extra earnings, for example − while others may well not search too diligently for work once accustomed to living on benefit. But every inquiry into the extent of fraud has shown it to be slight, amounting to well under 1 per cent both of the claims made and of the benefit money paid out. In contrast, there is evidence that many people do not claim the benefit to which they are entitled. The overwhelming majority of claimants for unemployment benefit and income support are genuine claimants who have to exist on a meagre income and cope with the stigma of the dole and the demoralization of being out of work. Unemployment and the present inadequate income maintenance system that exists to cope with it highlight the inequalities of contemporary society and perpetuate a vicious cycle of deprivation across the generations.

What could be done to improve this situation? Clearly the unemployed need more money than they can get at present. They are the worst treated of all categories of people depending on social security. But the very fact that there are currently nearly 3 million people unemployed makes it unlikely that they will be treated more generously unless attitudes and priorities change. During the 1960s when unemployment was at a low level, an earnings-related supplement was added to unemployment benefit. This meant, for those who were entitled to the supplement, that the drop of income in periods of short-term unemployment was less dramatic than it might have been. However, this supplement was dropped in 1982 with very little public outcry. It seems very unlikely that any similar or more generous scheme will be reintroduced by the present government, especially since, as just described, the recent changes in unemployment provision have had the effect of decreasing the level of benefits enjoyed by the unemployed.

Hopes for any extension of the period over which unemployment benefit can be claimed seem equally unlikely to be met. The present government is reluctant to take any measures that would increase the social security bill, and any extension of people's rights to benefit would increase costs. There is a case for extending entitlement to unemployment benefit, as of right, for as long as unemployment lasts. If a person is unable to work because of ill-health, then their right to invalidity benefit is without any time limit. Although it would be fair to treat the unemployed in a similar manner, it hardly seems politically feasible. Some increase in the level of unemployment benefit and income support can be argued for, but the level of such benefits tends to be set by the lowest levels of wages for unskilled work. It is always difficult to establish equity between low-paid workers and social security recipients and hostile media responses to the unemployed do not make it any easier to be fair to those out of work.

More generous family income maintenance could help the families of the unemployed without reducing the incentive to return to work or confusing equity between workers and non-workers. Many families would also benefit from more vigorous welfare rights campaigns and better information about benefits so that take-up of existing benefits improves. More generous disregards would enable those who cannot find permanent full-time work to increase their income if benefits were not too rapidly affected. At present there is little incentive for the unemployed or their spouses to try to earn what money they can to boost the family income: if they declare it they lose benefit and if they do not declare it they are liable to prosecution for fraud. Since the unemployed are frequently exhorted not to be idle and dependent, but to be full of energy and initiative, the response of the system to any entrepreneurial enterprise that falls short of achieving full independence for the unemployed is baffling and depressing. If high levels of unemployment are to be a permanent part of a new high-technology age in western industrial nations, then a new and flexible approach to income maintenance is required. Without a new approach the position of the have-nots in our society could deteriorate even further than it has at present.

Manpower and training policies

Providing an income to those who cannot find work is a major part of the social policy response to unemployment. However, governments have also considered how they could improve the labour supply and make it more relevant to the labour market. We have already noted that unemployment varies quite dramatically between different regions. People move to find work in more prosperous regions or countries and much recent migration (both immigration and emigration) reflects movements of the labour force in the active search for work.

Even before the first rudimentary insurance scheme was introduced to tackle the financial needs of the unemployed, a system of employment or labour exchanges had been introduced to help people find work. Labour exchanges held details of job vacancies reported by employers and they tried to match applicants to jobs and employers to suitable labour. When unemployment insurance was introduced it was made payable at the labour exchange when a claimant signed on each week for work. Labour exchanges were not the first responsibility of the central government Ministry of Labour: the original department was primarily concerned with questions of conciliation and arbitration in industrial disputes, as well as with the analysis of labour statistics. However, the labour exchanges and then the payment of unemployment benefit gradually came to dominate the work of the central department, particularly during the inter-war depression years. During the Second World War, the Ministry of Labour and National Service, as the department was then called, was active in the conscription and direction of labour and it took over responsibility for factory legislation as well as developing its training side.

The Ministry of Labour changed its name in 1968 to the Department of Employment and Productivity and in 1970 to the Department of Employment. In 1973 it was drastically altered by the establishment of the Manpower Services Commission (MSC), which took over responsibility for employment and training services, and in 1974 the Advisory, Conciliation and Arbitration Service was set up to work to solve industrial disputes.

The Manpower Services Commission was responsible to the Secretary of State for Employment and was a quasi-independent commission with a full-time chair and representatives of employers, trade unions, local authorities and professional training bodies. The MSC made arrangements to assist people to 'select, train for, obtain and retain employment', and had a general responsibility with regards to unemployment and training.

The setting-up of the MSC reflected a dissatisfaction with the role and image of the old Department of Employment and a growing awareness of the need to develop a comprehensive manpower policy. It had become clear, particularly as unemployment increased, but more generally as a consequence of failing economic performance, that the post-war boom had endured more by good luck than good management and there was no real manpower policy to seek to fit the labour supply to the changing labour market. Many new jobs had been filled in the 1960s by recruiting new members to the labour force – married women and New Commonwealth immigrants, for example – rather than by retraining or relocating those made redundant by changes in the labour market structure. Training for industry had been haphazard and uncoordinated, based on a variable pattern of apprenticeships and day-release work at technical colleges, with industry bearing a substantial proportion of the costs. A new approach to manpower training was clearly needed.

On the employment agency side, it was felt that the old exchanges had developed a 'dole queue image' and become identified more with the administration of benefit than with the provision of an active employment agency service. But the major concern was undoubtedly with unemployment, which in the 1970s was very noticeable in its impact on young people. Unemployment could have a positive impact, it was suggested, if it provided the impetus and opportunity for training, but it was utterly wasteful and damaging if it merely enforced idleness. The Employment and Training Act 1973, which established the MSC, also set up an Employment Service Agency and a Training Services Agency. These agencies were integrated as divisions of the MSC in 1978 and a further division was set up with responsibility for special programmes.

The MSC set about creating a new image for the employment exchanges. A new system of Job Centres was created and these aimed to provide a lively and positive placement service. They are often situated prominently in the local high street and try to offer a very personal and constructive service. Payment of unemployment benefit was separated into benefit offices so that the Job Centre could compete more effectively with the private agencies in attracting notices of job vacancies. It is no longer obligatory for all unemployed people to register at their local Job Centre. Unfortunately, the efforts of the Job Centres are hampered by the fact that the number of vacancies fell rapidly in the late 1970s, and only a third of such job vacancies as do exist are currently notified to the centres.

In 1988 the MSC became the Training Commission and then, later the same year, was renamed the Training Agency. The Training Agency continues to be responsible for increasing the relevance of education to employment, through the Technical and Vocational Education Initiative (TVEI) in schools. It is also responsible for other schemes, including Business Growth Training, the Enterprise Allowance and the Small Firms Service. In addition, the Training Agency runs the Employment Training Scheme (ET), which aims to help people gain skills and knowledge to enable them to compete more effectively for jobs. The training is both directed and practical, and is for a maximum of twelve months. A qualification is obtainable at the end of this period. This will be either a City and Guilds or other recognized qualification or, if none exist in the area of training received, a National Record of Vocational Achievement awarded by the TA. Trainees receive an allowance at least £10 above their normal weekly benefit, and whilst ET is open to everyone between 18 and 60, priority is given to 18–24 year olds.

YOUTH UNEMPLOYMENT

A disturbing feature of the present severe unemployment is its effect on young people. Youth unemployment is a major phenomenon: 10 per cent of male and 15 per cent of female unemployment is made up of unemployed 16–19 year olds, although these proportions have been reduced in recent years as a result of young people on YTS schemes no longer being registered as unemployed. More unemployed than employed young people are without qualifications.

Not surprisingly, the MSC was particularly concerned with these problems and it put a great deal of thought and effort into finding solutions to them. In terms of youth training the MSC launched into a series of publications and special programmes with rather bewildering speed. *Towards a Comprehensive Manpower Policy* was published in 1976 and the first schemes of Job Creation and Work Experience were established, concentrating mainly on the young. The Holland Report, *Young People and Work*, followed in 1977 and concentrated on the problem of unemployment among young people. On its recommendations the Job Creation Programme was phased out and the Youth Opportunities Programme was introduced. Most recently, the Youth Training Scheme and Employment Training have been implemented. It is difficult to know what is being achieved with such a rapid series of programmes. According to some critics the proliferation of schemes has more to do with an *ad hoc* reaction to crises in the unemployment situation than with the development of any really thoughtful manpower policy directed towards young people.

Basically the main thrust of the MSC's work, and now that of the Training Agency, has moved away from special programmes to create work towards new training initiatives. The Job Creation Programme ran from 1976 until it petered out in 1981. Job Creation schemes aimed to provide work for young people, and some older experienced unemployed people, in a variety of settings. Priority was given to projects that would contribute to environmental improvement, particularly urban renewal. Local authorities were the principal sponsors, with voluntary organizations the second most important group involved. Schemes ranged from derelict land reclamation to carpentry shops, and they provided a short-term but stimulating experience of work in a variety of settings for a range of young people.

Alongside the Job Creation Programme the MSC launched a Work Experience Programme, where the emphasis was on providing help to young people in the transition from school to work. WEP was available to youngsters under 19 and it provided, instead of temporary employment, opportunities to learn about work. Instead of a modest wage, the young people were paid a training allowance. WEP schemes were to provide, over at least six months, for induction, planned work experience under supervision, further education or off-the-job training and counselling on personal progress and problems. WEP schemes could be run by any employing organizations, but encouragement was given to private employers.

As Job Creation and Work Experience developed, it became clear that unemployment, particularly youth unemployment, was not going to be a temporary phenomenon. The Holland Report, *Young People and Work*, acknowledged the severity of the unemployment situation and outlined the need to think coherently about the range of opportunities for young people in work, in education and on special programmes. Following the report's proposals, two new schemes were introduced in 1978: the Youth Opportunities Programme and the Special Temporary Employment Programme.

The Youth Opportunities Programme (YOP) and the accompanying Special Temporary Employment Programme (STEP) were to be run by area boards: twenty-eight boards were set up in 1978 and a network of local consultative groups was encouraged. STEP was designed to create some temporary posts for young adults, particularly in the inner-city areas. It was replaced in 1981 by the Community Enterprise Programme, which later became the Community Programme. Young unemployed adults aged 18–24 were employed on community projects for a maximum of one year. Voluntary organizations made considerable use of this MSC funding of temporary jobs to expand a wide range of community services. The young adults became employees of the sponsoring organization, which was reimbursed for approved wages and a contribution towards running costs. Schemes provided for environmental improvements, energy conservation and local community amenities. The Community Programme no longer exists, which has severely affected many local community groups and projects.

Alternative training for 18–24 year olds is provided by Employment Training, in which this age group are a priority. ET represents a move away from using young unemployed people as a source of labour for voluntary and community projects towards training within industry and the service sector, with a qualification at the end of it. However, the true value of this training remains to be seen as the scheme progresses.

The Youth Opportunities Programme, like its predecessor Work Experience, aimed not to create jobs, but to link young people into the world of work by offering them a range of work experience and work preparation to equip them for finding jobs. Based on the experience of this programme, the MSC published, in 1981, a report entitled *A New Training Initiative*, which the government backed in its White Paper *A New Training Initiative: A Programme for Action*. This ushered in an ambitious Youth Training Scheme designed to provide, from September 1983, a full year's foundation training for all unemployed school leavers. It also aimed to develop the scheme to create more opportunities for training for young people in employment and to set a target date for recognized standards for all craft, technical and professional skills, to replace existing time-serving or age-restricted apprentice-ships. Further training needs for adults were also considered.

The Youth Training Scheme was operative by the end of 1983. It is an ambitious and contentious scheme described as 'a vocational preparation scheme for young people of all abilities designed to provide an integrated programme of training, planned work experience and further education'. It aims to be 'work based and focused on practical competence'. YTS aims to be a real bridge between school and work. It is open to all 16 year olds, unemployed or in employment, some 17 year olds and some young disabled people up to the age of 21. It offers up to two years of training in a wide range of skills: engineering, computing, catering, retailing, food manufacturing and farming are mentioned in the MSC promotional literature. YTS is not compulsory, though young people who do not participate may lose income support. YTS schemes aim to attract and train all the young unemployed and to provide a varied and flexible vocational education.

The schemes themselves are run by a large number of firms, colleges and organizations. Managing agents are responsible for coordinating local schemes, so that all the elements of induction, work experience, off-the-job training, skill training and assessment can be brought together, and schemes are approved by the Training Agency. There are two main types of scheme. Mode A provides financial support to employers in their training tasks. The idea is that if an employer, or group of small employers, agree to take on more school leavers than they would normally employ and train, the Training Agency pays not only for the extra trainees, but for some of the normal intake, in the ratio of 3:2. There is also some payment for the managing agents' time in organizing the scheme. Young trainees are paid an allowance during the training year, currently £29.50 per week in the first year and £35 in the second, which is payable out of the block grant. Mode B funding covers schemes that cater wholly for unemployed young people. Training workshops and community projects as developed under YOP are being continued and new schemes set up.

The Youth Training Scheme is clearly ambitious and comprehensive. Some of its supporters argue that it provides a stimulating opportunity for young people to get involved in the world of work instead of becoming apathetic and depressed on the dole queue. It equips large numbers of youngsters with skills of a varied nature and gives them the motivation to learn and to look for relevant work, while it provides industry and services with a better trained and organized potential workforce. Critics argue that it encourages employers to take on trainees for short-term schemes rather than young employees for permanent work, it subsidizes employers, underpays young workers, and fails to tackle the fundamental problem of shortages of jobs. YTS schemes were certainly under-subscribed initially though the take-up is improving.

The scheme is obviously, like the whole range of Training Agency activities, a costly growth area, and is subject to government pressure to concentrate rather more attention on the needs of industry than the interests of the young unemployed. Pressure groups, particularly Youthaid (the voluntary organization representing the interests of the young unemployed), are highly critical of the TA's lack of support for the Mode B schemes, run by local authorities and voluntary bodies, compared with the employer-based Mode A schemes. The whole scheme is thoroughly confused in its basic objective of helping industry *and* helping young people. Arguably it is better than nothing, and many individual YTS schemes are innovative and rewarding experiences for the trainees concerned. But to develop such schemes while education services are cut and jobs are reduced is bound to prove a controversial issue. Education does not, it is claimed, cater adequately for the vocational needs of young people, particularly the less academic young people. But it is not clear that the TA is better placed than further and higher education to improve the school–work link.

OTHER RESPONSES TO UNEMPLOYMENT

Income maintenance and placement and training services are the principal social service responses to unemployment. But unemployment clearly has an impact on other areas of provision. Because of the effects on health and family life, high unemployment needs to be considered by other services, but there is little focused response to it at present. Social service departments are well aware of the increase in family problems associated with unemployment: the poverty of the unemployed is evident in the increase in debt and financial difficulties, while the stress of being out of work plays its part in crises in family relationships. There is some response from the voluntary organizations, both to cater for the social needs of the unemployed and to use the unemployed in voluntary work with the old or handicapped, but the scope of this is slight. Many local authorities and recreational and cultural bodies now acknowledge the poverty of the unemployed by offering free or reduced fares or entry fees, etc., for the 'unwaged'. But there is still a marked tendency among service providers and the employed generally to ignore the unemployed and to avoid taking account of their problems.

Unemployment is a serious social problem, difficult to tackle at its basic causal level, and expensive to respond to at the level of impact on individuals and families. The present social policy to deal with the social impact of unemployment is inadequate: financial provision in particular is ungenerous and unimaginative. The need for those in work (and relatively well off), to share resources and living standards with those out of work (and relatively deprived), is imperative. But it is only likely to develop if there is a much greater understanding of the causes and problems of unemployment and a much deeper commitment to the welfare of the whole of our society.

SUGGESTIONS FOR FURTHER READING

Brenner, M. H., *Mental Illness and the Economy* (Harvard University Press, 1973).

Brown, M., *The Structure of Disadvantages* (Heinemann, 1983).

Burghes, L. and Lister, R., *Unemployment: Who Pays the Price?* (Child Poverty Action Group, 1981).

Harris, J., *Unemployment and Social Policy* (Oxford University Press, 1973).

Hawkins, K., *Unemployment* (Penguin, 1984).

Hayes, J. and Nutman, P., *Understanding the Unemployed* (Tavistock, 1981).

Piachaud, D., *The Dole* (Centre for Labour Economics, 1981).

Purcell, K. (ed.), *The Changing Experience of Unemployment* (Macmillan, 1986).

Showler, B. and Sinfield, A., (eds), *The Workless State* (Martin Robertson, 1981).

Sinfield, A., *What Unemployment Means* (Martin Robertson, 1981).

7

The personal social services

THE NEED FOR SOCIAL CARE

The need for social care is not easily defined or described. This is because there is no absolute need for care – it depends on what society acknowledges as reasonable at any point in time. The whole area of personal needs and social services is fraught with value judgements about the proper functions of the family or the responsibilities of the individual and woolly ideas about communities. Nevertheless, at a very simple level, it is accepted that some people need care because they cannot look after themselves and lack adequate family and neighbourhood support.

The reasons why people need care are many and varied. Some people have extra handicaps to cope with: physical disability, the frailty of extreme old age, mental handicap and such like. Children will need care if their parents are unable to provide it or do not do so to the standards society currently considers necessary. Many people become casualties of over-rapid social change and inadequate social provisions. People cannot cope on poverty-line incomes with housing shortages and unemployment. Single-parent families and immigrants face added difficulties in finding and keeping a home together, and many who have been ill or become redundant at work or who have been left socially isolated need help to rehabili-tate themselves in society. The individual problems vary enormously, but the need for some form of social care is common to them all.

Not only do some individuals and families need care; neighbourhoods and communities are often unable to function effectively. Industrial decline, slum clearance, and changing patterns of transport and communication can destroy or debilitate communities, leaving them vulnerable and disorganized, unable to adapt to change or to retain a fair share of resources.

Although the need for social care has long been recognized, only recently has it been perceived as a sufficiently discrete and coherent need to justify separate and distinct statutory provision. Traditionally, statutory concern with the need for social care was interwoven with provision for destitution, treatment or control. Provision was usually of an institutional nature and the care element was subordinate to the primary objectives of the workhouse, asylum, infirmary, hostel or reformatory that offered it. Gradually provision of care became a separate function, distinct from the provision of income, medical attention, education or reform. However, it was then limited to separate and distinguishable groups, such as orphaned children or the disabled, to meet their needs.

This fragmented provision focused attention on the problems of specific groups and made possible the development of some caring services to a very high standard. For example, local authority children's departments, responsible for children deprived of normal home life, provided a range of children's homes and supervised fostering and adoption with the help of specially trained child care officers. But the cost of specialization was considerable. Specialization tended to isolate groups from the rest of society and even from their families. It led to some overlap in services, confusion of responsibility, gaps in provision and awkward career prospects for the social workers concerned. Concentration on need groups meant that services tended to operate on a casualty basis, taking action only when there had been a failure in family or community support and unable, therefore, to work to prevent failures. The specialist services remained tiny, with insignificant budgets and no say in vital planning issues that affected the total community. In each area of concern there was increasing anxiety over the need to provide more preventive work and support to the family and community and it became clear that the specific orientation of social care services hindered developments along such lines.

Disillusionment with institutional solutions to the need for care and a growing interest in community alternatives, together with increasing concern for prevention, have helped to form a more general view of the problem. It is now accepted that individuals, families and communities need care because they have problems they cannot deal with on their own. The reasons why people need help vary enormously and so do the motives of the state for intervening in their lives. But the general need for social care is now considered an appropriate focus for the organization of services to meet that need.

The type of care needed varies considerably. Some people need a home, a place to live, an accepting and caring environment. In some cases they may only need a temporary shelter, in others a fairly permanent home. A need for residential care has long been recognized for certain groups such as deprived children, old people and those with mental or physical disabilities. Other groups such as homeless single persons, wayward adolescents, ex-prisoners or battered wives, have a need for care that is often less widely acknowledged.

Only small minorities need full residential care but many more people need a degree of help and support in the community. Many people have a home but need help in running it – practical help with maintenance or domestic work, or adaptations to take account of disabilities, or general advice and support, or help with meals, or simply company. Many handicapped individuals have families who do devotedly care for them but need occasional relief or regular support. Care can be provided during the day for children, old people, the disabled and so forth, to enable them and their families to cope without the necessity for a full residential placement and without unnecessary stress or neglect.

Some individuals lack family support and need a substitute for the care a family could provide, but many families themselves need support in order to keep together. Families are particularly crucial for the care and socialization of children and many need help in these functions if they are to survive and provide adequate standards of care. Families may need practical help and all too often material aid; advice on the bringing up of children and support through day care and services; help with a wide range of problems from housing to marital relations. Care of the family can be a valuable preventive measure, reducing the need of children or the handicapped for residential care. In both family care and individual care there is a need for advice and help in using other statutory services – in obtaining maximum benefits, adequate medical care, better housing and so on.

The needs of communities vary, though most share a need for better communication and involvement of people in the services and provisions that affect their lives. In some areas the need for greater self-determination is striking, as people have opted out of conventional democratic processes and succumbed to feelings of helplessness in the face of technological change and bureaucratic bullying. Communities need encouragement to greater political participation in local affairs, they need confidence to express their interests and demands, they need a renewal of hope and determination to improve community life. In deprived areas, community groups need active encouragement to become involved through better information, professional advice and support and practical services for aiding organization. In some communities there is a particular need to develop tolerance and improve race relations; in others the need is to reduce vandalism and violence; in others to develop a greater sense of neighbourly responsibility. At a time of increasing professionalism and bureaucracy, the power and responsibility of ordinary people as individuals and neighbourhood groups need emphasizing and developing. The capacity of society to care for its more vulnerable members and to contain violence and disharmony depends as much if not more on ordinary families and communities as it does on statutory services and expertise, but both families and communities may need professional support if they are to function effectively.

In the personal social services, needs are often elusive and intangible, and they are still very controversial. While the need for residential care is well established, the need for community development is much less accepted. But in fact the two are very strongly linked. It is easy to see a need for total social care when children are abandoned or old people isolated. However total care is not an adequate solution to such problems because institutions can themselves generate and perpetuate difficulties. If the need is seen as one of *preventing* family break-up or the isolation of the elderly, rather than one of coping with the consequences of such events, then the need for community development and family support becomes much clearer. In the pursuit of prevention a wide range of social needs for day care and domiciliary services have now become visible, and serious problems of urban deprivation and social injustice are being revealed. The need for social care cannot easily be described or quantified partly because in this sensitive area the interrelated nature of social needs is so apparent. A need for care may be the result of a need for better housing or it may be linked to the wider social problems of a whole area. Moreover, our perception of need is limited by our ability to respond to it, and it is easier to provide palliative care than to revitalize communities or achieve a better distribution of resources. We none the less have some idea of the dimensions of the problem and can see that it embraces an immediate need to provide social care and support to a variety of individuals and families; a longer-term need to develop more effective family and community life; and an ultimate concern with social justice. In response to this curious mix of needs, from practical things like gadgets or mobile meals services to a vague ideal of social purpose and community welfare, we have evolved the personal social services whose structure will now be described.

THE ADMINISTRATION OF PERSONAL SOCIAL SERVICES

The provision of personal social services is the responsibility of local authorities. Under the Local Authority Social Services Act 1970, the counties and metropolitan districts of England and Wales and the London Boroughs have to establish a social services committee. The committee appoints a director of social services – a local government chief officer – who runs a department of social services. The department is responsible for the provision of residential care services, a variety of day care facilities, domiciliary and advice services and social help to communities, schools and hospitals.

At central level, responsibility lies with the Department of Health, which has a Personal Social Services division. Professional advice is provided by the Social Work Service, which has a central establishment and twelve regional offices. The Social Work Service is responsible for the general development of the personal social services; its role is basically constructive rather than regulative, although it does retain some inspectorial duties. Within the Social Work Service is a development group responsible for generating new ideas and experimenting with best practice. The Secretary of State for Social Services has overall responsibility for this area of provision.

The Seebohm Report

The effect of the Local Authority Social Services Act 1970 was basically to unify the previously fragmented and specialized social care services that had existed for the elderly, the disabled, deprived children and the mentally ill and handicapped. The Act was passed following the recommendations of the Seebohm Committee which published its report, *Local Authority and Allied Personal Social Services* (Cmnd 3703), in 1968. The Seebohm Committee was set up in 1965 to review the organization of personal social services and consider what changes were necessary to create a more effective family welfare service. The personal social services existed to promote the welfare of different groups of people with special needs. They were services that made use of social work skills to help people cope with special problems and make full use of all available community resources from statutory services to neighbourly help; they provided such extra care through residential homes or day or domiciliary support as was deemed necessary. Most of the social care provided was a response to the dependencies created by social, physical or mental handicaps, but some was concerned with problems of social control, especially those arising from child neglect or delinquency. The main services were provided by local authority children's departments and welfare departments, but some were the responsibility of local health departments, which had particular concern for the care of the mentally ill and mentally handicapped and some families with difficulties. A good deal of specialized social care provision was also made by voluntary bodies sometimes aiding the statutory concern and sometimes pioneering with new services or new need groups.

As was noted in the previous section, policies of prevention and community care in all the services led to a renewed interest in family welfare. During the 1960s there was mounting concern at the lack of any clear statutory responsibility for the welfare of families and the consequent inadequacy, overlap and confusion of provision. Psychological and sociological studies were emphasizing the importance of the family and demonstrating its vulnerability in the face of social change. There was also a growing awareness of the need for coordination of policies and provision between services and of the need to strengthen the social care sector in local government. On the professional front, social workers were increasingly conscious of the shortcomings of fragmented provision and were moving towards professional unity and generic training.

There was accordingly considerable interest in the Seebohm Committee's deliberations, and evidence was obtained from a wide range of relevant organizations and professions. There was a fair degree of consensus on the need for administrative reorganization, and the committee's call for a unified personal social services department was generally welcomed. The Seebohm Report went further than suggesting fundamental administrative reforms, however: it put forward a radically different view of the role of personal social care services. To quote the opening phrase of the report:

> We recommend a new local authority department providing a community-based and family oriented service which will be available to all. This new department will we believe reach far beyond the discovery and rescue of social casualties: it will enable the greatest possible number of individuals to act reciprocally, giving and receiving service for the well being of the whole community.

So the objectives of the local authority social services departments derive from the Seebohm Report. The 1970 Act merely implemented the reorganization suggested by Seebohm and listed the legislative duties of the new departments, but the report attempted to establish a new philosophy for social care. It emphasized the importance not only of the family but also of the community. It envisaged a department concerned with the welfare needs of all people, not merely those minorities who had become casualties or had clearly definable handicaps. And it spelt out in some detail ways in which the social care services could be made more generally relevant and available so that they would become a genuinely universal and basic social service.

The legislative position

Under the 1970 Act, local authorities have established social services committees and departments and to these are referred a wide range of duties and responsibilities. Among the principal duties are the duty to receive children deprived of normal home life into care and duties to promote the welfare of children and to provide for children in trouble. Most of these duties are spelt out in the Children Acts and the Children and Young Persons Acts. Under the National Assistance Act of 1948, local authorities have duties to provide residential accommodation for the elderly and infirm and to promote the welfare of the blind, the deaf and the general classes of the handicapped, including those suffering from mental disorders. Various functions that derive from the National Health Service Act of 1946 are now referred to social services. These include the provision of home helps, and certain responsibilities formerly belonging to maternity and child welfare, including the provision of day nurseries. Social services also have responsibility for the registration of homes for old people and the regulation of nurseries and child-minders. They have a responsibility to act as adoption agencies and a duty to provide and maintain reception centres for persons without a settled way of living. Under the Chronically Sick and Disabled Persons Act 1970 they have a duty to obtain information on the need for welfare services and a duty to make such provision.

These are the principal legislative concerns of the social services departments: the full schedule of related enactments is more detailed. It can be seen that the legislative position is very complex, partly because of the background of social services in specialized and fragmented provision but largely because the needs they are responding to are so sensitive and variable. The list of statutory duties is long. It includes some very precise and inescapable responsibilities, such as those for providing homes and keeping registers, which still shape the output of social service departments and determine much of their allocation of resources and development of work. But it also includes some decidedly vague duties to 'promote the welfare' of certain groups, under which legislative sanction much preventive and community work is now being done and under which the Seebohm objective of a reciprocal community welfare service can be pursued.

STRUCTURE AND ORGANIZATION OF SOCIAL SERVICES DEPARTMENTS

Under the 1970 reorganization there was major structural change in the creation of new unified departments. There was also much concern to make those departments more efficient in the use of scarce resources and to create management systems within them that would assist in the development of a more universal service. Considerable interest in the application of management theory and technique to social service organization was manifest at this time. As a result the structure of many departments benefited from a conscious and informed intent to devise an organization that would match the objectives of the new service. There was concern to make the service more acceptable and accessible and to move away from the narrowness of specialist care. Accordingly, attempts were made to ensure decentralization of provision, to allow flexibility and discretion at field level, to facilitate the flow of communication throughout the organization and to create a truly generic social work service. There was also concern to create the potential for effective planning and involvement in local corporate management.

Obviously local variations do exist, but a typical social service department has some degree of decentralization through area teams and some division of responsibility along activity rather than need groups lines. Typically, assistant directors head sections responsible for fieldwork, residential work, domiciliary and day care services and research and development. A small number of area teams are established, each with an area office serving a given geographical area. The fieldwork services are usually decentralized, teams of social workers working with generic caseloads of families, children, old people, the handicapped or mentally ill as the need arises. The other main provisions vary, with residential provision largely run on an authority rather than area basis and some of the day and domiciliary services operating from area team level, while others serve the whole authority.

The area teams of social workers mostly work generically but some specialization does exist. In some authorities specialist intake teams concentrate on diagnostic work and intensive short-term care. In most areas one or more community workers will be active in supporting community groups and stimulating local action. Liaison with voluntary bodies is an important aspect of the job, as is the encouragement and use of volunteers. Area teams make contact with other social services, liaising with schools and community health services and working with the courts and hospitals.

The changes in social work consequent upon reorganization have been considerable. The move to generic work, the greater involvement in the community and the increased concern with prevention and social change led to much anxiety about the role of social workers. A constant and often vigorous debate has been carried on around the relative merits of case work or community work and over the whole position of social workers in our society. It seems appropriate that, at a time of reorganization, roles as well as structures should change and the debate is necessary. It might be helpful none the less to offer a brief and necessarily limited description of the social worker's role.

All social workers have basically two functions. One is to put their clients in touch with all the services and resources (statutory, voluntary, neighbourly and personal), that might be of help to them in coping with problems and to assist them if necessary in persisting with applications and appeals and understanding regulations. The other is to help clients to gain insight into the nature of their problems, to offer comfort and support in times of stress and to help clients to either adjust to their situation or move constructively to change it. These functions apply whether the client is an individual, a group, a family or a whole community. In all cases the social worker's aim should be to help with a mixture of practical assistance and the development of insight and understanding. Social workers therefore need access to extensive resources and must develop skill in the diagnosis of problems and in the helping process. Their work must always be demanding because human problems are always complex and often deceptive and contradictory. Their work is often depressing because human problems involve suffering and solutions are not easy. There is often conflict between immediate help and long-term prevention, and the more social workers probe into the causes of distress the less possible it becomes to find easy answers and the more necessary it becomes to respond on individual, community and societal levels in the search for solutions. Inevitably social workers must at times feel frustrated, impotent and unsure of themselves, but at other times they will feel they have helped and responded adequately to a need for social care.

Fieldwork is rightly regarded as the frontline service in social care because social workers should have the immediate and initial contact at the area office or in the client's home with the people they seek to help. However, it is now well recognized that a range of practical services must be brought into play to help people. Day and domiciliary services are of growing importance in social service departments. Day care may be provided for children whose mothers work, although it is now more often provided for mothers who are under stress. Day nursery provision is usually inadequate for the need and supervised child-minding is also provided. Encouragement is given to local groups to provide playgroups for the benefit of mothers and children, even where there is no absolute need for care because of a mother's absence. Day centres are provided for old people, offering a place to go, lunch, social and recreational activities and sometimes medical care. For the handicapped, day centres usually aim to provide occupation and sometimes rehabilitation. Domiciliary services include the highly important home help service, especially useful for the elderly and disabled, mobile meals services, practical help with the problems of disability, laundry services, aids and adaptations for the blind, deaf and handicapped. Peripatetic foster mother schemes help children to stay in their own homes, and, when a substitute home has to be found for children, boarding out with suitable families provides an alternative to the use of residential care.

The provision of residential care is still a major function of social services departments, even though the community care services have received more attention recently. In fact, residential provision still accounts for just over half the total cost of personal social services. Homes are provided for children in need of care and children in trouble. These are now known as community homes and local authorities are grouped in regional planning committees to provide a full range of homes from small family group homes to specialized assessment centres and schools. The largest group for whom residential care is provided is the elderly and physically handicapped. Again, a variety of provision exists, but the variation has much to do with the age and size of the buildings and less with different functions. Relatively little provision is made so far for the mentally ill and handicapped, as economies have held back the building programme that should have increased provision for these groups. For other groups such as the homeless or young unmarried mothers provision is locally extremely variable. The provision of residential care is costly in both capital terms and current costs. It has suffered, in a time of interest in community care, from unpopularity and consequent neglect. But its contribution to social care must always remain an important one and efforts have to be made to avoid the isolation of this aspect of care from other services and developments.

One of the major points emphasized in the Seebohm Report was the poor quality of many social care services and the gaps in provisions. Far too many services were of a low standard, having poor facilities, untrained staff, long waiting lists and inadequate coverage. There was a considerable lack of information about the extent of needs for different services and consequently little attempt at rational ordering of priorities. Too many services were provided without any attempt to evaluate their effectiveness, and shortfall in provision was largely guessed at. As a result, Seebohm recommended that social services departments undertake research into needs and attempt to monitor the effects of different policies and compare the success of different provisions. Accordingly, most, though not all, local departments have a research and development section. These sections collect data on their localities and assess needs so that the department is in a better position to plan its services and decide on priorities. They can evaluate provision, initiate and monitor change and examine the substitutability of different services. They are particularly important in the overall local government context to help give the social services department an effective say in the authorities' corporate planning. Research and development staff are also well placed to forge links with related services. Along with fieldworkers they can be involved on health care planning teams and contribute to such things as housing action areas and community development programmes.

THE DEVELOPMENT OF PERSONAL SOCIAL SERVICES

The Seebohm Report and the publicity over reorganization raised expectations of the new departments to unrealistic levels. Initially problems of structure and staffing were the main preoccupation, and then departments had to take stock of their inheritance of buildings and services and attempt to even up standards and fill in gaps.

The tasks of reorganization and improvement would themselves have been considerable, but several other new responsibilities coincided with the changeover. The Children and Young Persons Act of 1969 was to be implemented and this placed heavy new responsibilities on the social services departments, especially to provide court reports and supervision and also to develop new services of intermediate treatment. The

Chronically Sick and Disabled Persons Act of 1970 gave the departments an entirely new responsibility to assess the needs of the disabled and to ensure provision was available to meet them, and this resulted in enormous pressure of work. The White Paper, *Better Services for the Mentally Handicapped*, published in 1971, asked the local departments to take a much more vigorous part in providing community care for this neglected group.

As a result of these measures, and generally raised expectations, local social services were initially under considerable pressure. Inevitably there were some complaints of a deterioration in standards, especially from the courts and the medical profession. But in fact the scope of their work has increased steadily: more people are receiving more services than ever before, and the departments have tackled new challenges, such as the impact of high unemployment and the growing evidence of widespread child abuse.

Staffing problems

Clearly staffing is a major issue in social services departments as staff are the main resource. Total staff involved in 1985 in England amounted to 300,910 or 217,013 in whole-time equivalents. Of these numbers 29,721, (13–14 per cent) were social workers, nearly 55,000 were in the home help service, and 57,000 were in residential work.

Much thought has been given recently to the whole question of training. In 1971 the Central Council for Education and Training in Social Work (CCETSW) was established. The council has a statutory responsibility to promote education and training in all fields of social work and to recognize courses and award qualifications. It consists of members representing the employing bodies, educational establishments and professional associations.

The council recognizes courses that lead to the award of the Certificate of Qualification in Social Work (CQSW). This qualification is obtained after successful completion of either a two-year training in social work at a College of Further Education or a university training for graduates. University graduate courses are either two years, or one year for graduates who already have social science qualifications. In addition some universities now offer four-year degree courses in social work studies where students combine a degree and the CQSW. The CQSW is now the standard, basic generic training for social workers. A further qualification,the Certificate in Social Science (CSS), was introduced by the central council to encourage the development of an alternative, less academic training for workers in social services departments who are not CQSW trained. The CSS is available for the numerous workers who provide supporting services in day or domiciliary care or who carry out routine visiting and offer practical help to clients. Training is largely on an in-service basis. The residential field has always had a training problem, as the vast majority of workers have had no direct qualifications for their demanding jobs. A CCETSW report in 1973 asserted that *Residential Work is a Part of Social Work,* and argued for common training at CQSW and CSS levels for the staff of homes. All too often the particular needs of residential staff are neglected by the training courses, however, and this area remains a problem.

More recent debates within CCETSW have brought about a change in the training programme, to be implemented in the early 1990s. Much of the early debate focused on extending the training period for qualified social workers to three years, including an additional year for specialist training in one area of social work. Given the difficulty of obtaining government financing for such an extension, however, CCETSW have now agreed to a new two-year course leading to a diploma in social work, which will replace both the two-year CQSW and the shorter course for graduates with social science qualifications.

A major issue in staffing the personal social services concerns the administration of the department. Senior staff at director and assistant director level include many people with professional social work backgrounds. While this has proved important to the development of the services, it does mean that many lack specific management skills. Some attempts are now being made to offer courses to social workers in senior and middle management grades to provide some training in management and social planning. This cannot be covered in professional social work training and anyway benefits from the recruitment of older, post-experienced personnel. A neglected but related issue concerns administrative staff without professional social work training; they are barred at present from moving up to the highest level of management, however experienced they are in the delivery of personal social services.

The whole question of training for social workers is essentially bound up with the question of their role. The social work profession welcomed the move to create a unified social services department, and on the whole it has been enormously strengthened by it in terms of numbers and of influence. But the Seebohm development gave rise to confusion and uncertainty as well as expansion and growth, and social workers have proved extremely susceptible to anxieties about their role. They have been uncertain about the move to generic social work and loss of specialist skills, about the place of community work and community development in social services, about their involvement in administration and the management of local government, and about their role as client advocates and campaigners for welfare rights. The issue is a complex one and gives rise to strong feelings, and there is space here to touch on only some of its more controversial aspects.

The establishment of integrated social services departments offered new opportunities to social workers to provide a more community-based and preventive general welfare service. Community development approaches and the fostering of self-help groups were urged as more appropriate methods of social work for area teams. Working with individuals, largely through the development of psychological insights rather than the provision of material help, was condemned by some critics as at best irrelevant and at worst blatant social control. Increasing numbers of poor clients with financial problems meant that much social work time was spent in argument with income support offices and in dispute over fuel bills. Inevitably social workers found themselves confused by these changes, and the training courses overloaded students with new approaches and information, and argued over course content. Meanwhile older staff, trained and experienced in child care or mental health, resented the loss of specialist work. There was criticism from inside and outside the social work profession of the generic approach and allegations of falling standards. These allegations were fuelled by the public outcry and scapegoating that followed several tragic cases of child abuse during the 1970s. Social workers, torn by conflicting demands and contradictory advice, grew anxious about their identity and purpose, and endlessly debated the merits of case work versus community work and specialism versus genericism, and sought to define their function.

The Department of Health and Social Security joined the professional and public debate with the establishment of a Working Party on Manpower and Training for the Social Services. Its report, known as the Birch Report, was published in 1976. It sets out clearly the facts on numbers and levels of current training and made recommendations for its future development. The authors of the Birch Report admitted to being clearer about training itself than about what training was for, and some critics of the report were disappointed by its failure to define social work more clearly. The working party avoided most areas of controversy and concentrated on recommendations for expanding training to ensure that by the 1980s much higher proportions of staff in social services departments would be fully qualified by either CQSW or CSS courses.

An important contribution to the debate about role has been the publication of research findings on the actual work of social workers in the new departments. In particular the DHSS-sponsored investigation, reported as *Social Service Teams: the Practitioner's View*, which was published in 1978, provided a detailed commentary on the way social workers actually carried out their numerous duties and responsibilities. The research analysed the differences in ways of working between a sample of area teams. It revealed the range of factors - organizational constraints, geographical and demographic characteristics of the area, type of staff employed and their levels of skill and training, etc. - that influenced the structure and functioning of social work teams. It provided a good deal of thought-provoking information about methods of work and degree of formal and informal specialization. This kind of research does not provide instant answers to all the controversial questions about social work but it does provide the basis for a more informed and constructive discussion of role.

In 1980 a working party was set up at the request of the Secretary of State for Social Services under the chairmanship of Peter Barclay, Chairman of the National Institute of Social Work, to review the roles and tasks of social workers in local authority social services departments. The working party had a membership drawn from the social work and related professions and from academic bodies. It reported in 1982 and the Barclay Report, *Social Workers: Their Role and Tasks*, immediately became the focus of a lively debate among all those concerned with personal social services.

The bulk of the working party's conclusions, which endorsed the importance of local authority social work, were generally acceptable to the profession. But the majority of the Barclay members argued for a shift of emphasis in social work away from its traditional preoccupation with individual cases towards a more community-oriented approach to social care. They called for a clear partnership between the statutory services and the voluntary carers, including the informal carers. Community social work, they argued, would support and help ordinary people in their roles as carers rather than offer professional alternatives and undermine their efforts.

The majority view was vigorously repudiated in one dissenting minority report, while another urged that social work should become even more radically decentralized and local than the main report suggested. Fierce arguments developed among social workers who either wished to adopt the new 'patch and partnership' approach or preferred to stick to recognizable professional methods. It was feared by some that too ready an enthusiasm for community social work would result in a lowering of standards of service, particularly in the present economic climate.

Whatever the intrinsic merits of local partnerships, they must certainly not be used by a local authority as an excuse for cost-cutting or off-loading responsibility. Genuine community work is not cheap, nor should it be any less professional than individual case work. Skilled work is required from social workers if they are to work alongside the informal carers in truly generous, democratic, enabling partnerships, and a good deal of experiment will be required before every social services department has found an effective way of working in the community.

PLANNING AND PRIORITIES

The personal social services grew considerably in the decade following their establishment. This was hardly surprising since the Seebohm Report had pointed out many gaps and short-comings in the existing provision, and new duties, particularly those concerning the disabled and children, had been added to the wide range of responsibilities already carried by the new departments. Other factors added to the pressure to expand: high public expectations; increased knowledge about needs from a range of research findings; the new role of social services departments in local government; professional pressures; economic and social trends, particularly the overwhelming demographic trend of an ageing population structure.

In terms of overall costs the services developed rapidly, growing up to 14.5 per cent per annum (albeit from a very small base). In terms of staff and buildings the expansion was obvious: area teams of social workers were established and area offices opened, specialists in community development and intermediate treatment were recruited, day centres for the old or the handicapped were opened and researches into the needs of the disabled were undertaken. The DHSS asked all authorities to submit plans in 1972 for the development of personal social services over the next ten years, and issued guidelines showing the sort of numbers of staff and premises required. Growth was, for a brief and happy period, very much taken for granted.

Since 1976, however, the public expenditure crisis has dominated the provision of personal care services, and social services departments have had to cope with the cutbacks in budgets necessitated by financial constraints. In 1976 the DHSS issued its consultative document *Priorities for Health and Personal Social Services in England*, which has been discussed already in Chapter 3 (pages 79–80). The priorities document suggested giving priority in services to the elderly, the mentally handicapped, children and the mentally ill. In the further document, *The Way Forward*, the need to give priority to the disabled was added. Since it is from all these groups that the clients of the existing social services are drawn, these documents were hardly of much practical use for social services committees looking for ways of establishing priorities or making savings.

Indeed, whilst emphasis on establishing priorities for these groups has grown – in particular in increasing moves towards community care and maximizing 'ordinary life' for the elderly, mentally ill and handicapped – this has been at a time of funding cuts and crisis in the work of social service departments. Whilst demographic changes in the population – greater proportions of older people, handicapped and disabled surviving to an older age – have increased demands on the social services, so too have other changes. Inflation, recession and unemployment and the numbers of people struggling to survive on inadequate benefits add to the burden on social service departments, as do under-funding in housing, education and health programmes. Social services, like health services, need extra finance in the light of such changes in demand, simply to provide the same level of care as before. But cuts in services and current policies of cash limits on local government expenditure have prevented departments meeting new demands, let alone planning for innovative and preventive services or community development. In particular, the rising visibility of child abuse, both physical and sexual, has resulted in a heavy burden on field social work teams, who have a statutory responsibility to protect such children. The public outcry after cases such as that of Jasmine Beckford has increased the stress of such work, whilst funding and staff levels needed to cope with such a workload have not been forthcoming. As a result, many social work teams are finding that work with groups such as the elderly, mentally handicapped or people with a disability has had to take a lower priority, rather than a higher one.

Throughout this period, however, there has been increasing emphasis on the move towards community care for the elderly, mentally ill, handicapped and people with a disability. In 1981 the DHSS produced a consultative document *Care in the*

Community and Joint Finance, which increased the amount of money available for joint financing of community care projects by health authorities and local authorities, and which also extended the period of time over which joint finance would be paid. This was greatly welcomed, as the joint finance set up in the mid-1970s had proved too limited to aid the more long-term projects in the move towards community care. Even so, the increases were insufficient. The 1980s saw a growing consensus on the part of those providing the care that more priority should be given to the 'Cinderella services', and that community care should mean maximizing the individual's opportunities for 'ordinary life', yet at the same time there was a growing condemnation of the failure of health authorities and local authorities to achieve community care. Three reports in particular pointed to this failure, and suggested that reasons for this included poor collaboration between services, lack of overall control in one body and poor funding.

In 1985 both the Social Services Select Committee on Community Care and a report from a combined team of local authorities, health authorities and the DHSS suggested joint planning arrangements needed to be reinforced and given greater prominence in the delivery of services. In particular, the Select Committee observed that the run-down of hospitals far outstripped the provision of alternative care in the community, and that most of what is seen as community care was being provided, unpaid, by women within families.

In 1986 Sir Roy Griffiths was appointed to review community care with suggestions for improving the provision of care, and his report, *Community Care: An Agenda for Action*, was produced in 1988. The dominant themes of the report were poor coordination, failure of objectives and lack of clarity over division of responsibility for provision of care. Griffiths recommended a 'mixed economy' approach to community care, with care being provided by a mixture of private, voluntary and public sources. The private sector in community care had been stimulated in 1983 by a change in DHSS rules enabling eligible residents in a private residential home to claim their costs from the DHSS. The private sector grew rapidly in the years following this change, mostly in the provision of care for the older population, but to a lesser extent also in care for mentally handicapped and mentally ill people. The Griffiths Report envisaged a mixed economy of welfare encouraged by the local authority, which would retain overall responsibility for the coordination of community care.

Despite the cost saving implications of community care that is provided by the private and voluntary sector, in addition to public funds, the government did not respond positively to the Griffiths Report, largely because of doctrinaire opposition to any increase in local authority responsibilities. Not until mid-1989 did the government announce that the Griffiths recommendations were to be acted upon with overall control in the hands of social service departments. Meanwhile, the provision of care for the groups identified in the early 1970s as priority groups continues to be provided from a mixture of sources, under-funded and lacking in overall coordination and without a clear plan as to the future direction of such services.

The personal social services, established on an integrated functional basis only in 1970, have had a very challenging and formative period of growth. Although they have had their problems and their critics, the services have made dramatic strides forward in providing a caring response to the needs of the old, the handicapped and children with difficulties. They have not gone far enough, especially in the provision of community services and family welfare, and much specialist work with the mentally ill and deprived children, for example, still urgently needs developing. When departments are under stress owing to lack of resources, they tend to fall back on the provision of their familiar statutory duties because these alone are difficult enough to fulfil. However, some of the wider objectives of a preventive, community-based, reciprocal welfare service have been pursued despite constraints. The links between personal care services and general levels of employment and resources are clearer, and new ways of strengthening individuals and communities are emerging. The personal social services and social workers operate where change shows and often where it hurts, so they need to be flexible, variable, even uncertain of their role, if they are to move with it. It would be tragic if the gains of the 1970s were lost forever to the cuts of the 1980s, and personal social services were reduced to a residual and cautious response. For all their operational costs and difficulties, the social care services remain crucial to the quality of life in our society and they need to be passionately and vigorously defended at national and local level.

SUGGESTIONS FOR FURTHER READING

Brown, M., and Baldwin, S. (eds), *The Year Book of Social Policy in Britain 1978* (RKP, 1980).

Cooper, J., *The Creation of the British Personal Social Services* (Heinemann, 1981).

Fuller, R. and Stevenson, O., *Policies, Programmes and Disadvantage* (Heinemann, 1983).

Goldberg, M. and Hatch, S., *A New Look at the Personal Social Services* (PSI, 1981).

Hall, P., *Reforming the Welfare* (Heinemann, 1976).

Jones, H. (ed.), *Towards a New Social Work* (RKP, 1975).

Jones, K. (ed.), *The Year Book of Social Policy in Britain 1971* (RKP, 1972).

Parry, N., Rustin, M. and Satyamurti, C. (eds), *Social Work, Welfare and the State* (Edward Arnold, 1979).

Rodgers, B. and Stevenson, J., *A New Portrait of Social Work* (Heinemann, 1974).

Rodgers, B., Doron, A. and Jones, M., *The Study of Social Policy: A Comparative Approach* (Allen & Unwin, 1979).

Seebohm Report, *Report of the Committee on Local Authority and Allied Personal Social Services*, Cmnd 3703 (HMSO 1968).

Simpkin, M., *Trapped within Welfare* (Macmillan, 1983).

Walker, A. (ed.), *Community Care: The Family, the State and Social Policy* (Blackwell and Robertson, 1982).

Younghusband, E., *Social Work in Britain 1950–1975* (Allen & Unwin, 1978).

Part Two
Special need groups

8

Child deprivation and family welfare

THE PROBLEM OF CHILD DEPRIVATION

The need for children to have a stable home life and happy upbringing has long been recognized. Children are dependent on others for their very survival, and the quality of the care they receive, physically and emotionally, will go far to determine the sort of adults they will grow up into. It is therefore vital that they are given the right sort of care, so they can grow up to be well developed and strong physically, mentally alert, contented and emotionally stable. Only then can they grow up able to enjoy full lives, to become responsible and useful citizens and to make good parents in turn.

Most children are reared by their natural parents and most are cared for well. As recognition of the importance of the early formative years has deepened, however, the state has taken an increasing part in concern for child care. It has demonstrated its concern in three main ways: by aiding parents in their job of child-rearing through the provision of services such as maternity and child welfare, schooling, etc.; by taking care directly of children who have no parents; and by taking over the care of children whose parents are not providing properly for their physical and emotional well-being.

Aid to parents is provided mostly through the basic social services. Child benefits indicate the state's recognition of the financial implications of parenthood. As we saw in Chapter

2 on social security, however, these do not keep the very low-paid workers above the officially defined poverty line. But the aim is to help parents financially even though the actuality falls short of the intention of preventing family poverty. The maternity and child welfare services have been developed to help parents do their best for their children. Mothers are given ante- and post-natal care and children are medically inspected, vaccinated, etc., periodically. The health visitors at the clinics and on domiciliary visits offer advice and help on many aspects of child-rearing and can refer children for further specialized attention where necessary. Education services, of course, are a vitally important aid to parents in providing schooling and ancillary services.

The state, then, offers a fair amount of help to all parents in their task of rearing children. It also has to assume responsibility for those children who lack parents or are not receiving proper care. In the case of orphan children the position is relatively clear: a child without parents needs someone to care for it. But children, with parents, who are not receiving proper care are a more complicated category to define. The state has, in a sense, to define what proper care is, or at least what falls short of it. It has to take powers to intervene in family life and take into care children who are being neglected or badly treated. So the reasons why many children are in care depend on what the statutory powers and duties of the child care service are. These have tended to widen as our understanding of the needs of children has developed. Initially only orphaned, abandoned or destitute children were cared for by the state; then those who were cruelly treated or delinquent; and today any child who is deprived of normal home life on a temporary or permanent basis. Before looking more closely at the reasons why children come into care, and at the numbers involved, it is necessary to look briefly at the main legislation in this field and the powers and duties of the child care service.

CHILD CARE

The main legislation relating to the care of children is the consolidating Child Care Act of 1980, the Children Acts of

1948 and 1975 and the Children and Young Persons Acts of 1933, 1963 and 1969. However, at the time of writing, a new Children Bill is making its way through the legislative process, and will, once enacted, form the basic legislation relating to childcare in the 1990s. Central responsibility for child care rests with the Department of Social Security through the Personal Social Services division. Responsibility used to lie with the Home Office and there was a separate Inspectorate for child care and a Central Training Council in Child Care. Following the Local Authority Social Services Act 1970 responsibility was transferred to the DHSS when child care became part of personal social services. Responsibility for development and inspection was taken over by the Social Work Service and the work of the training council has been absorbed into the Central Council for Education and Training in Social Work.

At local level, responsibility for child care rests with the social services committees of the local authorities. Counties and county boroughs became responsible for child care under the 1948 Children Act. This gave them a statutory duty to appoint a committee and a chief officer specifically for the care of children. Local authority children's departments were established following the report of the Curtis Committee in 1946. This recommended the creation of a specialist children's service to replace the existing provision, which was fragmented among various departments, including public assistance. The report of the Seebohm Committee recommended the creation of unified social services departments which, from 1970, have been responsible for work under various Children Acts.

The Child Care Act of 1980 was a consolidating Act replacing the Children Act 1948. Under part 1 of the 1980 Act, local authorities first have a duty to promote the welfare of children by making available such advice, guidance and assistance as may diminish the need to receive children into care. Then, as section 2 of the 1980 Act, they have the duty, originally spelt out in section 1 of the 1948 Act, to receive a child into care where it appears that a child under 17 'has neither parent nor guardian or is lost or that his parents or guardian are, for the time being or permanently, prevented by reason of mental or bodily disease or infirmity or other incapacity or any other circumstances from providing for his proper accommodation, maintenance and upbringing; and in either case, that the intervention of the local authority under this section is necessary in the interests of the welfare of the child'.

A very wide variety of cases are received into care under this section. Children are also taken into care when they are committed by the courts under the 1969 Children and Young Persons Act. The major reasons for a care order are that the children have themselves committed an offence, they are in need of care, protection and control, or they or another child of the same family have been victims of an offence or are in the same household as a person convicted of a serious offence such as manslaughter, cruelty or suchlike.

Most of the children coming into care under section 2 of the Child Care Act do so at the request of their parents, and their parents can take them home whenever they wish. Indeed, the local authority has a clear duty to restore the child to his or her natural parents as soon as this is consistent with the child's welfare. In the minority of cases in which the child does not return home, he or she will remain in care up to the age of 18 if necessary. In some cases, where the parents are dead or permanently unable to care for the child the local authority assumes parental rights over the child. Children who are committed by the courts to the care of the local authority cannot, of course, be taken home by their parents whenever they wish. The authority is given parental rights over the child by the court order and unless this is revoked these remain in force until he or she reaches 18. However, children over whom the local authority exercises parental rights may be allowed to return home on trial if this seems to be in their best interests.

Social services departments thus receive children into care for a variety of reasons. The bulk of receptions are under section 2 of the Child Care Act. Some of these are children who have no parents or who have been abandoned, and these will be long-term cases. The majority, however, are children who have come into care because their parents are unable to look after them. A large number of cases are received because of the short-term illness or confinement of the mother. Other circumstances in which children come into care include long-term illness, particularly mental illness, the imprisonment of the parent, the death or desertion of the mother, homelessness of the family through eviction, and unsatisfactory home conditions.

Not all requests for admissions into care are complied with, of course. Parents are encouraged to make their own arrangements where possible, and are helped by such means as the admission of younger children to day nurseries. Concern for the prevention of break-up of families has greatly increased since the Children Act of 1948 and local authorities now have a statutory duty to develop preventive work, as the next section will show.

Where children do come into care, close contact is maintained with the parents and they have to pay towards the cost of their children's upkeep according to their means. Children who come into care through the courts are committed to the care of the local authority either because they are themselves offenders, or because they are the victims of offences or because they are found in need of care. Children are found in need of care, protection and control if the court establishes that they are not receiving the sort of care a good parent may reasonably be expected to give and they are falling into bad associations, are exposed to moral danger, or the lack of care is likely to cause suffering or seriously affect their health or proper development, or if it establishes that they are beyond the control of their parents. Obviously children who have been neglected to the point that they are the subject of care proceedings are likely to be difficult and sometimes very disturbed. They are likely to need very careful handling if their substitute parents are to establish a happy relationship with them. Older children who are beyond control and difficult or delinquent will not take easily to substitute homes and will often cause a good deal of trouble there. They might need a less emotionally demanding environment in which they can recuperate and relax before they are able to tackle relationships again.

While the children sent by the courts are likely to be, on average, more disturbed than those received under section 2, the differences are not too noticeable. All children will tend to suffer from separation from their parents, siblings and familiar surroundings. Short-term cases are often small children to whom the separation is so alarming that its temporary nature is irrelevant to them. Children tend to come into care after upsetting events at home, such as a mother's illness or following the trauma of eviction and homelessness. And often they come from homes where there have been difficulties – rent arrears, marital troubles, sickness and so on – for many years, before a further crisis causes the children to be taken into care. Many of the children will have experienced poverty and insecurity, if not actual neglect, and may well have been known to the health or education authorities as children at special risk before they come into the care of the social services department.

In short, some children will come from relatively stable homes for temporary care, others have had very damaging and painful experiences and come from permanently broken homes and are likely to require long-term care. All will be disturbed and unhappy to some extent at the loss of familiar surroundings and some will be deeply hurt in their capacity to trust and respond to the people who endeavour to provide substitute homes.

There are currently nearly 67,000 children in the care of the local authorities in England and Wales. The total has grown since the present service was set up in 1948, although in fact the proportion of children in care per thousand of the total population under 18 has not altered so much. But the turnover is very great, the vast majority of children in care being short-term cases.

The type of care offered to children must vary according to their needs. But in most cases the aim of the social services departments is to find the child a substitute home as near to a good, normal home as possible, until such time as he or she can return to their own home. While good standards of physical care, hygiene, nutrition and so forth are clearly vital, it is now realized that the most important need is for the child to receive personal attention and genuine affection. Only in a secure and loving atmosphere can the child cope with the shocks that have preceded and accompanied their coming into care, and develop to their full potential. This realization has led to the abandonment of the large institutional type of children's home and a policy favouring the boarding out of children in ordinary homes where possible. Boarding out (or fostering) has been practised for many years and the Curtis Committee on the care of children strongly urged that this should be the first choice in finding substitute homes. Under the Children Act of 1948 the local authorities were given a duty to place a child in foster care unless this was not practicable or desirable in the child's best interests. Where it is not possible, children's homes are kept as small as possible and are not isolated from the community around them.

The range of substitute homes offered by the local authorities varies considerably and it is of course essential to try to match the different children coming into care to the most appropriate home. Accordingly, all authorities must provide facilities for the initial and temporary reception of children with the necessary skilled staff for observing and assessing their physical, mental and emotional condition. These reception centres are also used for the temporary care of children where it is necessary to change the foster or other home. In cases where it proves very difficult to place a child, the reception centre might end by providing relatively long-term care, but this is not usual or desirable.

After assessment by the child care officer or reception centre, the child is placed in a suitable substitute home. This is, as already indicated, a foster home where practicable. About one-third of the total number of children in care are in foster homes, but the proportions of children boarded out vary between different areas. Foster parents are paid a weekly allowance that covers the basic costs of maintaining a child, but care is taken to see that fostering does not become a materially profitable exercise. In selecting foster homes social workers interview and assess would-be foster parents for their general suitability, then great care is taken in placing a particular child in a particular foster home. Where the arrangement works well, children obtain a secure substitute home. They are able to form a good relationship with their foster parents and they have the advantages of remaining in a normal setting, going to school, making friends and generally participating in the life of the neighbourhood. However, fostering does not always work out so well. The reasons for the success or failure of fostering are not well understood. Clearly in some cases the parents expect to lavish care upon a poor, neglected child who will respond with gratitude and affection. They receive a child who has been badly let down in the past, who has to learn, painfully, how to care and trust again. Far from experiencing simple gratitude, such children will most likely feel terribly torn and anxious when faced with their foster parents' offer of affection. If they come out from their defensive withdrawal and hesitantly accept the affection they are likely to need to test it out, to see whether it can withstand some heavy strain or whether, like past ties, it can be broken. So a hurt child will be moody and often intensively provocative, testing out the validity of the proffered affection and expressing some of the pent-up anger and agony from the past. Not surprisingly, some foster parents are bewildered by the bad behaviour.

It is the skilled job of the social workers to help the foster parents cope by understanding their anxiety, explaining the child's difficulties and helping them to get along together. It is hard for foster parents to cope with very demanding and disturbed children and no less hard to part with them once they have learnt to love them. Foster care is not permanent and many children will return to their natural parents, and here again foster parents will need support and help in easing a parting.

It is not easy to find enough foster parents to care for very difficult children; all too often fostering breaks down and the child has to be returned again to the reception centre. Repeated failures in fostering are obviously very damaging to a child to whom it means repeated rejection. So for some children it is deemed better to place them in small homes where it is easier to maintain continuity of care. Most local authorities now run small family group homes instead of the larger children's homes common before the 1948 Act. These typically cater for up to a dozen boys and girls of various ages, and they are run by a houseparent with some assistance by day. Often the houseparent is a married woman whose husband goes out to work but acts as a father to the children in the evenings and at weekends. The home will usually be a converted older house or even a large council house on an estate, and the children will go to the schools, churches and clubs in the neighbourhood. At some small homes children from the same family can be kept together, whereas fostering would entail splitting them up. Also, various children deemed unsuitable for fostering – because of behaviour problems or physical handicaps, for example, or because there are strong ties with the natural parents – can be accommodated, together with those who have had a foster placement breakdown.

Following the 1948 Act efforts were made to foster a deprived child where possible and homes were regarded on the whole as second best. But in recent years the wisdom of fostering in all cases has been questioned and the merits of a less emotionally demanding atmosphere, which a home can provide, have been increasingly accepted. Some authorities now favour homes taking fifteen to twenty children, particularly for the difficult medium-term cases where the child is away from their natural home for more than a few months. Practice varies quite widely in different areas, of course. In addition to the provision already described, some authorities still retain some of the older-type large homes and several run residential nurseries. But most authorities have been closing down their residential establishments in recent years.

Broadly speaking, the aim is to provide, whether by fostering or small family group homes, as much individual attention and as near normal an environment as possible for the child who has to come into care. Alongside this aim is that of returning the children to their natural home wherever possible. This is a duty in respect of section 2 cases, and, even with children committed by the courts, efforts are made to ensure their eventual return to their own homes. This involves allowing the children home on trial, a practice that has increased sharply since 1948, and taking whatever steps are necessary to rehabilitate the family so that full parental responsibility can be resumed.

Since the implementation of the relevant sections of the 1969 Children and Young Persons Act, social services authorities have integrated the previously separate system of approved schools and remand homes for delinquent children with their ordinary children's homes. They now aim to provide a full range of community homes, including not only the family group homes already described but also larger homes with educational facilities. Some authorities provide hostels for older children who need some care but not the full care of a family group home, but on the whole the needs of young workers and older school children are not well catered for. A growing proportion of children in care of the local authority are not actually placed in homes or boarded out but are left under the charge of parent, guardian, relative or friend with some supervision from the social workers.

Apart from their major tasks of receiving children into care and providing substitute homes for them, local authority social services departments have various other responsibilities in the child care field. One of these concerns the supervision and arrangement of adoptions. For children permanently deprived of their natural home, adoption provides a secure alternative home. Under the 1958 Adoption Act, local authorities have a duty to secure the well-being of children awaiting adoption. Persons who wish to adopt a child may contact their local social services department, which may either place children for adoption itself, or contact a registered adoption agency, or make direct arrangements with the child's parents. The social services departments supervise the child during the statutory three-month period that elapses between the notification of adoption proceedings and the making of an adoption order by the court; a social worker is usually appointed as a guardian *ad litem*, i.e. for the duration of the case, to interview the prospective adopters, investigate the relevant circumstances and report to the court. Attempts are made to consider the best interests of the natural parents and the would-be adoptive parents, but the interests of the child are, of course, of paramount importance.

Following mounting concern about some of the problems of adoption and fostering, a departmental committee was set up to investigate. Its report on the *Adoption of Children* was published in 1972. This recommended a change in procedures so that adoptive parents would be assured that no changes of mind by the mother at a late stage could result in the removal of a child. Moreover, it suggested that foster parents who had had the care of a child for five years or more should be able to apply for an adoption order without risk of removal by parents before a hearing. Despite considerable controversy, a Children Act was passed in 1975 based on these recommendations. It aims to improve adoption procedure and provides for more say from the child, as well as from the adults in a disputed case. But, however much care is taken, there are situations where it proves extremely difficult to be fair to both natural parents and prospective adoptive parents and this will always be a sensitive and emotional aspect of child care work.

Another function of the departments is that of child protection. Under the 1958 Children Act, local authorities have a duty to ensure the well-being of children who are fostered privately. The social work staff visit and inspect and offer advice and guidance where necessary in the interests of the child. Social services departments also provide care and after care for older children, by running hostels for working boys and girls and helping with the costs of further education and training, or simply by offering friendship and advice.

Social services departments cooperate closely with voluntary organizations concerned with the welfare of deprived children. They can place children in homes run by voluntary organizations and make contributions to their costs, and they have certain powers to inspect voluntary homes. Voluntary effort has been prominent in the development of services for deprived children. Organizations such as Dr Barnardo's, the National Children's Homes and the Catholic Rescue Society pioneered methods of child care during the nineteenth century and still play a very active part in the child care service. Approximately 12,000 children are currently being cared for by voluntary organizations.

PREVENTION: FROM CHILD CARE
TO FAMILY WELFARE

As the preceding paragraphs have shown, child care is, until the Children Bill becomes law in the early 1990s, based on the Child Care Act 1980, under which one major duty of the local authorities is to receive children into care and provide them with adequate substitute homes unless or until they can be returned to their natural parents. The majority of children come into care at the request of their parents, because they are temporarily unable to look after them, and they will return to their own homes in due course. However, a substantial proportion of the long-term cases are children who have been taken into care against the wishes of their parents because they have not been receiving adequate care or control.

The 1948 Act initiated many changes in child care. The terms under which children could be received into care were considerably widened, the methods of care were made more sensitive to the needs of children and the unified administrative structure ensured more uniform standards of care over the country. Moreover, major advances were made in training child care staff both for residential work and for the fieldwork of finding substitute homes, supervising fostering and keeping contact with parents. Nevertheless, the twenty years following the Act were ones of such rapid development in policy in the child care field that by 1968 the Seebohm Report recommended the absorption of the child care service by unified social services departments and the merging of specialist child work into generic social work. The emphasis had shifted radically from the child-centred approach of 1948 to the Seebohm concern for family and community. This change was essentially the outcome of concern for prevention in the child care field.

Interest in prevention of the break-up of families was discernible from the inception of the child care service. There are several reasons why it received greater emphasis as the years went by. More knowledge of the emotional needs of children demonstrated the importance of maintaining a warm and continuous relationship between a child and his or her mother or mother substitute. The study of sociology began to show the importance of the family and class and cultural factors in child development. The increased use of trained child care officers who had studied the growth and development of personality meant that more people were aware of the difficulty, if not the impossibility, of compensating a child for the break-up of his or her natural home. Practical considerations, such as the difficulty of finding enough foster placements and adequate staff for children's homes, also lent weight to arguments in favour of preventing children from coming into care. Moreover, there was some evidence of a feeling in the country that the state must not too readily take on the care of children lest it undermine the responsibilities of parents.

So efforts were made to prevent children from coming into care. Essentially this meant working with families at risk of break-up. In some cases it meant helping families who had applied for their children to be taken into care to find an alternative solution. But it also meant trying to contact families and individuals – doctors, schools, health visitors, housing departments, etc. – when they felt a family had too many problems. This resulted in the children's department undertaking general family case work and finding they lacked the power to provide much constructive help in many cases. Their powers were accordingly widened by the 1963 Children and Young Persons Act, which gave local authorities a duty to prevent and forestall the suffering of children through neglect in their own homes. Under this Act they were given responsibility 'to make available such advice, guidance and assistance as may promote the welfare of children by diminishing the need to receive children into or keep them in care'. Assistance could include assistance 'in kind or, in exceptional circumstances, in cash'. Preventive work now had full legislative sanction.

Children's departments were not the only agencies involved in family welfare, however. Within the local authorities, health departments were increasingly concerned, especially through the work of the health visitors, who were often closely involved with families in difficulties, and also welfare departments through their responsibility for homeless families, and education authorities through the education welfare services. Voluntary bodies also played, and still do play, a prominent part in family welfare, especially in the larger towns and cities. A description of some of the more prominent of these will indicate the scope and style of their contributions.

In many centres of population there exists a Family Welfare Association. These associations can often trace their origins back to the nineteenth century when they were, under different names, primarily concerned with giving relief in cash and kind to families in distress. In London, the Charity Organization Society (COS) did pioneer work in developing a casework approach to the families who came to it for aid, helping them to solve their problems and help themselves rather than become dependent on charitable funds. The COS became the Family Welfare Association shortly after the Second World War and its functions have widened in scope as the need for basic relief has been reduced by the growth of statutory income maintenance services. The story is similar in other areas, with an older organization or group of charities coming together as a local Family Welfare Association. Today the organization and staffing of the local FWAs vary, but they have roughly the same aim: to promote family welfare by helping families overcome their problems. They still have funds to dispense and many clients initially come in financial distress, but social workers are also available to give advice and support.

Another very important, but very different, family service is provided by the Family Service Units, a national organization. The FSU operates through local units, many of which are generously grant aided by local authorities. All the major conurbations have units which provide an intensive case-work service to families referred by other statutory and voluntary social agencies. The FSU was founded in 1947, and was based on the experience of the Pacifist Service Units, which had helped families who were overwhelmed by the destruction, separation, chaos and strain of the war years to cope and re-establish themselves. This experience showed that the problems of many families had little to do with the actual wartime conditions which were only an additional stress for families already overwhelmed by financial, housing and emotional problems of their own. The need for help did not, therefore, end with the war, and FSU continued the work subsequently. The essence of the FSU approach consists of the family caseworkers having very small caseloads so that they can visit families frequently – several times a week if necessary – and help directly with the practical as well as emotional problems the families face.

In London, Family Groups were started by the London Council of Social Service, now the London Voluntary Service Council. Family Groups consist of a network of small local groups mostly of mothers and young children, meeting regularly under the guidance of locally recruited group and play leaders. Through mutual help and group development, local families are able to share their problems and pool their resources, and develop skills and confidence. Family Groups are a major preventive approach, strengthening families in their capacity to cope with the stresses of financial difficulties, urban living, family life and child-rearing. The work of fostering and supporting such groups has now been taken over by a national organization called Cope, which works closely with local social services departments and adult education departments to spread the approach across the country.

The National Society for the Prevention of Cruelty to Children is increasingly concerned with helping families to cope better with the demands of rearing children. Various bodies concerned with the particular problems of the unmarried mother or with single-parent families also increasingly see their role as contributing to family welfare. At national level, the National Council for One Parent Families acts as a central organization drawing together the various statutory and voluntary bodies concerned and generally offers advice and information in this field. At local level, voluntary welfare organizations, usually run on a diocesan basis, often act as agents for the local authority in providing facilities for the reception of unmarried mothers and some provide long-term accommodation for mothers and their growing children or general social work help as long as it is necessary. Increasingly evident in this field are self-help organizations such as Gingerbread or Mothers in Action. Relate (formerly Marriage Guidance), is a voluntary organization with a national council, coordinating the activities of local councils, which aims to promote successful marriage and parenthood and thereby helps to maintain family welfare by improving marital relationships.

The list of all the voluntary agencies concerned directly or indirectly with family welfare would be too long to provide here. Facilities vary considerably from area to area. For example, in some areas, in addition to statutory departments and the main voluntary agencies, there are family rehabilitation units or holiday and recuperative homes for mothers and children. So it is impossible to generalize about the extent of the provision. Suffice it to say that in this field voluntary effort has long played a considerable part and there are signs that it intends to increase its contribution to this field.

In 1980 a Family Forum was established bringing together representatives of many of the voluntary bodies involved in family welfare. The forum exists to facilitate a coherent expression of the needs of families and to act as a pressure group to improve provision for them.

From the experience of voluntary bodies and of the different local authority departments concerned, much was learned about the difficulties of families and of the ways in which they could be helped. Initially it had been felt that some families failed to take advantage of the services offered by the welfare state and, despite the basic social services, they fell into poverty and sickness, remained ignorant of the skills and attitudes needed to cope with life and failed to find accommodation for themselves. Subsequently, especially during the late 1960s after the mounting evidence of shortcomings in the basic provision, there was a contrasting tendency to blame the services and society for forcing people into intolerable situations.

It is undoubtedly the case that poverty and bad housing conditions are still very much in evidence, that the poor have alarmingly inadequate provision of health care and educational opportunity and that homelessness is a very real threat. It is also the case that people who live with financial anxieties, poor health, and insecurity of employment income and accommodation are rarely happy and usually suffer not only from the actual privations of poverty or homelessness but also from a demoralizing sense of failure. Society makes certain demands and assumptions and, when families cannot live up to them, they can be made to feel outcast and inadequate and this does not help their ability to cope. It is humiliating to be living in debt and squalor in the midst of affluence and bewildering to feel helpless in the face of laws, regulations and procedures that one cannot understand. The strain and tension created by constant difficulties can lead to other problems and it can be hard to sort out which came first; it is all too easy to blame the surface symptoms of child neglect or indebtedness on irresponsible parenthood rather than on an unjust social system.

In fact, there are many reasons why families fail to stay together or to provide for their children adequately, reasons that include the stress of ill-health, unemployment or irregular employment, low pay, poverty and deprivation, bad housing and a poor environment and low levels of social support. These circumstances are found more often amongst poorer groups in society – single-parent households, those in lower-paid occupations, large families, those dependent on social security benefits, and so on – and, whilst it is at times difficult to determine patterns of cause and effect in such situations, structural and environmental factors are clearly of great importance in being able to care for children. One essential paradox is that it is those groups who are poorest in terms of resources to cope with difficulties who are beset with the greatest problems. For example, it is often women in poor health, living in poor and crowded conditions, on a low income and without private transport, who are trying to bring up and cope with the demands of small children on their own. Many families who get into difficulties have been struggling with problems that would daunt the most energetic and resourceful of people. So it is not surprising that those suffering the greatest stress – who are disadvantaged in terms of income, housing, environment, and health – are also those most likely to need help. And as stress increases, so too does this vulnerability. For example, as the housing situation worsens (in terms of shortages, high rents and insecurity of tenure), the first to become homeless are precisely those suffering greatest difficulty in other respects – large families and single-parent households.

Some families in difficulties appear to have had long histories of problems, and often the parents themselves have suffered a difficult childhood. The problem of the physical and sexual abuse of children, which has become a dominant theme of family studies and of the work of the social services in the 1970s and 1980s, is increasingly seen as one that replicates itself across generations.

Child physical abuse emerged dramatically as a major problem in the 1970s with the death of a child as a result of such abuse. Headline hitting cases such as those of Maria Colwell and Jasmine Beckford, for example, led to in-depth investigations into the action of the social workers and other professionals responsible for the children's welfare, and also alerted both professionals and society in general to the existence of child abuse on a wider scale than hitherto acknowledged.

Similarly, in the 1980s greater attention from both professionals in the field of child care and the media has increased our awareness of child sexual abuse, and the numbers of reported cases have grown considerably over the past decade.

In both physical and sexual abuse, the abusers have often experienced such abuse themselves as children, and this in part is seen as an explanation. However, sexual abuse of children clearly differs in nature from physical abuse: the perpetrators are mostly male, the victims mostly female, (although the number of cases of boys being abused in this way is growing), and understanding the origins of such abuse must lie within an understanding of sexuality and the distribution of power within our society. Sexual abuse is found across all classes and all circumstances, whereas physical abuse is often related to stresses such as poverty, bad housing and overcrowding. One of the greatest difficulties in discussing both forms of abuse, however, is that of knowing the true extent of the problem. Many children are unable to tell of their abuse, and some who do are not believed – it may be that abuse is more widespread than currently thought, whilst those families already under supervision by the social services for other difficulties are not more likely to abuse, but are simply more likely to be found.

What can be done to help families and prevent, not only their break-up and the admission of children to care, but also the problems of child neglect and abuse and the general unhappiness of those who feel overwhelmed by problems? Just as the causes of family failure are many and varied, so too the approach to family welfare must be on a wide front. In so far as the causes lie in faulty social provision, there must be action to change such things as the social security provision and to improve housing. In so far as the causes lie in individual problems, help must be made available to families, help that not only is relevant but is made accessible and acceptable even to those who are very angry or demoralized or despairing.

In terms of official policy the movement from child care to family welfare resulted in demands for the creation of a more effective family service. There was a desire to create a single referral point and a truly accessible and localized service that everyone would know about and use. The growing concern for a unified approach meant that when the Seebohm

Committee concluded its review of personal social services it recommended the creation of a single local authority welfare department. This has already been described in Chapter 7. One of the major tasks of the social services departments is that of helping families in difficulties.

Help starts with social work and this is now more readily obtained locally through the area team structure. Social workers must first diagnose the problems and then help with such practical aids as they have at their immediate disposal. They can now offer some material aid, including at times of emergency some cash assistance. They have a major part to play in helping clients get their rights from other social services. As services have become more selective the importance of the welfare rights movement has increased. There are now several benefits – family credit, free school meals, housing benefit and grants from the Social Fund, for example – that can help families in financial need, but the processes of application and appeal for these are complex enough to warrant the assistance of social workers in many instances. In particular, the operation of the Social Fund – a benefit offered as a loan – often calls for social workers to provide support for a particular case, given the limited budget of the fund and the rationing that must be applied as a result.

A vital part of family welfare involves help with housing by social workers taking a client's part in helping them get an application for council housing considered or encouraging the formation of community housing associations. The day and domiciliary services of the local authority can be brought to bear if relevant – day care of small children can help enormously in many family problems where the welfare of children is at risk. Liaison with other agencies and people concerned with families and children remains important. Where, for example, children are considered at risk of physical harm it is important that medical authorities pass on relevant information about non-accidental injuries and teachers report cases of obvious neglect, or comprehensive risk registers are compiled.

Despite many years' experience of child care and family case work there is still a lively debate about the causes and extent of family failure and about what further measures should be taken to reduce it. In 1974 the DHSS, with the academic and administrative help of the Social Science Research Council, funded a seven-year programme of research into these questions. Numerous research projects were set up to investigate patterns of transmitted deprivation where families appear to hand down problems from generation to generation. From the evidence it appears that narrow intergenerational patterns of deprivation have been exaggerated: family failure is best understood in the context of the larger problem of social class. There is a network of disadvantage in society in terms of income, access to housing, educational and employment opportunities, etc., and large numbers of families caught up in this network are relatively deprived and vulnerable to breakdown. The DHSS/SSRC initiative, which at the outset looked for explanations of deprivation within families, ended by acknowledging the importance of structural factors.

Whatever the cause of failure, help to families has to operate on a wide front. There is room in family welfare both for the development of effective social policies in housing and income maintenance and for sympathetic support and individual help with particular problems. Social services departments and voluntary bodies can help with a wide range of services and approaches: playgroups, money advice centres, family or women's groups, nurseries, support for child-minders, counselling and case work, all can play a part in preventive work with families.

The work that social workers, and other professionals such as paediatricians and GPs, do with families, however, has become a difficult question of balance between policies of prevention that involve family and community support and policies of intervention where the immediate interests of the children are given priority. Social services departments were strongly criticized in the 1980s for not taking more effective action to protect children at risk. The distressing case of Maria Colwell, who died whilst under local authority supervision in 1974, was sadly followed by similar cases of child deaths in the 1980s. These cases led to profound questioning in social services departments, and in the inquiries that ensued, of the desirability of attempting to keep the family together wherever possible. Clearly the social services must be flexible in their attitudes and responses to such problems. However, the inquiries also revealed the difficulties of social service departments in terms of staffing levels, training and supervision of inexperienced social workers.

More recently, the problem of child sexual abuse has been highlighted, and here too difficulties for social workers in protecting the children may sometimes be in conflict with other interests. This was most graphically illustrated by what has become known as the Cleveland Controversy, where there was a very rapid increase in referrals of cases of suspected child abuse in the summer of 1987. These referrals became the focus of national attention when some of the parents fought the court decision for the removal of their children to a place of safety. In fact, only a minority of the children were returned to their parents and in a large number of cases suspected abuse was subsequently confirmed. However, the debate highlighted again the difficulties for those working in the field in getting the right balance between protecting the child and supporting families, particularly in an area so emotionally fraught and where evidence of abuse may be intangible.

Legislation in the field of child protection has emphasized the role of the local authorities. The 1980 Child Care Act placed the duty of promoting the welfare of children as the first responsibility of social service departments. The new Children Bill of 1988 repeals the 1980 Child Care Act, along with other relevant Acts such as the 1975 Children's Act. However, the Bill retains the duty of local authorities to protect children at risk. In effect, the Bill, when enacted, will be the major legislation governing the care of children. The focus of the Bill is on the protection of children, and in particular it replaces the concept of parental rights with that of parental responsibilities in relation to the care of children.

The first major change in the structure of child care law is the introduction of the concept of paramountcy – that is, that the child's welfare must be seen as paramount in all decisions relating to the care of the child, residence, access, and so on. Under section 7 of the Bill, four types of court order relate to the child's upbringing. These concern residence, the exercise of parental responsibility in specific instances, access, and steps that are prohibited in the care of the child without the court's approval.

The Bill also replaces the idea of voluntary care – where parents have asked to have children taken into care because of specific problems – with the duty of local authorities to provide care and accommodation for any child who needs it. One further important change is the replacement of place of safety orders with what are to be called emergency protection orders. These, obtainable from the court, last eight days, but the parents will have the right to appeal after 72 hours. The new emergency protection orders also allow courts to order a medical examination of the child, whilst parents may, after 72 hours, challenge any medical evidence as a result of this examination and request an alternative examination.

The new Bill reflects the dilemma over protecting the children, the difficulties in obtaining medical evidence to substantiate suspicions of abuse, and the need to meet demands for parental rights in the wake of the Cleveland affair. In many respects it fails to answer these issues satisfactorily, although allowing the court to order medical examinations without parental consent legitimizes a position well established on an informal basis amongst the professionals involved. Perhaps the most important advance is the recognition of the need to place the child's interests and welfare above any other considerations – although this may prove simpler in the abstract than it is in practice.

CHILDREN IN TROUBLE

The development away from specialist child care to unified social services was the result of an increasing awareness that the family must be supported and assisted if child deprivation was to be avoided. The importance of the family for the prevention of delinquent behaviour was also recognized and it is now widely accepted that the delinquent child and his or her family are in need of the same kind of attention as the deprived child and his or her family. There were accordingly several moves to bring services for the young offender closer to those for the deprived child. These culminated in the 1969

Children and Young Persons Act, which brought about some radical changes in the treatment of young offenders.

The arguments for treating disturbed, delinquent and deprived children alike are based on the assumption that the child is the product of his or her home and not a totally separate responsible individual. Deprivation at home can lead to various forms of maladjustment, including delinquent behaviour, and court procedures and punishment are seen as an inappropriate response to the situation. It is considered better to work, over a period of time, with the family as well as the child, providing whatever support, training or care appear to be appropriate at different stages of development. In this approach a court order following an isolated offence is regarded as too rigid a way of tackling a complex problem and one that fails to involve the family adequately.

In the mid-1960s, when these arguments were much canvassed, there was some pressure to abolish the whole system of juvenile courts and to rely instead on family councils and family courts. Radical proposals were put forward in the 1965 White Paper, *The Child, the Family and the Young Offender*. These proved too controversial and modified proposals appeared in the 1968 paper *Children in Trouble*, which formed the basis of the 1969 Act.

Juveniles who break the law have been dealt with by separate courts since 1908 and since 1933 the courts have been specifically charged to have regard to the child's welfare in all their dealings. The courts had a variety of treatment orders avai'able in respect of the children brought before them, including placing children on probation and sending them to attendance or detention centres or to approved schools. The juvenile courts also had powers to place children in care, and the former children's departments had to receive children in need of care and protection and find them substitute homes. Child care authorities were also involved in running remand homes and approved schools.

The 1969 Children and Young Persons Act retained the juvenile court system but reduced the effective powers of the juvenile magistrates. Action to deal with offenders was to be taken on a voluntary rather than a court basis where possible. Prosecution of children aged 10 and under 14 was to cease, though this has never been implemented. If a child has committed an offence *and* the parents are not providing adequate care, protection and guidance, or the offence indicates the child is beyond parental control, then they can be brought before the court as in need of care, protection and control. For the age range 14 and under 17, prosecution is only possible for a limited number of offences on the authority of a magistrate, and the extended care, protection and control procedure is used in most cases. The courts must now make care orders committing children to the care of the local authority. The local authority (now the social services departments), must decide on the most appropriate form of care. For all children in care, a comprehensive system of community homes is now being developed, organized on a regional basis and managed by local authorities or by voluntary organizations in collaboration with local authorities. Community homes include former remand homes and approved schools and former children's homes.

So children sent from the courts, whether they were offenders or offended against, can now be placed in whatever type of residential care is deemed most appropriate to their needs at the discretion of the social workers of the local authority. This part of the Act has been strongly criticized and to some extent misused for a minority of very difficult cases. Since magistrates are no longer able to make approved school orders, it appears that some are sending children to the higher courts for possible custodial sentences. Another problem is remand for very difficult children. At present, too many young offenders are being remanded in prisons because local authorities lack enough secure accommodation for them. Steps are being taken to provide more secure places for the unruly and disturbed children who would otherwise disrupt community homes and reappear before the courts.

The local authority also undertakes supervision of children and this replaces the previous probation order. Supervision is by a social worker, who can make certain requirements such as that the supervised person resides in a specified place or participates in specified activities. Under these provisions local authorities are expected to provide Intermediate Treatment, which is designed to replace attendance and detention centres.

Intermediate Treatment is meant to help not only children in trouble but those at risk of getting into trouble. The idea was that a wide range of activities would be developed for groups of young people that would allow them to gain a sense of personal involvement and achievement. Children under supervision could be directed to such projects as appeared appropriate to their needs although the projects would not be exclusively for young offenders. Projects would be run by youth groups and voluntary organizations as well as local authorities. Many social services departments have appointed special Intermediate Treatment organizers to develop suitable projects, but progress has been slow. Intermediate Treatment needs enormous enthusiasm, imagination and energy in the design and carrying out of projects, and the necessary resources of staff and funds have not been forthcoming. This has seriously weakened the therapeutic and remedial potential of supervision orders and it is to be hoped that greater priority will be given to this area in the next few years.

Essentially the 1969 Children and Young Persons Act involved a transfer of responsibility from the courts to the local authorities. This meant in practice that magistrates had less say in determining what happened to children in trouble while social workers gained more say. This was in accordance with the expressed intention of the Act to merge the previously separate concepts of 'delinquent' and 'deprived' into one category of 'children in trouble'. The changeover has not proved easy. Local authorities have had to implement a controversial Act, involving a considerable increase of responsibility for them, at a time when the creation of the new social services departments preoccupied the child care and social work staff. As a result the magistrates, never very happy with the Act, were quick to criticize the way it was carried out. They claimed that the courts were inadequately served by the new social services departments. More fundamentally they criticized the reduction of their power to make residential orders and the merging of treatment for delinquent and non-delinquent children.

Many people feared that the 1969 Act was too radical and would make life too easy for the young delinquent. The increase in juvenile crime throughout the 1970s appeared to confirm the critics' views. Others felt that the implicit emphasis on home and family as formative influences on young people denied the importance of sociological explanations of delinquency. They demanded an even more radical approach to delinquency that would tackle not the individual offender but the wider deprivation and social injustice of which they considered him the product. In the event, the law and order lobby proved the more powerful of the two approaches.

An inquiry was held into the working of the 1969 Act and a White Paper, entitled simply *Young Offenders* (Cmnd 8045), was published in 1980 with proposals for 'strengthening the law relating to juvenile and young offenders in England and Wales'. For juvenile offenders the White Paper contained proposals for the courts to add a residential care order. This would apply only to a juvenile already in care of a local authority and then found guilty of a further imprisonable offence, and would be for a fixed period of not more than six months. Further proposals included the retention of the detention centre, the introduction of a new sentence of youth custody to replace borstal training, and the power for juvenile courts to impose community service orders on offenders aged 16.

The White Paper proposals reflected the magistrates' views that the 1969 act was too soft on young offenders. The Criminal Justice Act of 1981 implemented the proposals, despite some opposition. Youth custody is now a single determinate sentence for young offenders and the courts have much greater discretion in ordering the punishment or treatment of offenders. This is despite research evidence that has shown how ineffective much custodial treatment of young people tends to be.

Basically the 1969 Act, despite the controversy that has surrounded it and the resource problems that have hampered its implementation, must be seen as a notable step forward and one consistent with a renewed general acknowledgement of the importance of the family. It extended society's consideration for deprived children towards those groups that had previously excited anger rather than compassion and as such it was a progressive and humanitarian measure. It merits a vigorous defence in the face of developments such as the 1981 Criminal Justice Act, which threatened to encroach on its humane vision with the clamour of the law and order lobby.

SUGGESTIONS FOR FURTHER READING

Bowlby, J., *Child Care and the Growth of Love* (Penguin, 1953).

Brown, M. and Madge, N., *Despite the Welfare State* (Heinemann, 1982).

Children in Trouble, Cmnd 3601 (HMSO, 1968).

Coffield, F., Robinson, P. and Sarsby, J., *A Cycle of Deprivation?* (Heinemann, 1981).

Curtis Report, *Report of the Interdepartmental Committee on the Care of Children*, Cmnd 6922 (HMSO, 1946).

Donnison, D. V., *The Neglected Child and the Social Services* (Manchester University Press, 1954).

Finer Report, *Report of the Committee on One-Parent Families*, Cmnd 5629 (HMSO, 1974).

Heywood, J., *Children in Care* (RKP, 1959).

Holman, R. (ed.), *Socially Deprived Families in Britain* (Bedford Square Press, 1970).

Ingleby Report, *Report of the Committee on Children and Young Persons*, Cmnd 1191 (HMSO, 1960).

Jordan, B., *Poor Parents* (RKP, 1974).

Judge, K., *Rationing Social Services* (Heinemann, 1978).

Kellmer Pringle, M., *The Needs of Children* (Hutchinson, 1974).

Madge, N. (ed.), *Families at Risk* (Heinemann, 1983).

Packman, J., *Child Care Needs and Numbers* (RKP, 1968).

Page, R. and Clark, G. A. (eds), *Who Cares?* (National Children's Bureau, 1977).

Rutter, M. and Madge, N., *Cycles of Disadvantage* (Heinemann, 1976).

Sainsbury, E., *Social Work with Families* (RKP, 1975).

Timms, N., *Social Casework* (RKP, 1969).

Wendelken, C., *Children in and out of Care* (Heinemann, 1983).

Zimmerman, S., *Understanding Family Policy* (Sage, 1988).

9

Services for old people

THE PROBLEM OF OLD AGE

Simply to grow old is not in itself a problem. The urge to survive is fundamental to our nature and inherent in our fight against disease and poverty and in our attempts to control the environment. In a sense, then, survival into old age is a triumph, but a triumph that brings with it many problems, problems that tend to increase the longer one survives, the greater age one attains. The problems arise because old age is a period of increasing dependency – materially, physically, socially and emotionally. If the special needs that arise from these states of dependency are met fully and promptly then the problems will be kept to a minimum and on balance old age will be experienced as a time of contentment. If they are not met, old age may become a problem both to the individual and to society.

Material dependence arises because the old cannot earn their living and financial arrangements must be made to see that they have an income that is adequate to their needs. Physical dependence arises because for most people the process of ageing involves a general physical and sometimes mental weakening. The old are more frequently ill than the rest of the population and more frequently suffer from physical disabilities such as partial loss of hearing or arthritic joints. Gradually their capacity to care for themselves fully is reduced so that they require help with heavier cleaning jobs or gardening, then help with routine tasks such as shopping and cooking and finally, in some cases, help even with feeding, washing and dressing themselves. Many of the aged, therefore, need help in the home, or perhaps residential care, and a considerable number will require intensive medical and nursing care at some stage.

These material and physical states of dependency are fairly widely recognized since, for example, increasing frailty is a fairly easily discernible consequence of growing old. Less readily acknowledged are the social and emotional problems that ageing can bring. Old people cannot get out so much, for physical or financial reasons, or both. They have less opportunity to make new friendships and tend to depend for companionship on the continuity of longstanding relationships. As spouses and relatives and friends of their age move away, or die, old people look more and more to their few surviving relatives and neighbours for affection, friendship and reassurance and can easily become very dependent on a small number of people for social contact. Moreover, growing old often involves very considerable adjustments for the individual, who has to accept increasing physical dependency and consequent loss of autonomy and status. Many find it hard to accept a dependent role and fight to assert an independence that they lack the means to substantiate, often, in the process, alienating and exasperating the very people they depend on. The old have to accept changes in patterns of living and cultural standards that they cannot understand, and cope with rejection by the younger generations, as well as a good deal of sentimentality and shallow stereotyping in private and public references to themselves. Adjustment to their changing role and position in society can be so painful that some old people fail to achieve it satisfactorily and live at odds with society in bewildered but proud withdrawal.

If these social and emotional needs are to be met, the old must have every facility for preserving their contacts with relatives and friends and possibilities for some compensatory relationships when deeper ties are ultimately broken. They deserve a more sensitive environment that does not so harshly relegate them *en masse* to the category of 'old people' and does not emphasize, in attitudes and actions, their increasing dependency; many need help, too, in coming to terms with the process of ageing and the major adjustments it entails – to retirement, to relinquishing their home, etc.

It is a fundamental point about the aged, and one that is applicable to any group of people who need special help, that they will differ very widely in their capacities and in their needs. Old age begins officially on retirement but the majority of people in their sixties and many in their seventies remain reasonably fit, independent, active and content and in many cases they will remain so until the end of their lives. For some, though, some of the problems are evident from the point of retirement, or even before, and for very old people, in their eighties and nineties, the chances of considerable dependency are clearly rather high. Not all of these dependent old people can rely on consistent family care. So, although many old people cope smoothly with the problems of ageing, others fail in varying degrees to obtain the special help they need. As a result they suffer from poverty, physical hardship, neglect, sickness and disability, loneliness, humiliation and fear. Old age becomes something to be dreaded and endured rather than enjoyed by the individual.

In Britain today we tend to consider old age as a social problem. We know from research and investigations and general observation that many old people are desperately poor and neglected, appallingly isolated and lonely. At the same time we are worried about the mounting costs of the social services intended to meet the needs of the aged There are several reasons why the problem appears to l e particularly acute at the moment and some of the more important ones need stating. First, the proportion of old people in the population is rising fast. In 1900 the proportion was 4.7 per cent, in 1950 it was 10.8 per cent and today it is over 18 per cent. This means that there are more old people needing special help and proportionately fewer people of working age to provide for them. Old people also live much longer nowadays. This is one reason why the proportion of over 65s has risen, but it also means that many more old people will grow very old, with much higher chances of becoming very dependent and physically feeble. Average life expectancy was only 43 years in 1880; it had risen to 62 years in 1939, and by the 1960s it was over 70.

At the same time as the number of old people in the population is rising, several factors are operating that have tended to reduce the ability of the family to cater for the needs of old people, especially their needs for care and companionship. Prominent among these factors are increased social and geographical mobility consequent upon greatly increased educational opportunity and a rapidly changing economy; the marked trends over recent decades towards smaller families, higher marriage rates and earlier marriage; and the growing numbers of women continuing in or re-entering full-time work. The greatly increased life expectancy of both men and women today means that the children of many of them may themselves be entering old age when they, the parents, are really in need of care.

A further problem of ageing, which in part follows from a greater life expectancy, relates to retirement. In the past, this has been seen as most relevant to men, although now that more women work in paid employment it is a problem for both sexes. However, there is evidence to suggest that women may have fewer problems in adjusting to retirement than men. Men, if they are still fit on retirement, will have another fifteen years of life ahead of them, whilst women will mostly outlive their husbands and have a further twenty or more years ahead. Apart from the possible financial hardship of retirement many find it hard to adjust to having little to do. They are bored at home and yet feel ill at ease in their former places of enjoyment – pubs and sports grounds and so on – and with their former friends if these are still working. They feel useless being no longer productive workers and yet having little to do at home. This problem is much worse for those who are forced into premature retirement through redundancy. The sense of uselessness and the boredom of empty days, the abrupt, often humiliating change of status from worker to 'old age pensioner', can lead to severe depression and consequent physical and mental deterioration. There is a real need here both for a more flexible employment situation, which could absorb older people in less arduous or part-time work if they required it, and for more efforts to prepare people for retirement, helping them to develop time-consuming, absorbing and possibly profitable hobbies in advance of finishing work.

The problem, then, that old age presents is partly inherent in the process of ageing, and partly the consequence of certain current demographic and social trends. In 1987, 10.4 million people in Great Britain were over retirement age. The vast majority need pensions to meet their financial needs, almost all will be registered with a doctor and will make use of the health services, and many require special housing or residential accommodation and some degree of help in coping with the problems arising from increasing frailty, social isolation and their dependent role. Clearly the social policy required to tackle the problem must be comprehensive in scope and its instruments flexible and imaginative in application.

SERVICES FOR OLD PEOPLE

There is no one social service designed to meet all the needs of old people. Society has accepted responsibility for seeing that their needs are met in a piecemeal fashion, tackling the most obvious needs first – those for financial provision, medical care and residential accommodation. A considerable part of the total range of need is met through the basic social services of income maintenance, health, housing and personal social services. In special welfare services for the aged, voluntary organizations play a prominent part. This fragmentation of concern for the aged is sometimes criticized, but clearly when we are considering a particular *group of people*, like the aged, rather than a particular *problem*, like sickness, it would not be possible, or desirable, to provide all that is needed through one statutory service. The aged, like any other group, have special needs that arise because they are aged, but they share the basic needs of all human beings. It is quite appropriate that they utilize the health services and income maintenance services which are provided generally, and also utilize the special services provided particularly for them.

Financial provision

A fundamental need of the aged is for adequate financial provision, since the vast majority are unable to earn their living. In endeavouring to meet this need numerous problems are encountered, notably how to find enough money to provide adequately for the increasingly large proportion of the population who are in retirement, and therefore by and large non-productive, and how to define 'adequate' in this context. In Chapter 2 the present social security system was described and it was noted that the bulk of the work of social security is concerned with pensions and benefits for old people. In principle we accept that people should be helped to provide for their own needs in old age by contributing throughout their working life to a pension scheme. This method of financing old age is widely practised through the media of private insurance and occupational superannuation as well as that of statutory National Insurance. Because of this it is particularly important in devising an effective social policy to meet the financial problems of old age to consider both the long-term and the short-term aspects. We must try to meet the needs of those people who are in retirement now, and try to create an effective scheme whereby those who are working now will be able to retire with financial security in the future. The effectiveness of retirement pension schemes is greatly threatened by increasing longevity, the problem of keeping pace with the cost of living in an inflationary economic situation, and the problem of rising standards of living which bring new affluence and expectations.

At the present time, the majority of old people claim retirement pensions under the National Insurance scheme. The basic rate at April 1989 is £43.60 per week for a single person and £69.80 for a couple, but some pensioners are entitled to somewhat higher rates because of graduated contributions or deferred retirement. Some old people who were not included in the scheme as contributors receive a lower rate of pension. Many old people receive occupational or private pensions in addition to their basic retirement pension and a large number have personal savings or private incomes of widely varying amounts. Those old people who are dependent on the retirement pension and who find it does not meet their needs can claim a supplementary pension from income support. This means that all people over pension age who are not in full-time work have a statutory right to have their income brought up to a guaranteed weekly level. This consists of income support allowances and premiums, which add up to £46.10 for a single person, and £71.85 for a couple, plus the actual cost of rent and rates. In addition, older pensioners may get a slightly higher premium, marginally increasing their total weekly amount. Income support is, of course, only paid on test of need, but in assessing a person's means certain forms of income such as disability pensions and a reasonable level of capital are to some extent disregarded.

When the present National Insurance scheme was introduced in 1946 it was hoped that the benefits paid under it would be adequate for subsistence. This has proved impossible, partly because of the wide variations in need imposed by disparate rents, and partly because of the steady rise in the cost of living. Accordingly, a substantial number of today's retirement pensioners need to claim assistance and submit to some form of test of need. Through pride or ignorance many people fail to do this. A deliberate attempt was made in 1966 to make assistance known and acceptable, when it became known as supplementary benefits. Now, it is hoped that all who need a supplement to their basic pension obtain it, but there is still evidence that many do not. In addition to income support many old people can claim housing benefits but there is always anxiety that some of the most needy old people will fail to take advantage of their rights. As a group, today's old people are still relatively deprived in our society and this must be seen as a major failure in social security policies.

Policy changes in the 1970s moved the provision for people over retirement age towards a wholly wage-related scheme of insurance. In the years since 1945 occupational pension schemes outside the state scheme flourished, particularly for the higher-income groups. Attempts to provide a similar scheme related to earnings, but as part of state provision, resulted in the 1975 Social Security Pension Act 1975, which came into operation in 1978. The main provision was that of State Earnings Related Pensions (SERPs), which was an earnings-related pension scheme provided by earnings-related contributions made by both employees and employers. Originally the scheme allowed for pensions to be calculated on the best twenty years of earnings, which at least went some way towards enabling women, who spend some time out of the labour market caring for dependants, to maximize their future pension. However, SERPs has become a more marginal system as a result of recent changes in the legislation relating to pensions.

In particular, the 1986 Social Security Act and the Finance Act (Number Two), 1987, have introduced a more complex pension position. Since 1988 employees can contract out of SERPs and also out of their employer's occupational pension scheme, by choosing to opt for an 'appropriate personal pension' instead. APPs are mostly money purchase schemes, that is, they do not have a guaranteed final pension, unlike most occupational pension schemes, nor are they index-linked up to retirement age, unlike SERPs.

The position is now much more complex for individual employees, for whom the best choice may be one of several options. In addition, the provisions in some occupational pension schemes and APP schemes for dependants, especially widows, may be very poor. What does seem certain is that SERPs will as a result of these changes become more of a marginal scheme, whilst the government has offered several 'sweeteners' to individuals choosing to leave SERPs for APP-type plans. The schemes that do exist in the private market for pensions are related to purchasing power – so inequalities in earnings will be reflected in life after retirement, whilst those without the power to buy a pension will become increasingly dependent on the low rates obtainable from state pensions and means tested benefits. In addition, it seems likely that some, at least, of those who choose to opt out of the state or their employer's scheme may end up dependant on state benefits at a later date, as the benefits from the money purchase schemes are unpredictable for both employee and dependants.

For the present-day old age pensioners, however, the problem of financial insecurity remains. Retirement benefits are not enough to live on, so nearly 2 million pensioners have to claim income support. Pensions are essentially low incomes and low incomes are especially vulnerable to the effects of inflation. Certain costs, particularly fuel costs, fall heavily on old people. Fuel costs increased dramatically during the mid-1970s and have remained high ever since, and this adversely affects many old people. Compared to other social groups, pensioners spend more of their budgets on fuel, partly because they need to heat their homes all day and are less active than younger households, and partly because they often have antiquated and costly heating systems to run. Some attempts were made to provide specific aid with fuel costs by providing supplementary benefit recipients with a discount or rebate, but these were scrapped under the 1986 Social Security Act, so the problem remains a serious one for many elderly households. Pensions have increased in real terms over the last twenty years, but not as fast as real personal disposable incomes. Although they are now regularly increased in November every year, a government pledge to increase the rates in line with the rise in either earnings or prices, whichever was higher, was dropped in 1980. As a result, the pension rise in November 1980 was effectively reduced and increases in current pensions no longer keep pace with rising costs. The real value of current state pensions has been eroded, whilst means tested support on which older people increasingly rely has similarly suffered cuts in real value. At the same time, the effects of inflation, the recession and financial cutbacks in other services in the 1980s have led to increased poverty amongst this vulnerable group in society.

Health services

Old people make considerable use of the full range of services provided under the National Health Service Act. Even if those who are living in institutions are excluded, it is estimated that half of old people under 75 and about two-thirds of those over 75 are suffering from a long-standing illness in addition to normal minor ailments. Large numbers of the elderly suffer from some degree of disability or impairment of physical or mental function. It is not surprising, therefore, that old people make fairly heavy demands on medical care.

General practitioners spend a good proportion of their time with elderly patients and this is acknowledged in the rates of payment for different categories of patients on the GP lists. Some have adopted a system of routine visiting of all the old people on their lists in order to check that health is maintained and to ensure that diseases and disabilities are tackled at the onset. Many GPs cooperate closely with the community health services, which are particularly valuable for the old. Health visitors call to give advice and help on the problems of increasing infirmity and the management of disability, and encourage the maintenance of adequate standards of hygiene and nutrition.

District nurses can continue treatment at home for elderly people who have been hospitalized or provide long-term treatment and care for those with chronic ailments. Community psychiatric nurses provide a vital service to the elderly mentally infirm enabling them to carry on living at home through the provision of medication and support.

Despite the general practitioner and domiciliary medical services many old people have to enter hospital for treatment or care. As old age advances this can become a very disturbing experience and even where the medical problem is not grave the hospitalization itself can accelerate confusion and frailty among old people. In recent years this has been more widely recognized and both doctors and nurses have increasingly made a specialty of the care of the aged. Geriatric units are being established and consultant geriatricians appointed. Efforts are made to rehabilitate patients after treatment to ensure that where possible their hospital stay is temporary. Nevertheless, a large number of elderly patients do come into hospital with terminal illnesses or chronic diseases, including mental disorders, and they require long-term care. They do make heavy demands on the resources of the hospital service, so steady efforts are being made to improve the preventive aspects of geriatric care. However, the 1989 White Paper, *Working for Patients*, has caused some concern that an unprofitable and expensive service like geriatric provision may be reduced if hospitals and GPs are encouraged to become self-managing budget holders, whose first goal must be to contain costs.

Social care

Under Part III of the National Assistance Act of 1948 local authorities have a duty to provide residential accommodation for old people who need care and attention. This is now the responsibility of the social services department, but until 1970 it was the job of welfare departments. Residential care is provided by local authorities for about 105,000 old people in England and Wales. A further 25,000 are cared for in homes run by voluntary organizations and 78,000 are cared for in private residential care.

In 1948 local authorities had a variety of old premises used for accommodating the elderly, mostly old public assistance institutions. The aim of the new welfare authorities was to provide homes rather than institutions and so private houses were acquired and converted and then modern purpose-built homes were constructed. These accommodated about thirty old people, which was originally considered the optimum size, but over the years purpose-built homes grew larger and up to seventy places became quite common. The bulk of local authority homes are now purpose-built and accommodate thirty to seventy old people. There are still some larger homes in existence and a small number of old premises used jointly with the health authorities but it is planned to close these eventually.

The 'ideal' old people's home has about fifty beds, mostly in single rooms, and accommodates both men and women. There is usually a large dining room, several lounges and a sheltered garden area. Accommodation for residents is on the ground floor or well-serviced by lifts. Staff have separate self-contained accommodation if resident. The home is situated within easy access of shops and other facilities and in the heart of the residential area from which the old people come. The furnishings will be modern and colourful and residents will be encouraged to bring small items of their own furniture with them to give individuality and interest to their rooms. All meals and full care, including night attendance, will be provided and visiting strongly encouraged. The aim of the staff will be to make people feel as much at home as possible. Residents pay for their care according to their means and all will have at least a minimum amount of money for personal use.

Naturally homes differ. Ideal standards are not always achieved. Many homes are too large to be homely. Some still have dormitories, lack space for pleasant sitting rooms and have poor staff accommodation. Some of the converted premises are isolated and inconvenient to run. Some of the modern homes are too clinical, impersonal and routinized for comfort. The quality of the staff, from matrons to cooks, is probably the biggest single factor determining whether a home has a happy atmosphere, and good staff are hard to get for the demanding, albeit rewarding, job of residential care. Residential staff have tended to become isolated from field staff and their training and pay have lagged behind those of field social workers. Efforts have been made to improve the training and conditions of employment for residential care staff, in the light of increasing emphasis on community care in the 1970s and 1980s. However, in the face of increasing restraint on public expenditure, these have not been notably successful. The provision of homes for old people by local authorities is still for only about twenty places per thousand old people in an area, and many of these will be for very old and frail disabled people. For this minority, residential care is a vital service. For others it could be a pleasant existence if places were available and there was room for flexibility and experiment in provision.

When welfare departments were created in 1948, their major concern as regards old people was with residential accommodation. Gradually this concern was widened to include the provision of a broad range of services for old people who remain, and wish to remain, independent in their own homes. This wider concern was of course shared with health authorities, voluntary organizations and housing departments, and it is now explicit policy in the unified local authority social services departments. From 1963, with the publication of the command paper *Health and Welfare: the Development of Community Care*, local authorities have been encouraged to see as their principal responsibility the provision of services to enable the aged to live independently in the community. From the 1968 Health Services and Public Health Act they have had the powers to promote the welfare of old people.

Social services departments now have a variety of services available to promote the community care of old people. Social workers in the area teams visit the elderly to assess their needs and provide such services as seem appropriate and are available. One of the principal domiciliary services is that of home helps. Home helps, often recruited within an area by a home help organizer at area office level, call regularly on old people and provide domestic services such as cleaning. They also provide a friendly contact, which is extremely valuable for detecting and referring any other needs. Mobile meals services can be provided or luncheon clubs for the more active old person, where company and entertainment can be obtained as well as a meal. Telephones can be installed, emergency call-card systems operated and local neighbourly help recruited to reduce the isolation of many old people. Most authorities now run day centres where old people can obtain care and recreation, and most use their residential homes for temporary admissions where necessary. Transport is sometimes made available and clubs, holiday schemes, outings and social evenings encouraged. Many of these services help old people living alone, but some also help old people living with their families and reduce undue burdens on relatives.

The scope of day and domiciliary care has grown sharply in recent years, although it is still woefully inadequate in relation to the demand for services, particularly the home help service. Coverage is still uneven between authorities, but most are overburdened. One response to this and the funding crisis in the early 1980s was to introduce charges for the home help service, up to a weekly maximum, which varied from authority to authority, but was in the region of £2. In most local authorities, claimants of benefits such as income support are exempt. Even so, the introduction of charges had the immediate response of reducing demands on the service, although this does not mean that all those who needed help were now able to get it, or that those withdrawing demand did not need help. In addition, local authorities may have difficulty in knowing which old people need help and of getting help to them in time. Home helps and domiciliary care of all kinds remain an important, and under-provided, form of care for older people in the community.

Housing and the elderly

Clearly, if old people are to continue to live alone they need not only the support of domiciliary health and social care services but also suitable premises. Size, location and quality of housing are important to all people, but clearly the old, with their reduced mobility and increasing frailty, have a special need of decent accommodation. The sad fact is, however, that in Britain the old have the worst housing of any group. Higher percentages of the elderly than of the general adult population live in accommodation built before 1919 that is often poorly maintained. Higher percentages of the old lack fixed baths, indoor WCs and adequate heating arrangements. There is, therefore, a real and urgent need to improve the housing conditions of the elderly.

Recognition of the importance of housing, especially for community care policies, led to the building of an increasing number of small dwellings by local authorities including one-bedroomed flats and bungalows. Attempts have also been made to provide sheltered housing – that is, groups of small dwellings with some communal facilities and a warden in attendance. Sometimes small bungalows have been built in the grounds of residential homes, in other developments they have been linked to a warden's bungalow by means of alarm bells. Groups of bed-sitters with communal lounge facilities have been tried, and in some places the shared lounge has been available for social facilities for the old people of the neighbourhood. Housing associations as well as local authorities are involved in the provision of sheltered accommodation.

The essence of good housing for old people is that it should be easy to run (easy to heat, clean and move around in), conveniently situated, afford independence and privacy to the occupant, with opportunity for sociability and the security of regular contact. Most sheltered housing schemes are extremely successful and together with the domiciliary services allow some old people to retain their independence and their interest in life. The trouble is that there are just not enough places available at the moment, and in recent years local authorities have been unable to provide more owing to the shortage of funds and the cash limits imposed on local authority expenditure by central government. With the changes in housing association operation as a result of the 1988 Housing Act, it seems unlikely that these organizations, in the past an important supplier of accommodation for older people, will be able dramatically to increase their share of provision. In the owner–occupied and privately rented housing sectors old people do not often have the means or the energy to make use of improvement grants. They remain very vulnerable in privately rented accommodation as they can often be ignorant of their rights. Efforts are now being made to ensure that more old people are using housing benefits where these apply, but there is a need for constant vigilance to protect the most vulnerable groups of old people from the worst aspects of bad housing.

The voluntary contribution

Voluntary organizations are particularly active in the care of old people. They play a large part in the provision of welfare services, especially in running clubs and recreational activities and helping with the provision of meals, and they make a substantial contribution to the demand for residential care. Too many organizations are involved to list them all, but nationally organized groups such as Red Cross and WRVS are prominent, and were frequently pioneers in the provision of meals services. The National Old People's Welfare Council, now known as Age Concern, coordinates and encourages the activities of a vast number of local groups concerned with old people's welfare. These local committees offer, either directly or by coordination and encouragement of local effort, a wide range of services such as visiting, holidays, social clubs and even sheltered workshops for the elderly. Age Concern acts also as a pressure group on behalf of the elderly, publishing information on their needs and on services available. The Centre for Policy on Ageing is primarily a research organization funding inquiries into the needs of old people.

Many schemes for housing old people have been developed on a voluntary basis. They include schemes like that of the Abbeyfield Society which aims, by converting large older-type houses, to provide old people with the personal security and independence of their own room and furnishings, combined with the advantages of the degree of companionship and care that a communal dining room, the provision of main meals and the friendly attention of a resident housekeeper afford. Another area of voluntary activity is the provision of classes on preparation for retirement. These can help many people to adjust more happily to the changes retirement brings about in their lives.

Not only are voluntary organizations active among the aged, the aged are also active in voluntary work. The relatively young old person is free to contribute a good deal of time, energy and experience to voluntary action, and large numbers take advantage of retirement or reduced family responsibilities to increase their participation. Many younger old people run clubs for the elderly and help organize meals services. A very large number help, informally, their neighbours and relatives older than themselves. This activity is doubly advantageous in that it helps to meet the needs of the more elderly for a variety of services and also helps to give the younger elderly person a sense of usefulness, a strong interest and in some cases a degree of insight and preparation for the inevitable transition to a greater ageing that must be faced.

NEW INITIATIVES

In 1978 the DHSS issued a discussion document entitled *A Happier Old Age*, which considered the needs of the elderly in society. Following the response to its various questions a White Paper was published in 1981. *Growing Older* (Cmnd 8173) considered the needs of the elderly for financial support and opportunities during retirement, for housing, care and support and health services. The general message of the paper was that care of the elderly should concern and involve the whole community. It was a useful review of services but not a profound analysis of problems in this field and it makes for rather bland reading.

That same year also saw the publication by the DHSS of a consultative document on *Care in the Community*. This was followed by a circular of the same title which set out proposals to help long-stay hospital patients to return to the community. Many long-stay patients, it was suggested, particularly those in hospitals for the mentally ill and mentally handicapped, but also many elderly and chronically disabled patients, could move out of hospital if appropriate facilities for their care and support in the community were made available. The circular acknowledged that the main burden of providing such care would fall on the local authorities and it aimed to ease this by extending provision for the transfer of NHS financial resources to those local authorities or voluntary bodies that offered to develop community care projects specifically for long-stay hospital patients.

Local authorities have been cooperating with the health authorities in the provision of community care schemes for several years under special arrangements for joint finance. The 'Care in the Community' initiative sought to extend this cooperation to help people who have been hospitalized for long periods. Since April 1984 health authorities have been able to make continuing payments to local authorities providing social care, and to give grant aid to education and housing departments as well as social services and voluntary organizations.

The alteration in 1983 in DHSS benefit rules that enabled older people living in private residential care to claim their fees from the DHSS brought dramatic increases in the number of private residential homes, and in the number of older people living in them. However, even with this growth in numbers, the vast majority of the older population live either in their own homes or in those of relatives. The 1980s saw a number of reports on community care that cited low funding and poor planning and coordination of projects as being responsible for the lack of a developed community care initiative to support all people, including the elderly, in the community in their own homes. As it is, a large part of the caring that is carried out for older people, both those living at home and those living with relatives, is carried out by women, mostly daughters and daughters-in-law. The 1988 Griffiths Report, *Care in the Community: An Agenda for Action*, described once more the problems of community care as being poor planning and control, and poor division of responsibility for different areas of concern. It recommended a stronger role for local authorities coordinating a range of services provided by the private and voluntary sectors as well as by the local authorities themselves. After a considerable delay, the government has agreed to implement the Griffiths' recommendations, but in the meantime health services have remained overburdened and unable to care for many older people, and there is a question mark over the future of geriatric care as a result of the 1989 White Paper on health services. The personal social service departments of local authorities are similarly stretched, with priority in many areas going to statutory work with children, and more and more older people are living in the community either without support or with help from relatives increasingly burdened by this caring role.

Perhaps more depressing than actual shortages of provision is the tendency to alienate the old in contemporary society. This occurs when too much provision becomes labelled as especially for old age pensioners. Administrators of services do need to be careful not to isolate recipients too much. The old need help but they do not necessarily need a massive range of old people's services.

Clearly, some of the needs now met by social services departments would be better met by the old people themselves if they had the financial means to preserve their own independence. It is worth remembering that most people cope quite adequately with the practical problems of old age if they have financial security and decent housing, and it is on the provision of these we should concentrate. Moreover, despite the importance of professional social care, it is families who still play the major part in meeting the social, emotional and general physical needs of the dependent old. The role of the state in services for old people should be to create conditions that maximize the ability of the individual, families and the community to cope independently. There are, after all, many aspects of the problem of old age that no formal statutory provision can deal with. Only families, the community and above all the old people themselves can solve the need to belong, to have a place, meaning and dignity in life. The role of the social services here is the vital but subordinate one of enabling them to meet this need effectively.

The importance of this enabling approach is, happily, gaining greater recognition. The role of families and of informal neighbourhood care is much more widely acknowledged and various projects to support the carers and stimulate neighbourhood networks are under way. Much of this is welcome but it has to be looked at critically when public expenditure cuts dominate the policy discussions. Families, which essentially means women, already provide massive, unpaid, largely unrecognized care and it is vital that policies of decentralization and community care do not too readily shift an even greater burden on to both the elderly themselves and their caring relatives. What is required is a genuine enabling partnership between the formal and informal sectors in which people and their families receive relevant and generous support from income maintenance and the health and social services of their neighbourhood.

SUGGESTIONS FOR FURTHER READING

Goldberg, E. M., *Helping the Aged* (Allen & Unwin, 1970).

Hicks, C., *Who Cares – Looking after People at Home* (Virago, 1988).

Meacher, M., *Taken for a Ride* (Longman, 1972).

Mortimer, E., *Working with the Elderly* (Heinemann, 1982).

Phillipson, C. and Walker, A. (eds), *Ageing and Social Policy* (Gower, 1986)

Shanas, E., Townsend, P., Wedderburn, D., *et al.*, *Old People in Three Industrial Societies* (RKP, 1968).

Shaw, J., *On Our Conscience* (Penguin, 1971).

Tinker, A., *The Elderly in Modern Society* (Longman, 1981).

Townsend, P., *The Family Life of Old People* (RKP, 1957).

Townsend, P., *The Last Refuge* (RKP, 1962).

Tunstall, J., *Old and Alone* (RKP, 1966).

Wicks, M., *Old and Cold* (Heinemann, 1978).

10
The physically disabled

THE PROBLEM

The terms 'physically disabled' and 'physically handicapped' cover people with a wide range of disabilities: the blind and partially sighted, the deaf and hard of hearing, people with congenital deformities, those who have suffered serious injury, those who suffer from crippling diseases such as arthritis, tuberculosis, 'organic nervous disorders', and so on. Clearly the needs of each person, and the problems they present, will differ according to the nature and severity of the disability and according to the individual's personality and social and economic situation. But all the physically handicapped have one need in common – the need to be helped to overcome their disabilities and live as near normal a life as possible, being a part of, and contributing to, the life of the community.

It is perhaps useful, in considering the problem, to differentiate between a disability and a handicap. It is possible, within limits, to assess a physical disability. Blindness can be ascertained, the degree to which a person suffers from loss of hearing can be measured, and the extent to which an injury or disease is physically disabling can be assessed in a fairly precise manner. But the extent to which a given disability will *handicap* a person in education, work, social relationships, enjoyment of leisure, etc., will depend on their social as well as their clinical state, and on the timing of the disability. A person born severely disabled will need a great deal of help in overcoming the effects of the disability, but they will possibly be able to adjust to it better than the person who has enjoyed perfect health and led a full, normal life and is suddenly injured or crippled by disease. Someone who has acquired skills in early life for a job involving considerable strength and mobility will be more handicapped in finding work if they become wheelchair-bound than someone similarly afflicted who has qualifications and experience in a field that allows them to do a sedentary job demanding intellectual skills. Similarly, the person who has a great love of music might find blindness less of a handicap in obtaining pleasure than would the person who had a passion for football. Various factors will strongly affect the extent to which disability leads to handicap, primarily the ability of the disabled person and their family to cope with disablement. The family may encourage independence, or they may stifle it; the individual may rise to the challenge, but may equally be overcome with bitterness and despair.

It is still difficult to indicate the size of the problem of physical disability in Britain, as there are no exact records. At present we have to rely on several sources of information, which sometimes overlap, and which definitely leave great gaps. We have registers for certain groups of disabled people – those registered with local authorities, those who are listed as disabled with the Department of Employment, records of certain groups receiving treatment or pensions, and so on. The total picture is incomplete, partly because not everyone who is disabled is necessarily in receipt of a pension or special welfare service and many of those on the disabled persons employment register, for example, include those with mental handicap as well as those with physical disabilities.

A survey carried out by the Office of Population Censuses and Surveys between 1985 and 1988 estimated that there were more than 6 million adults in Britain suffering from one or more disability. OPCS used a scale of 1–10 to measure disability, where a score of 1 was the least severe and 10 the most severe, in terms of level of incapacity and suffering. The survey estimated that 2.7 million people were in the top five categories, that is, suffering the most severe disabilities. They also discovered that more women than men were classified as having a disability, and that the rate of disability and the number of disabilities suffered increased with age. Many of these disabilities found in the older age group were related to loss of hearing and sight, and increasing mobility disability, related to such problems as rheumatoid arthritis. Clearly, these categories of disability blur the border-line between what is generally considered as disability and what is considered the increasing frailty of old age. It proves impossible to keep to rigid categories when examining this issue.

Although it is not possible to give any exact statistics of the physically disabled, it is possible to give some indication of the extent of the problems they face. We have already noted that these will differ according to the actual disability and according to the individual's circumstances. This simple fact cannot be overstressed and it accounts, in part, for the continuing lack of precise data on the numbers of physi-cally handicapped in Britain: we do not know exactly how many people are physically disabled because they are not a clear homogeneous group that can be counted. Neverthe-less, we need to consider what problems might arise and make provision accordingly, accepting that such provision should be very flexible if it is to cope with the range of need presented by the disabled. Some problems are fairly obvious: whether the disability is congenital, or the result of an accident or disease, the maximum amount of medical care available is required, in order to minimize the effects of the disability, or arrest the causative condition. Advances in medical science have made possible extensive treatment, by medical, surgical and rehabilitative techniques, which can remedy some defects and compensate for others. Some of the disabled will need, despite medical treatment, intensive care and regular nursing all their lives, others will need steady attention from their doctors even if they are relatively mobile and independent.

For many of those who are disabled from birth or during childhood, special education is obviously necessary. Clearly the blind, the deaf and the crippled cannot be expected to make do with ordinary educational provision but require spe-cially adapted teaching methods, and in some cases peripatetic teachers if they are confined to their beds at home. On leaving school most of the disabled will need help in finding suitable employment; some will need a permanently sheltered working environment; many will need financial assistance as they are unable to earn a living. The majority of severely handicapped persons need some help in the routine of ordinary living, as travel, shopping, housework, catering and so on are bound to be difficult and sometimes impossible. Because of their restricted mobility and their sense of difference, many will need assistance in establishing social contacts and suitable leisure activities.

Finally, all the physically disabled, however seriously or slightly they are handicapped in obtaining education, work, financial security and so on, do have one need in common: the need for understanding and acceptance. For many of the disabled the greatest hardship they suffer is not the frustration and practical problems of lives that are limited by disability but the sense of being in some way segregated from the rest of society. They feel, and in many cases they are, stigmatized, rejected, objects of disgust or pity in other, normal, people's eyes. They feel, in a world that tends to cultivate an oversimplified and idealized image of normality, members of an abnormal, deviant group. This is a very great hardship indeed, and only a very determined effort by society will ensure that the disabled achieve real acceptance and integration. The disabled may sometimes need help themselves in overcoming feelings of bitterness, despair or resentment towards the rest of society, and help in adjusting to and accepting the consequences of disablement without succumbing to a withdrawn resignation or unnecessary isolation.

PROVISION FOR THE HANDICAPPED

The special needs of different categories of the physically handicapped were recognized first by individual philanthropists and this led to the establishment of numerous national and local voluntary organizations aiming to promote the welfare of the disabled. Many of these pioneer voluntary bodies still exist, and they have been joined by large numbers of organizations that have arisen in recent years to tackle the needs of particular groups among the disabled, so that voluntary effort continues to play a major part in meeting the needs of the handicapped. It is only during this century that statutory services have been developed and they came in a very piecemeal fashion. For example, some educational provision was made for the handicapped child once the universal state education system showed the need. Rehabilitation services were boosted by the world wars, which greatly increased the numbers of severely disabled persons needing help in adjusting to their handicaps and finding suitable employment. After the Second World War the coverage of the needs of the disabled became fairly comprehensive in scope, although there was no attempt to set up a single department or authority to be responsible for their needs. Instead the various statutory authorities concerned improved their provision, and the voluntary effort was further encouraged. There was not, however, much discussion on the overall needs of the disabled, and research into how the needs could best be met was minimal.

Only very recently has there been a development of more comprehensive concern for the disabled. This was precipitated by the Chronically Sick and Disabled Persons Act of 1970. This Act generally strengthened and added to the welfare powers of the local authorities. But it had a particularly important clause in section 1, which laid a duty upon the authorities to inform themselves of the numbers of disabled persons in their areas and to make arrangements to meet their needs. In carrying out this duty, local authorities found themselves attempting to assess the numbers and needs of the disabled on a scale never before attempted. The Act occasioned a considerable debate about the needs of the disabled and as a result much publicity was given to their cause and many of their problems received greater critical attention. Particular reforming efforts have been made in the areas of welfare services and of financial provision. The general position remains one of fragmented concern; years of relative neglect of this group cannot, of course, be easily compensated for by debate and good intentions. But at least the issue is now more lively and from 1974 the disabled have had a special Minister for the

Disabled, at the Department of Social Security, to champion their cause and coordinate provision for their needs.

Medical provision

All aspects of the National Health Service are involved here. The maternity and child welfare service contributes by ensuring early diagnosis of problems, such as deafness, through its system of regular medical examinations and the observation of health visitors. It also plays a prominent part in preventive work through the vaccination and immunization programme designed to give children protection against crippling diseases such as poliomyelitis and the damaging effects that can follow relatively mild diseases such as measles. General practitioners are available to identify problems and refer them for further investigation, and to cooperate with the hospitals for long-term treatment.

The hospitals play a major part in treating diseases, in dealing with the victims of accidents, and their rehabilitation. The largest groups of persons registered as suffering from general handicap are those who suffer from organic nervous diseases, which include polio, multiple sclerosis, epilepsy, and so on. Arthritis and rheumatism are prominent crippling diseases. Hospitals provide not only active treatment, by surgery and medicine, but also long-term care of the very severely afflicted, research into the causes and treatment of disabling disease, and the rehabilitation of patients, both those recovering from diseases and those disabled by accident. Through such techniques as occupational therapy and physiotherapy, and by the inspired use of artificial limbs, walking aids, powered wheelchairs and so on, many severely disabled persons can be helped to adjust physically to their situation, develop compensatory skills and achieve considerable mobility. Medical rehabilitation units attached to some hospitals specialize in helping disabled patients maximize their potential and overcome their disabilities, and rehabilitation is increasingly seen as an integral part of a full treatment programme. Under the NHS patients can obtain artificial limbs, wheelchairs, special vehicles and various other aids and appliances, while hearing aids and spectacles are available where necessary, though, ironically, only on a means test. The community health service provides home nursing, which can be very useful to handicapped persons, and in some areas physiotherapy classes and transport are available.

Educational provision

As was noted in Chapter 4, local education authorities have for a long time had a duty to provide special education for handicapped children. Under the 1944 Education Act they have had a duty to provide this for numerous categories of children: the blind, partially sighted, deaf, partially hearing, physically handicapped, delicate, maladjusted, epileptic, educationally subnormal, children with speech defects, and the autistic. By 1987 nearly 140,000 children were receiving special education in England and Wales. Nearly three-quarters of these children were educated at special schools, often in special classes. More than half the total number were categorized as educationally subnormal.

Special education has been subject to considerable controversy for many years. On the one hand, educationalists have argued that segregation of handicapped pupils is wrong and they ought to be taught in ordinary schools, albeit with special lessons and equipment provided, in order that they do not lose touch with ordinary children. On the other hand, it has been argued that in order to maximize the benefits of special education it should become even more specialized, with schools focusing attention on a particular problem and designed and equipped exclusively with this in mind.

A committee of inquiry was set up in 1974 to consider the whole question of the education of handicapped children and young people and to review existing provision. The committee, known by its chairman's name as the Warnock Committee, reported in 1978. Its report, entitled *Special Education Needs*, contained important recommendations for bringing the education of handicapped pupils into line with that for ordinary children. The committee urged that the emphasis should henceforth be on the special needs for education of certain groups of children – those with learning difficulties – rather than on various categories of handicap. The special educational needs should be met as far as possible within the normal educational system, and parental views should be taken into account in making provision for particular children.

While the Warnock Committee was sitting, the 1976 Education Act established in principle that handicapped children should be educated in ordinary schools wherever practicable. An Act was passed in 1981 to pursue this aim and establish the new framework for special education suggested by Warnock. The Act provides for the local education authority to ensure that a child identified as having special educational needs is given education within an ordinary school as long as that is compatible with efficient use of resources and efficient education, both for the child concerned and for other children at the school. Local authorities have the power to make special educational provision for the under 2s and will have a duty to make such provision for children aged 2–5 and 16–19 as well as for those of compulsory school age. The Act also provides for the setting up of new procedures for the identification of children with special educational needs and for the establishment of a new definition for the term.

However, although the Education Act 1981 shifted the emphasis in education from handicap to special educational need, based on assessment of curriculum requirement rather than on the child's disability, there has been little progress in the integration of the handicapped in education. Meanwhile, within the special schools more thought is being given to providing a varied educational experience to meet the needs of pupils who might share a common handicap but whose aptitude, intelligence and aspirations vary widely. There remains a shortage of specially trained teachers and of real secondary education facilities. Access to further and higher education has been unduly restricted for handicapped children and this should be improved. More help should also be available for the parents of younger handicapped children under the new legislation.

The physically handicapped youngster faces severe problems in finding employment. A report entitled *The Handicapped School Leaver*, produced in 1964 by the British Council for Rehabilitation of the Disabled (now merged with the Central Council for the Disabled as the Royal Association for Disability and Rehabilitation), highlighted the problem of this group and urged that more youth employment officers have special training for working with the handicapped. Handicapped school leavers are frequently behind their peers in educational attainment owing to loss of education through time spent either under treatment or overcoming disabilities affecting learning, and they also have special difficulties in finding suitable employment. Even where a suitable job is found, a handicapped young person is likely to have difficulties with getting to and from work. Far too many handicapped young people have been condemned to operate at a lower level of education and achievement than their abilities warrant because of lack of facilities for further and higher education.

Since the report, the local education authorities' career service has generally improved its provision of specialist careers officers for helping the handicapped, but more still needs to be done in this area. The disabled face much frustration and discrimination in their lives and it is vitally important that they receive the maximum help through education, careers guidance, training and help with obtaining employment so that at least they have a real chance to find and keep satisfactory work.

EMPLOYMENT NEEDS AND SPECIAL PROVISION

A wide range of facilities is available to help the disabled overcome the difficulties they face in finding and keeping suitable work. These are mainly provided under the Disabled Persons (Employment) Acts of 1944 and 1958 and are run by the Department of Employment. A disabled person's employment register is kept at local offices of the division, and the disabled can register themselves and obtain the special attention of the disablement resettlement officer (DRO). It is the DRO's job to find suitable employment for the disabled and this entails building up a knowledge of suitable work available in the locality and of sympathetic employers, as well as discussing the individual disabled person's particular problems and inclinations. The DRO can follow up a placement to discuss any problems that may arise between the disabled worker and his employer. The Acts also provide for a quota scheme, which makes it compulsory for every employer of more than twenty people to take on a quota of at least 3 per cent registered disabled, although few firms adhere to this scheme and monitoring is poor. Further, certain occupations can be designated as reserved for registered disabled. At present only two jobs, car park attendants and lift operators, have been so designated.

The DRO may recommend that a disabled person attend a course at an Employment Rehabilitation Centre (ERC). He will liaise with the medical rehabilitation teams and with the ERCs to know something of the overall picture of the person's employment problem. The ERCs provide short courses for men and women who need help in regaining their confidence and fitness for work. They offer no specific training, but they assess a person's capacity and carry out vocational aptitude tests as well as offering a working routine to re-accustom the disabled person to the demands of a normal working day. The ERCs can, if necessary, be followed by periods of vocational training at training centres and colleges which teach the disabled new skills so that they can obtain work again.

If they cannot immediately find open employment the DRO might find them a place in the government-run sheltered employment scheme which is known as Remploy. There are currently nearly ninety Remploy factories up and down the country which employ disabled people in productive work that earns them a reasonable wage. Remploy factories produce a wide range of goods from kitchen furniture to overalls and they also do contract work for other manufacturers. They are, however, subsidized to some extent, and although the Remploy workers do a full day's work they do not have quite such demands made on them as they would encounter in open employment. A considerable number of Remploy workers do move on to work in open conditions but many remain semi-permanently in the sheltered environment. Some local authorities and voluntary organizations also run workshops for disabled people.

The disabled person's employment services are reasonably comprehensive, and the Piercy Report on *The Rehabilitation*

Training and Resettlement of Disabled Persons (1956) expressed general satisfaction with the scheme. Nevertheless there is room for improvement and change. It has been argued that the scheme is geared too closely to the needs of the industrial worker disabled by accident or disease in middle life, who, following full medical care and rehabilitation, needs help in returning to the routine of work, in adjusting to disability and in finding new skills within his or her capacity. The scheme is less helpful for the person who is handicapped from youth and has no experience of work, and it is not always suitable for those who are unused to and ill-suited for industrial work, for example, those from clerical work or service trades. In particular, the ERCs fail in some cases to rehabilitate the men and women who pass through them largely because it is not their physical disablement but their attitude that is handicapping them in returning to normal working life, and the ERCs are not really equipped to change these attitudes. Their routine is quite demanding and in some ways it expects a level of determination on the part of the rehabilitee that would probably be high enough to get him back to work without a course of formal rehabilitation.

Criticism of the retraining schemes is often that they train people for jobs that are not always available to them and they expect too much mobility from people who have further reasons, in their disability, for being reluctant to move from their familiar surroundings. There has been discussion over whether the DROs should not be better trained, possibly in other social work, in order that they can help the disabled adjust psychologically to their change of status as well as help them in practical ways. There is, too, a need for a greater awareness of the changing demands on the scheme. For example, there are today many fewer tuberculosis cases and far more mentally handicapped persons using the services than there were in the 1950s and this means new demands are placed on the staff that they are not always able to meet.

The establishment in 1974 of the Manpower Services Commission to run the public employment services and training services, formerly the responsibility of the Department of Employment, helped to some extent to revitalize the employment services for the disabled – for example, with special facilities for disabled people on the Training Opportunities Scheme run by MSC. However, in 1988 the responsibility for the employment of disabled people was returned to the Department of Employment, whilst schemes such as TOPs no longer exist.

Overall, the employment position of the disabled is still far from satisfactory. Generally mounting unemployment severely affects the disabled in particular. Unemployment of registered disabled is always at a much higher rate than unemployment generally and so the recession has severely damaged the chances of large numbers of disabled people obtaining work. And yet it is estimated that two-thirds of companies fail to employ their quota of registered disabled and only two government departments employ 3 per cent disabled. Local authorities and nationalized industries have an equally bad record of neglect of the disabled. The Disability Alliance argues that the quota system should be enhanced and properly enforced and the number of sheltered employment opportunities rapidly expanded. However, it remains a hard task to convince society that much more should be done to create fairer employment opportunities for the disabled.

FINANCIAL PROVISION

Obviously most severely disabled persons are likely to have financial problems as they have either a limited earning capacity or even none at all. Moreover, disability can itself make extra demands on financial resources because the disabled need extra care and special services. State financial provision for the disabled is very complex and patchy. It has operated on the rather inequitable basis of paying different amounts of money or none at all according to the source of disability rather than its extent. Persons disabled by war or in the armed forces and those disabled at work as a result of injury or prescribed industrial disease have for many years enjoyed reasonable financial provision. Those normally at work but disabled by non-industrial illness have had a limited cover under National Insurance, and those who have never been in the workforce have very limited special provision and must rely on income support if they lack resources. The result of this anomalous position has been that the majority of the disabled have had to suffer great financial hardship. Only in the last few years have real efforts been made to equalize provision for different groups of the disabled and there is still a long way to go before we can claim to have adequate social security in this area.

Provision for the industrially disabled comes under the 1946 National Insurance (Industrial Injuries) Act and it is operated alongside the main insurance scheme. Injury benefit is payable to anyone injured or disabled at work regardless of contributions. Sickness benefit is payable for up to twenty-eight weeks if a person is incapacitated for work at the rate of £33.20 a week, together with £20.55 for an adult dependant. If incapacity for work continues thereafter, a person can obtain invalidity benefit at the higher rate of £43.60 plus £26.20 for an adult dependant and £8.95 for each child. In addition, people who become unfit for work more than five years before pensionable age may receive an invalidity allowance. People who become disabled as a result of industrial injury or disease may also claim disablement benefit, which is paid in compensation for the disability itself, and is calculated in relation to the assessed level or percentage of disability suffered as a result of employment. At 100 per cent assessment, the weekly rate of benefit is £71.20. Additional allowances that can be paid include a constant attendance allowance, exceptionally severe disablement allowance, and reduced earnings supplement, which is paid to those who are unable to work in their normal occupation as a result of industrial accident or disease, and can be claimed either in addition to or separate from disablement benefit, payable where appropriate.

The industrial injuries scheme is reasonably fair and sensible. It recognizes the basic need of the severely disabled for maintenance and the special needs for nursing care and attendance. It also takes into account the actual disability and, whether or not it handicaps a person in working, it provides some financial compensation for it. Similarly the war pension scheme pays out relatively flexible and generous pensions for disability arising from service with the armed forces or wartime civilian casualties. These schemes are regarded as models that should be extended to those whose disability is congenital or arises out of non-industrial disease or accident, for whom cover, though recently improved, is still only partial.

Insured workers who are off sick are entitled to draw sickness benefit. If they remain chronically incapacitated for work they can now claim invalidity benefit at a higher rate. Under the 1975 Pensions Act, invalidity pensioners will eventually qualify for inflation-proofed earnings-related pensions. Invalidity benefit is paid according to the usual contribution conditions and dependants' benefits are added where appropriate.

For those who are not in the workforce there are now some non-contributory invalidity benefits. The severe disablement allowance of £26.20 per week, plus an amount for adult and child dependants, is payable to the chronically sick and disabled who are incapable of work. The severe disablement allowance replaces the non-contributory invalidity pension and the housewives' non-contributory invalidity pension (HNCIP), which was payable to married women who were unable to take paid work but who did not have sufficient contributions to claim invalidity benefit itself. To qualify for the HNCIP, a woman had to satisfy stringent conditions regarding her incapacity to carry out normal household duties. This was deemed to be discriminatory according to the European Directive on payment of benefits, and it was replaced with the severe disablement allowance for all claimants in 1984. Most of the applicants for the non-contributory disablement allowance are dependent on income support for their income maintenance, and it is automatically deducted from their benefit. But at least it is a benefit as of right and without means test. Those who benefit from the non-contributory disablement allowances are allowed to earn up to a prescribed amount, similar to the benefit, without loss of pension.

The introduction of the non-contributory disablement benefits was regarded as an important step towards helping to right the long-standing injustice of the financial provision for the disabled. Disabled housewives in particular had been totally left out of previous schemes. This caused considerable hardship because the disablement of a wife and mother, apart from the suffering involved, can lead to financial burdens and/or neglect of home and children.

Most of the above benefits are towards the maintenance of the disabled and their dependants when they cannot earn. There is now some provision to meet the extra costs of the disability itself. In 1970 an attendance allowance was introduced, payable to a person in need of substantial care and attention. This is payable for adults and children over the age of 2. There is a higher rate for the more severely disabled and a lower rate for those less severely incapacitated. Claims are submitted to an Attendance Allowance Board. Currently the rates are £34.90 for the higher allowance and £23.30 for the lower. Recipients are free to decide how to use the allowance, either as a contribution to general household expenses or to buy extra care. An invalid care allowance is a benefit for people of working age who are unable to go out to work because they have the care of a severely disabled relative. The current rate of invalid care allowance is £26.20. This is deductible from income support, but is worth claiming even by those on income support as recipients are credited with insurance contributions.

Mobility allowance was introduced in 1976 to help disabled people whose walking ability is severely restricted. It is a weekly non-means-tested cash benefit of £24.40 and it can be spent on any aspect of mobility, from payment for holidays or taxi fares to help with the costs of buying a car. The allowance is intended to replace the old scheme whereby special invalid trikes or a private car allowance were made available, and that scheme is being phased out. Linked to the mobility allowance is a voluntary organization called Motability, which helps disabled people make the best use of their allowance to acquire a private car by leasing on hire purchase. Mobility allowance beneficiaries are entitled, like members of the old vehicle schemes, to exemption from payment of road tax on cars.

War disablement pensions remain payable to those disabled during the wars, and they carry a range of additional allowances similar to those under the industrial injuries scheme.

The financial position of the disabled has improved dramatically in recent years. There are still many anomalies and too many disabled persons are dependent on income support, but at least the attendance and mobility allowances go some way towards acknowledging the financial burdens of disability.

Children who are disabled cause an extra financial burden to their parents and there have been some moves to acknowledge this. Following discussion of the settlement of private claims for compensation for thalidomide children, a special fund was set up to help other congenitally handicapped children. The fund is administered by the Joseph Rowntree Memorial Trust. Set up in 1972 it was established with £3 million to help parents with the costs of some special provisions. It is, however, more in the nature of a charitable gesture than a true extension of state responsibility for this area of need.

The financial hardship of the disabled has recently aroused considerable protest, particularly from among the more articulate of the disabled themselves. A pressure group known as the Disablement Income Group (DIG) was formed to campaign for better provision. Disappointment with the 1974 proposals led to the formation of the Disability Alliance, a consortium of groups concerned with the disabled, to continue to fight for a better deal. The ultimate goal of the pressure groups is a universal disability allowance, paid on assessment of disability and not related to age, income, working position or marital status. This would involve some acceptance by society of compensation to the chronic sick and disabled, not just of a responsibility to maintain them. It seems unlikely that this will occur in the near future. Although there are now many benefits available, they all have fairly stringent qualifying conditions. Vast numbers of people, especially among the elderly, receive no financial recognition of their moderate disability. Difficulties in defining disability, together with powerful limits on society's generosity towards handicapped groups, seems likely to continue to restrict the scope of financial provision for the disabled for many years to come.

WELFARE AND PERSONAL
SOCIAL SERVICES

Local authorities were made responsible for the welfare of the handicapped under the National Assistance Act of 1948. Initially they had a duty to promote only the welfare of the blind but from 1951 they had power to promote the welfare of the deaf and of the general classes of the physically handicapped. From 1960 this power became a duty.

The services that the authorities developed for the handicapped followed the model already established for the blind. They included: keeping registers; providing help to the handicapped in overcoming the effects of their disabilities and obtaining any available general, preventive or remedial medical treatment necessary; advice and guidance to handicapped persons on personal problems and also on any relevant statutory or voluntary social services; encouragement of handicapped people to take part in social activities; and arrangements for voluntary visitors. The services also included practical help by way of aids and adaptations to the homes of the disabled, provision of recreational facilities and travel and holiday schemes. For the blind, the services offered included the teaching of Braille, and the home teacher of the blind was a specialist social worker who provided this service. For the deaf, welfare officers had to provide a communication and translation service where necessary.

The pattern of provision was based on a partnership between the local welfare authorities and a wide range of voluntary organizations, many of which acted originally as agents of the local authorities in discharging their responsibilities. Provision for the blind and deaf was reasonably comprehensive as a result, although often rather isolated, but provision for the heterogeneous general classes of disability was very slight and uneven between authorities.

From the start of welfare provision for the disabled it was recognized that social workers would have a key role to play in putting the handicapped in touch with the provision available. Since 1959, when the Younghusband Report on *Social Workers in the Local Authority Health and Welfare Services* appeared, there have been systematic training courses for social workers designed to include the welfare of the disabled in their scope. Gradually the idea of welfare work for the physically handicapped has become more professional. Social workers were trained to perceive the psychological as well as the practical problems facing the disabled. Disablement arouses severe anxieties and strong resentment in people. Not surprisingly, a disabled person, suddenly threatened by a role change from head of the family to dependent invalid, can become frustrated and bitter. Social workers should be able to help people with a disability express their feelings, adjust to new roles, find new sources of strength and generally cope with the psychological impact of disability.

However, the most striking developments in welfare services have been on the delivery side rather than the personal counselling aspect. As with the elderly, the aim of welfare became the provision of community care. For the disabled, who by and large do not live in institutions, this meant services to help them become a more effective and integrated part of the community. Community care services include provision of places in occupation centres, development of transport services, encouragement of self-help groups and voluntary action, the provision of aids, adaptations and holiday schemes, and liaison with other bodies such as health authorities, housing departments and social security offices. Local authorities gradually developed such services, but the extent of their coverage and the quality of their provision was remarkably uneven. Some authorities maintained up-to-date registers and a full range of services, even if not enough of each, while others barely acknowledged the need at all.

In 1970 there were two major developments. Welfare services for the disabled became part of the new local authority social services departments and the Chronically Sick and Disabled Persons Act was passed. The first meant that people with a disability can now hope to enjoy more generic provision of social work, day care and residential care; a generally extended and localized service; the greater use of home helps and meals services; and the more effective encouragement of community work. The second meant that local authorities became heavily involved in researching into the numbers of disabled and attempting to assess their needs, and the public became much more aware of the whole problem of disability.

Research findings in this field have often proved depressing reading. Most local surveys on the prevalence of disability indicated that existing registers were badly understating it. Surveys of provision have indicated that this still falls short of a desirable level. In most areas there are simply not the resources to meet the expectations that the 1970 Act raised.

The gap between provision and need is too great to be bridged rapidly and many shortcomings have continued to be revealed by the considerable glare of publicity directed at the local authority services for the handicapped.

More seriously there was, and still is, great confusion about need and demand for service. The 1970 Act, for example, gave local authorities power to install telephones and television sets in the homes of the disabled, but the social services departments have been bewildered by how to decide on priorities between services and between individuals needing services. In the absence of explicit rationing devices, various undesirable practices that obscure or delay demand have developed. As a result there has been bitter criticism of the local authorities and much disappointment among the disabled and their families. With a more sober view of what is possible, local social services departments are now beginning to plan for the provision of more comprehensive and effective welfare services for the disabled. It will take time for the resources and expertise to build up, but it is hoped that the will and intention to provide a first-class service now exists.

ACCOMMODATION

The need for accommodation is a real one, as many of the disabled are clearly handicapped in the ordinary housing situation. At present the local authorities have a duty to provide residential accommodation if this is required for anyone who needs it by reason of age or infirmity. However, many authorities lack separate provision for the younger disabled, who have to join old people in residential homes. More separate provision is being provided and many authorities make good use of the facilities made available by voluntary organizations.

As part of the growing concept of community care, spelt out in the 1963 *Health and Welfare: the Development of Community Care* plans, many authorities have recognized that the physically disabled, like the elderly, usually want to retain their independence and avoid entering homes as long as possible.

Also, when families are providing care for a disabled relative they usually want to continue to do so if this is at all possible. Local authorities have, therefore, begun to help the disabled in their own homes by providing meals services, domestic help and so on, and in some cases they make arrangements to take the disabled person on holiday to give the other members of the household a break, although all of these services are restricted by cash limitations on local authority expenditure.

A further logical step is to consider the provision of specially adapted housing. As mentioned earlier, social services departments can and do make adaptations to premises to make life easier for the disabled person. They can put in ramps instead of stairs, widen doorways, fix rails in bathrooms, lower working surfaces in kitchens, extend tap handles, place electric points within reach, etc. All these things can make life much easier and increase the independence of a disabled person, though clearly it would be simpler in many cases to provide bungalows or flats designed especially for the disabled, in particular those confined to wheelchairs. Some authorities are now doing this; in others ground-floor accommodation in blocks of flats is reserved by the housing departments for disabled people. Some areas have made some provision for sheltered housing, that is, specially built flats with some services provided by a warden. This is an area of provision that needs urgent expansion, since proper living accommodation is essential for those who are restricted in their mobility.

The Department of the Environment issued a circular in 1974, *Housing for People who are Physically Handicapped*, which gives guidance to local authorities on how to assess the need for special housing and advice on provision over such things as design and siting. This should have served as an encouragement to the authorities to develop this important aspect of community care. However, again, the impact of restraint on public sector expenditure and the increasing emphasis on the private housing market have resulted in poor provision overall for this group in society. Whilst housing associations have in the past provided some, albeit limited, accommodation to enable people with a disability to live independently, the

1988 Housing Act restricts the ability of housing associations to provide this kind of low-cost housing.

THE VOLUNTARY CONTRIBUTION

Voluntary effort has already been mentioned, but a further comment is required to underline the very large contribution of voluntary agencies in this field. They cannot all be named, but examples of different types of organizations will indicate the scope of the effort. In many aspects of work for the disabled the voluntary agencies were pioneers. Many organizations such as the Royal National Institute for the Blind (RNIB) and that for the deaf (RNID) provide services on a national basis, aiming to promote better understanding of and provision for the needs of the people they represent. The RNIB produces Braille literature, the talking book library, and educational aids. It runs specialized homes and schools for the blind, such as a social rehabilitation home for the newly blind, and several training establishments and workshops, and a placement service. The RNID runs similar services for the deaf, and in both fields there are large numbers of local and several regional welfare organizations that cater more immediately for the welfare of the blind and deaf of their localities. The Central Council for the Disabled is a coordinating national body that encourages the development of voluntary effort for the disabled, and the British Council for Rehabilitation of the Disabled conducts research into their needs and problems and acts as an information body.

A large number of societies and associations promote the welfare of different groups of disabled people – large societies such as the Spastics Society and small spontaneously formed groups of, for example, muscular dystrophy sufferers. Some provide extensive facilities and pioneer new methods of treatment, education and care; others are small social clubs meeting in members' houses for companionship and leisure activities. The range of effort is very great and its contribution extremely important, not least in quickly meeting new needs as they arise – for example, the special needs of thalidomide children.

It was noted at the start of the chapter that not least among the needs of the physically disabled was the need for under-standing and true acceptance in society. The provision of the services already described is important, but this must take place in a society that fully accepts the implications of disability, otherwise the disabled feel they are rejected and discriminated against. Rejection of the physically dis-abled is not uncommon, for disfigurement and malformation have been associated with evil in earlier, superstitious times. Today few people would openly express any repugnance for the disabled, but many probably feel it, and it is implied, for example, in over-solicitous or embarrassed responses to people in wheelchairs. Many deaf people complain, with some justification, of being treated as stupid simply because they cannot hear, and many crippled people complain of being avoided, or pitied, and rarely accepted for themselves.

There is, therefore, a real need for the development of a more aware and accepting society, since this rejection – obvious, implied or felt by the disabled themselves – is a great handicap in their struggle to feel part of the community and to lead normal lives. To overcome this discrimination, public education is needed, and less segregation of handicapped peo-ple, so that acceptance is increased by widening the concept of normality. If attitudes are hard to change, it is at least possible to create an environment less hostile to the disabled, for example, by a vigorous campaign to improve access to public buildings. The extent to which society is prepared to divert resources of money and skilled manpower to the treatment, education and care of the physically handicapped is always a telling indication of the extent to which society accepts them and truly cares about their welfare.

SUGGESTIONS FOR FURTHER READING

Blaxter, M., *The Meaning of Disability* (Heinemann, 1976).

Boswell, D. M. and Wingrove, J. (eds), *The Handicapped Person in the Community* (Tavistock, 1974).

Fulcher, G. *Disabling Policies?* (Falmer Press, 1989).

Hunt, P. (ed.), *Stigma: the Experience of Disability* (Geoffrey Chapman, 1966).

Lees, D. and Shaw, S., *Impairment, Disability and Handicap* (Heinemann, 1974).

Sainsbury, S., *Registered as Disabled* (Bell, 1970).

Sainsbury, S., *Measuring Disability* (Bell, 1973).

Topliss, E., *Provision for the Disabled* (Basil Blackwell and Martin Robertson, 1975).

Walker, A. and Townsend, P., *Disability in Britain* (Martin Robertson, 1981)

11

The mentally disordered

THE PROBLEM OF MENTAL DISORDER

Mental illness and mental handicap are grave social problems. Any form of mental disorder is a serious problem for the *individual*, since it can involve great suffering and prevent him or her from living a full and satisfying life. But the *social* problem posed by mental disorder is a particularly awkward one: on the one hand, facilities for care and treatment are necessary and on the other, some form of control may be required, because the more serious states of mental illness and mental impairment involve some failure to live a responsible and well ordered life that conforms to the demands of society. Since control means some infringement of individual liberty, great care has to be taken to ensure that the control is not abused, and also that it does not clash with the other needs for care and treatment.

It would not be appropriate in a book of this kind to go into details over the clinical manifestations and classifications of mental disorder, although the booklist at the end of the chapter contains some introductory reading on the subject. But some brief description of the nature of mental illness and handicap is necessary before the social implications, with which we are largely concerned, can be fully grasped.

'Mental handicap' is the term that has come into general usage to describe a condition of arrested or incomplete development of mind. It replaced the term 'subnormality', which itself replaced 'mental deficiency' as the formal description of a wide range of conditions in which some degree of subnormal intelligence is the only common factor. In some cases of mental handicap there are recognizable clinical abnormalities as well as low intelligence. Children born with Down's Syndrome, a condition caused by a chromosome abnormality in which those affected show distinctive 'mongoloid' features from birth, provide one example; others are cases where the handicap results from disturbances in metabolic or hormonal functioning or from brain damage at birth. In most of these conditions mental handicap is accompanied by physical handicap, sometimes of extreme severity. In other cases there are no apparent pathological attributes and no clear clinical causes so mental handicap cannot be deduced from appearance or symptoms but is diagnosed gradually from performance and development in early childhood. In many of these cases the handicap is only diagnosed on starting school on the basis of educational tests. Because poor educational performance is related to emotional disturbance and physical handicap and even cultural diversity, the diagnosis of actual low intelligence is not always a precise or accurate process. There is some evidence that parents of low intelligence tend to produce children of low intelligence but this is not invariably the case and, where it is, it is just as likely to be as a result of environmental deprivation as of heredity. Although poverty, deprivation and low intelligence tend to go together, it is hard to disentangle cause and effect.

The causation of much mental handicap is, therefore, obscure, and diagnosis of many cases must rest on social and educational grounds rather than on clinical criteria. Cases range from the severely handicapped person who may be physically helpless and incapable of coherent speech, to the highly acceptable, responsible person, earning a living, looking after themselves, obtaining considerable enjoyment from life and from relationships but generally regarded as not very bright. The needs of the mentally handicapped vary accordingly. Some cases are susceptible to medical treatment, some require intensive nursing care, most respond to education and training and a small minority may be so severely impaired that they may be detained in hospital or placed under guardianship. In most cases of mental handicap, even of severe mental handicap, there is considerable potential for learning and development, although the pace may be slow. Large numbers of mentally handicapped people are willing and able to lead relatively independent lives if they are given the opportunities, support and encouragement they need.

Mental illness, unlike most mental handicap which usually dates from birth or early years, may occur at any stage of life and may be chronic or acute, mild in form or severe. Some forms of mental illness are linked to organic disturbances, such as brain tumours; others to physical deterioration such as the senile psychoses. But most mental illness lacks any clear physical symptoms and is recognizable only from the patient's abnormal behaviour. This is why some forms of mental illness are confused with criminality – for example, because they are manifest largely by anti-social behaviour. Some definitions of mental illness beg the question of what constitutes normal behaviour.

It has gradually come to be accepted that there are no clear lines dividing normal and abnormal behaviour, only several continua on which people might be placed that shade very gradually from the recognizably normal to the clearly disturbed. Mental illness is a very complicated subject, and psychiatry (the study and treatment of it) is not yet well enough developed to permit of an easy, agreed classification. To oversimplify, the more obvious (not necessarily more serious) illnesses, generally regarded as 'madness', are often referred to as psychotic disorders. These illnesses are manifest by a wide variety of symptoms from paranoid delusions or auditory hallucinations to total withdrawal from normal communication into silence or bizarre, apparently meaningless jargon, and they have in common some degree of loss of contact with reality. Neuroses, in contrast, are often extreme forms of normal behavioural or emotional patterns, such as depression or anxiety, and the patient usually retains some insight into their condition. Personality disorders are conditions where the individual's whole personality appears to be permanently warped rather than that they are suffering from some actual illness at any given time. These distinctions are necessarily very loose and easily blurred when actual diagnosis is attempted. They do, however, give some indication of the very broad spectrum of behaviour grouped under mental illness, which tends to confuse public reaction and policy in regard to this problem. Where the mentally ill person is potentially violent, the social problem is quickly perceived; where they are withdrawn and depressed, the individual agony may be overlooked.

It is not easy to assess the size of the problem that mental disorder poses. Not only does mental disability vary so widely that it ultimately defies definition, but the extent to which a given mental disability, in so far as it can be measured in clinical terms, handicaps a person will depend not only upon the disability itself but on the patient's social circumstances as well. This is true of all the special need problems discussed in this book, but particularly so in the case of the mentally ill and handicapped when a breakdown in normal social relationships is often part of the actual disorder. Some examples might help to clarify this. If a child is born with some degree of mental impairment and has parents able to handle the situation calmly, without undue guilt or anxiety, creating a relaxed home atmosphere, encouraging the child's full development however slow it is, making use of the best educational facilities available and providing a stable, reassuring, affectionate home, then such a child might well not be severely *handicapped* by the disability, but grow up relatively independent, sociable and self-confident. If, on the other hand, a child with a roughly similar basic disability is a cause for acute anxiety to the parents, who either make excessive demands or over-protect, and fail to make use of the available care and educational facilities, rapidly rejecting the child altogether as unrewarding and unmanageable, such a child might find low intelligence a severe handicap. The same is true of mental illness. If a person is suffering from a fairly severe mental disorder and has close friends or relatives who sympathize, encourage early treatment and make full rehabilitation possible by providing a tolerant but secure home after hospitalization, then the person has a fair chance of ultimately coping with their illness without it handicapping their general performance in life too severely. But if a person with a roughly similar disability is socially isolated, or the home environment has actually precipitated or exacerbated the illness, then they will be gravely handicapped in attempting to return to normal life after a period in hospital.

In fact, social and economic circumstances such as poverty, poor housing or unemployment are highly associated with onset of some forms of mental illness, and serve to act as triggers precipitating episodes of depression, anxiety and, in some cases psychotic illnesses. Often, however, patients may find social or economic problems accentuated by treatment for psychiatric illness, particularly as an in-patient in hospital. For example, an individual may lose their job as a result of becoming depressed, a person suffering agoraphobia will be unable to go out to their place of work as usual, and so on. The relationship between cause and effect in mental illness is complex, but social and economic circumstances play an important role in both precipitating and prolonging difficulties.

Clearly it is not easy to be precise about the numbers of mentally disordered persons who need help, but some figures of those actually receiving care or treatment are a rough guide to the size of the problem. In 1986 there were about 34,000 beds in mental handicap hospitals and 60,000 beds for psychiatric patients in separate hospitals or wards of general hospitals. In addition 3,000 mentally handicapped and 200,000 mentally ill people were seen as new out-patients that year. At the same time, substantial numbers of mentally handicapped and mentally ill persons were receiving some attention from the community services. However, a great many people with some degree of mental disability were not receiving any formal care or treatment.

The needs of the mentally disordered vary as much as their disabilities. Treatment is necessary as far as the advance of medical and psychological knowledge permits. In some cases this will involve hospitalization. If the disorder is severe the patient may also require full care and, very occasionally, physical control. In many cases mental disability will prevent a person benefiting from normal education or from earning a living and therefore special education and financial help will be needed, even if care in an institution or home is not actually necessary. For those who are able to work, special help might be needed in finding suitable employment or creating a sheltered working environment.

However, the needs of the mentally handicapped are perceived differently at different times according to prevailing attitudes towards mental disorder and the extent to which it is understood. At the start of this century it was generally accepted that the care and control of the mentally ill and subnormal should be a public responsibility. But little was known of the nature and causation of mental disorder and so provision for treatment was minimal. Informed opinion considered that care was best provided in hospitals for the mentally ill (the old lunatic asylums) and institutions or colonies for the subnormal. Total care within a segregated institutional setting was seen as the best answer to the social and individual problems arising from mental disorder. Today, however, the value of care within the normal community wherever possible tends to be emphasized. This change of policy, which reflects a growing understanding of the nature of mental disorder, and the development of the social services generally, means that the needs of the mentally ill and the mentally handicapped are perceived in a different light.

The attempt now is to provide care on a community rather than an institutional basis, on the assumption that it is good to retain the mentally disordered within the community as far as possible and help to rehabilitate and reintegrate those who have had to go into hospitals for treatment. So today the needs of the mentally ill and handicapped are seen as demanding a wide range of facilities: homes, centres, clinics and so forth, served by doctors, nurses, teachers, psychologists, psychotherapists, speech therapists and residential care workers, linked by a body of trained social workers and placed within a tolerant, accepting and truly caring community.

THE MENTAL HEALTH SERVICE

The main provision of mental health care comes jointly under the National Health Service, responsible both for the psychiatric and mental handicap hospitals and for the community health services, and the local authority social services departments. The local education departments and the Department of Employment also have parts to play, as do many voluntary organizations concerned with the needs of the mentally ill and handicapped. Up to the creation of the National Health Service in 1946 responsibility for the mentally ill and subnormal was carried largely by the local authorities, which ran hospitals and institutions for the mentally ill, and organized some care and supervision in the community for the mentally subnormal. Their powers were laid down by the old Lunacy and Mental Deficiency Acts, which were concerned with the definition, ascertainment and commital of mentally disordered persons as well as with the administration of the services. In 1948 the National Health Service took over all the hospitals and institutions as psychiatric and subnormality hospitals under the regional hospital boards, while local health authorities continued the provision of community services.

Meanwhile, in addition to these administrative changes, important developments were taking place within the hospitals as knowledge of mental disorder increased. More patients received voluntary and out-patient treatment and the social aspects of mental welfare were acknowledged. It was increasingly apparent that the old laws, which were particularly concerned with the legal procedures for certification of patients, were obsolete in a period when the medical and social concern for mental disorder was of much greater importance. In 1954 a Royal Commission was set up to investigate and its *Report on the Law Relating to Mental Illness and Mental Deficiency*, published in 1957, was followed by the 1959 Mental Health Act. This Act, which was concerned with definitions of mental disorder, the administration of hospital and community services and the procedures for admission and discharge to and from hospital, became the statutory basis of the Mental Health service.

The 1959 Mental Health Act defined mental disorder as: mental illness; arrested or incomplete development of mind; and psychopathic disorder – the last a controversial category further defined as 'a persistent disorder or disability of mind . . . which results in abnormally aggressive or seriously irresponsible conduct . . . and requires, or is susceptible to medical treatment'. Responsibility for the administration of services had been laid down by the National Health Service Act 1946 and the 1959 Act further defined the powers and duties outlined there. Basically it provided for the care and treatment of the mentally disordered through the NHS under the central direction of the Minister of Health. Hospital care remained a central feature of provision but its role was changed. Regarding the admission and discharge to and from mental hospitals the object of the 1959 Act was to make admission as informal as possible. Patients could be admitted for care and treatment without any formalities and without liability to detention. Where compulsory admission was necessary, three types of admission orders were defined. These orders for observation or treatment were made either on the recommendation of two medical practitioners or, in the case of an emergency order, on the initiative of a relative or friend or a mental welfare officer with the backing of only one doctor. New Mental Health Tribunals were set up in each health region to deal with any complaints arising from compulsory admission procedures.

At local level the responsibilities for the prevention, care and after-care, set out in the 1946 NHS Act, were emphasized, and shortly after the Act was passed they were made a duty. Local health authorities were to provide residential accommodation, training, guardianship, mental welfare officers and any other services that might benefit the mentally disordered in the community.

The 1959 Mental Health Act, in essence, laid stress upon informality of treatment and hospital admission and on the development of a community care approach to the mentally disordered. It has been argued that it did not actually initiate any changes in the mental health field, rather it endorsed the developments that were already taking place within hospitals and in the community. But it did give considerable encouragement to the growth of services, particularly community services, and to the improvement of public understanding of the problems of mental disorder, and it was, accordingly, widely welcomed.

Despite enthusiasm for the 1959 Act, criticism of its operation developed, particularly during the 1970s. This reflected in part a widespread criticism of psychiatry as paternalistic and socially controlling and a growing interest in the civil rights of under-privileged groups. Both the Royal College of Psychiatrists and the voluntary organizations MIND (the National Association for Mental Health) and MENCAP (the

Royal Society for Mentally Handicapped Adults and Children) became active in pressure for change. The Butler Committee on Mentally Abnormal Offenders, in producing its report in 1975 on the law and services for this particularly difficult group of patients, made recommendations for changes to the Mental Health Act. The British Association of Social Workers was also strongly critical of the Act and joined its criticism to that of the other pressure groups. In response to these demands for change, an interdepartmental committee was set up to consider the criticisms and evaluate the suggestions for alternative procedures. A consultative document was issued in 1976 and a government White Paper in 1978. After further argument and discussion, an Act was passed to amend the 1959 Mental Health Act. Following this Mental Health (Amendment) Act in 1982, a further Mental Health Act was passed in 1983 to bring together, in one statute, the 1959 Act and the 1982 amendment.

THE MENTAL HEALTH ACT 1983

The basic principles of the 1983 consolidating Act remain the same as those of the 1959 Act: to provide treatment and care of the mentally disordered on an informal basis and in the community, wherever possible. The Act covers mental disorder, i.e. 'mental illness, arrested or incomplete development of mind, psychopathic disorders or any other disorder or disability of mind'. Mental illness is not further defined. New terms 'mental impairment' and 'severe mental impairment' are introduced, the latter defined as 'a state of arrested or incomplete development of mind which includes severe impairment of intelligence and social functioning and is associated with abnormally aggressive or seriously irresponsible conduct on the part of the person concerned'. 'Mental impairment' is similarly defined but involves a less than severe degree of impairment. Psychopathic disorder is 'a persistent disorder or disability of mind . . . which results in abnormally aggressive or seriously irresponsible conduct on the part of the person concerned'. Mental disorder shall *not* be construed as covering promiscuity, sexual deviancy or dependence on alcohol or drugs. Compulsory admission to hospital is possible under certain circumstances and much of the Act, like its predecessor, is concerned with the rights of the minority of patients who require to be detained in hospital or placed under guardianship.

Admission for assessment for twenty-eight days (section 2) is possible where a person is suffering from mental disorder and it is considered that he or she ought to be detained in the interests of his or her own health or safety or with a view to the protection of other persons. Two medical practitioners, one an 'approved' doctor, have to agree and state the grounds for their recommendation. Application for admission may be by the nearest relative or an approved social worker. The doctor in charge, the hospital managers or the nearest relative may discharge the patient, who has a right to apply to the Mental Health Review Tribunal within the first fourteen days of detention.

Compulsory admission for treatment (section 3) is possible, but the conditions are now more stringent than formerly and the periods of initial and subsequent detention have been reduced to six months, a further six months and then for one year at a time, and the patients' rights of appeal to the Mental Health Review Tribunal have been strengthened. Again, applications may be made by the nearest relative or an approved social worker and two medical recommendations are required.

Emergency Admission (section 4) for up to seventy-two hours is possible on the application of the nearest relative or an approved social worker who must have seen the patient personally within the previous twenty-four hours, but it requires only one medical recommendation.

Basically the amended Act seeks to improve the rights of patients and the safeguards against abuse of compulsory powers, though it is also concerned with the issue of protection of staff and public.

Much of the Act was fiercely argued over because of the very real conflicts of opinion that exist in these areas. In addition to tightening up the compulsory admission and detention procedures, the new Act tries to deal with the difficult issue of consent to treatment. It used to be considered that, if a patient was compulsorily detained, treatment was then at the discretion of the psychiatrist in charge of the case because such a person was not always able or willing to give informed consent. This was challenged and, after various proposals were fought over, the 1983 Act laid down detailed principles about consent and procedures for their application. Under the relevant sections it states that the patient's informed consent is required before certain designated treatments can be carried out. If it is not possible to obtain informed consent, the opinion of a second, independent psychiatrist must be obtained, backed by consultation with non-medical members of the clinical team. Some treatments of special concern require the endorsement of an independent panel as well as the patient's informed consent. The section concerning treatment requiring *both* consent and a second opinion refers primarily to psycho-surgery and hormone implantations; that concerning treatment requiring either consent *or* a second opinion refers primarily to electro-convulsive therapy and to the use of medication after three months regular administration. Consent means that the patient must be capable of understanding the nature, purpose and likely effects of the proposed treatments.

Mental Health Review Tribunals were set up under the 1959 Act. There is one tribunal for each NHS region and one for Wales and they contain medical, legal and lay members. Under the 1983 Act their powers were extended and the rights of patients to make application were increased. A further development under the Act was the designation of 'approved social workers'. Local authorities were given a duty to appoint sufficient numbers of them, which means that social workers must have relevant training in order to demonstrate their appropriate competence in the mental health field. Finally, the Act established a Mental Health Act Commission with a general protective function for all compulsorily detained patients. The Commission is multi-disciplinary and it exists to provide independent medical opinions to consent to treatment; to keep the powers of detention under review; to prepare a Code of Practice; and to visit and interview detained patients and investigate individual complaints.

The Mental Health Act 1983 has stirred up a good deal of argument and controversy, which is, arguably, a very good thing in an area where individual liberty is at such risk. It has increased the responsibilities of social workers, challenged the authority of psychiatrists, and extended the rights of patients and their relatives. It has also intensified interest in the role of mental hospitals and increased the overall commitment to the general policy aims of community care and informality of treatment.

HOSPITAL PROVISION

Looking now in more detail at the actual provision of services, hospitals are still, for both psychiatric and mentally handicapped patients, of the utmost importance. It is still considered necessary to have centres for the active treatment of the mentally disordered and for the long-term care of chronic cases.

The actual form that hospital provision should take is very much a controversial issue. The present psychiatric services have to work with many large old hospitals that were built during the nineteenth century as lunatic asylums. These are generally considered unsuitable for modern treatment of the mentally ill, but so long as demand for beds is high it is difficult to do more than try to upgrade and improve them. However, during the 1950s the introduction of new drugs, popularly known as tranquillizers, brought about a 'therapeutic revolution' within the hospitals. It became possible to control, if not cure, the symptoms of many psychiatric disorders by the use of drugs, and therefore it was possible to discharge patients after fairly short stays in hospital, continuing their drug therapy, in many cases, as out-patients. This made feasible an open door policy in the hospitals, in the sense both that patients were out quickly and that within the hospital a more relaxed atmosphere could be achieved as drugs controlled the excessive behaviour of severely disturbed patients.

The coming of new and dramatic types of treatment, however, only heightened rather than diminished the controversy over the old hospitals. Some people argued that it should be possible to run down the existing hospitals almost entirely, replacing them by short-stay psychiatric units at general hospitals and long-term care within the community. It was certainly true that many of the older hospitals needed running down. They were often structurally unsound and costly to maintain, hard to staff because of their physical isolation and far too big. Above all, the hospitals actually impeded the patients' treatment and rehabilitation because they were the object of contempt and fear in the eyes of many people in society – the high walls and isolation symbolizing that the hospitals held society's rejects. The patients felt stigmatized and ashamed upon entering them. Moreover, their vast size, around 2,000 patients in many instances, together with their past custodial traditions, tended to produce a form of organization that was rigid and hierarchical and threatening to the patient. It was argued that a lengthy period within a mental hospital could itself produce symptoms of social disorientation, apathy, loss of initiative and so on, which amounted to institutional neurosis, an illness that could persist long after the original illness had cleared up. In short there were considerable grounds for arguing that the old hospitals should go.

There was, however, no agreement over what should replace the mental hospital. Against those who advocated the end of any separate provision for the mentally ill were those who argued that some patients could best be helped by care within specialized institutions provided these were not huge, obsolete in design and rigidly organized. Some patients truly did require an asylum from the strains of the world. For their best treatment a place with grounds for walking in, and space to develop occupational therapy, away from the atmosphere prevailing in a well-run general hospital, was probably necessary. Indeed, some psychiatrists had developed a whole approach to treatment in which the hospital itself, the total environment, was organized therapeutically. Various names are used, such as administrative therapy, but the technique is most generally referred to as the therapeutic community approach. It aims to involve all the members of the hospital – doctors, nurses, ancillary staff and the patients themselves – in the healing process. These ideas, pioneered in this country by Maxwell Jones, among others, were in part the outcome of studying the mental hospital as a social organization. It was seen that the traditional system, in which the patients were at the bottom of a communication and status hierarchy and were denied autonomy or participation in the running of the institution, exacerbated the problems many patients had, or produced the characteristic 'institutionalization' which was to be deplored. Further, it was seen that the same institution that was so damaging could be therapeutic if it was organized deliberately to foster social confidence and responsibility in the patients. In other words, many mentally ill people were defined as ill because of a breakdown in their social relationships; drugs might relieve some of the symptomatic tension but help was needed to remedy the causes by encouraging patients to participate in a community that improved the capacity of all its members – patients and therapists – to relate in a meaningful way to one another.

It is obvious that those doctors who practised the therapeutic community approach had doubts about the complete integration of psychiatric patients into general hospitals, which must perforce be organized and run in a radically different manner. The more telling critics of those who advocated the end of the mental hospital argued on a more immediately practical basis. They pointed out that large numbers of patients, especially among the old, were unlikely ever to be really fit to enter normal community life, and that for many others the community care services were still woefully inadequate. However much one wanted to run down the existing hospitals, demand for beds would keep them open unless patients were quite unscrupulously discharged while still needing considerable care.

It can be seen that the role of the present-day psychiatric hospital is a very controversial issue, one in which official policy is very much involved. The 1962 Hospital Plan aimed at a reduction in hospital beds for the mentally ill of roughly one half the total, together with a move towards more provision within general hospitals. After the publication of the plan, numbers were reduced, though not at the anticipated rate and only in the face of strong criticism from some quarters.

Despite the controversy it is becoming increasingly clear that there is no real ground for argument between hospital and community care and that they should complement rather than rival one another. A blurring of the distinction between hospital and community medical care was one of the aims of the 1974 reorganization of the health service. There is a place for psychiatric units at general hospitals, for separate, perhaps isolated, specialized hospitals where a therapeutic community approach can be implemented, and for effective community mental health services. A flexible array of services is called for that can meet the very varied needs of different groups of the mentally ill. Meanwhile, the present position is that there are a few small modern psychiatric hospitals, able to make good use of a wide range of therapeutic techniques, some psychiatric units at general hospitals, many doing excellent work with the short-term cases, rather too many old, large institutions and the beginnings of day hospital care and community psychiatry.

Many of the large old psychiatric hospitals have succeeded in making good use of their facilities, in breaking down the whole organization into smaller, semi-autonomous units, and in ensuring generally that the emphasis is on the treatment and rehabilitation of the patients rather than simply on their care and custody. But some hospitals and some wards of other hospitals have failed to cope with the demands of too many chronic patients, and lack adequate staff, money and enthusiasm to prevent them becoming mere dumping grounds, especially of the psycho-geriatric cases. Shortages of professional staff are very severe in some places and over-reliance on foreign staff is not always in the patients' best interests in an area where personal communication is so important. So, despite much that is progressive and encouraging in psychiatric hospital provision, there is still much room for improvement.

A White Paper, *Better Services for the Mentally Ill* (Cmnd 6233), was published in 1975. This outlined the familiar and depressing picture of existing services dominated by large, old, isolated hospitals with shortages of staff and amenities and with inadequate day and out-patient psychiatric facilities, and put forward plans for an overall improvement of services. The training of more specialists and the provision of more day hospital care was duly set out. Other plans were for the expansion of community care facilities, including support for families caring for a mentally ill relative, and more hostels and day centres. Nothing was new in this White Paper: it was emphasized that it provided an outline of a long-term strategy rather than a programme of rapid action, so it was generally regarded as a due statement of concern and good intentions, and little more.

There has been some of the same controversy over the role of the mental handicap hospitals as over the psychiatric hospitals, but on the whole the issue is clearer: they ought to be replaced by smaller units, ranging from hostels and homes to specialist hospital units able to provide intensive nursing for the severely handicapped minority. The whole idea of large hospitals for the mentally handicapped is indefensible: there is evidence that many patients do not need, and do not receive, treatment, and a hospital routine is wholly damaging to them. There has been an undercurrent of anxiety about the hospitals for many years and lip service has been paid to the idea of replacing them with community hostels. But in recent years criticism has become intense.

In 1967, following allegations of ill-treatment of patients, an official inquiry was instituted into the conduct of certain members of the staff at Ely Hospital, Cardiff. The report of this inquiry found that some ill-treatment of patients had indeed taken place but also it found much to criticize in general: lax standards of nursing, inadequate medical care, poor conditions and bad management. Other highly critical reports were subsequently published following inquiries into conditions at what were then known as subnormality hospitals. In all these inquiries the main conclusions were that abuse of patients where it existed was the consequence of acute shortages of staff, overcrowding and lack of facilities for patients and that general neglect pervaded in subnormality hospitals.

As a result of the first inquiry the Hospital Advisory Service (now the Health Advisory Service) was set up in 1969 to visit, assess and criticize hospitals constructively and to help bring about improvements in their general standards. A further outcome of the scandals was renewed pressure to replace outmoded hospital care by care in the community. This culminated in the publication of a White Paper in 1971, *Better Services for the Mentally Handicapped* (Cmnd 4683), and a renewed commitment to community rather than hospital provision.

For both the mentally ill and the mentally handicapped, therefore, official policy favours the extension of community facilities. However, hospitals cannot be closed down overnight and there is a need for a more positive approach to hospital care. The condemnation of the large hospitals for the mentally disordered has been well founded and well meant, but it has, to some extent, made the problem worse. Staff in such hospitals have become increasingly demoralized by criticism and standards have easily declined as a result. For many mentally ill and handicapped people the hospital is likely to be their sole environment for many years to come. Hopes for alternative provision must not be allowed to stifle any change or improvement within existing hospitals. With dedication and enthusiasm from staff at all levels, humane and therapeutic regimes can be developed and the boundaries between hospital and community care broken down. But there is a need for constant vigilance to avoid abuse and for much greater resources to be channelled to hospitals. At present not even the minimum standards for food, clothing and accommodation are being met, and the staffing picture is depressing, particularly for the mental handicap hospitals. Under the DHSS priorities consultative document, issued in 1976, there was provision for the improvement of hospital standards, and it is important that the long-standing neglect of hospital services should be reversed.

The need for constant vigilance and the vulnerability of mental handicap hospitals were underlined in 1978 by the publication of yet another critical report, that of the Committee of Inquiry into Normansfield Hospital. Staff conflict and industrial action were new features of this depressing case, but the report again underlined the physical shortcomings of the buildings, poor standards of nursing care, and lack of clothing and other facilities for the patients, so typical of earlier reports.

The work of the Hospital Advisory Service relating to mental handicap hospitals was taken over in 1975 by a new body at the DHSS, the Development Team for the Mentally Handicapped. A National Development Group was established at the same time to advise on policy. Following the Normansfield Report, the Secretary of State announced that the development team would henceforth have an inspectorial element added to its advisory service function, and health authorities were to be asked to review their arrangements for monitoring performance at individual hospitals.

It remains to be seen whether such measures will go far to avoid a repetition of the basic abuses, however. Shortage of resources remains a crucial determinant of standards of care, particularly at long-stay hospitals, and there is little sign that resources will improve much if at all in the next few years. The particular need for nursing staff in the mental handicap field was the subject of a DHSS Committee of Inquiry. The Jay Committee reported in 1979 and recommended that nursing staff working with the mentally handicapped should be replaced by holders of a new social work qualification, that numbers of staff should be doubled and care transferred from hospitals to homes. These were somewhat unrealistic proposals in the light of the existing staffing and resource difficulties already facing the mental health service.

COMMUNITY CARE

It is currently the accepted policy in the mental health field to provide more services in the community for the mentally ill and mentally handicapped. Provision of community mental health is divided between the health authorities and the local social services departments, so there is no one, coherent, community mental health programme to describe. Community care is partly a reaction against a policy that overemphasized hospitalization and saw the institution as the answer to most social problems. It is also a practical answer to the difficulties of continuing to maintain and staff isolated institutions in an age when few people are prepared to make a career in residential work. More positively, it is the recognition that all people should have the right to live within the community – to contribute to it and benefit from it, and simply to be a part of it, except in very rare circumstances.

The hospitals themselves make a very important contribution to the care of patients in the community. Most have out-patient clinics, which enable many patients to be treated while remaining in their own homes. In some areas day hospitals are run for patients who need considerable care but who can still return home at night. In others, there are facilities for helping patients to bridge the gap between total hospital care and complete independence in the community. Hostels or discharge units within the hospital grounds enable some patients to go out to work daily and have a relatively autonomous and responsible life, while retaining some of the security of the hospital environment. Rehabilitation is fostered by developing workshops at hospitals that aim to give patients confidence in their working ability and experience in social relationships and responsibility. Psychiatric social workers work with doctors, obtaining reports on the patients' home situation and helping patients retain contact with the outside world. They can provide a vital link between hospital and community, although many hospital-based social workers have traditionally concentrated on team work within the hospital setting. Community psychiatric nurses help many patients return home and cope without the need for hospitalization, and their role has developed markedly in recent years as the emphasis has shifted towards the community.

The bulk of community care work is now the responsibility of the local authority social services departments. They took over the statutory duties and provisions of the old mental health departments.

Social services provision for the mentally disordered is through the full range of social work, day care and residential services. Social work help is vital in all community care services and can be part of the total treatment programme for the mentally disordered. Social workers are needed to help the families of mentally handicapped persons as well as the mentally ill or handicapped themselves. A family with a severely handicapped child will have many problems. The parents may be tied to the house, they will usually be financially disadvantaged, and the mother is likely to be overworked, trying to cope with the responsibilities of a normal housewife and mother and the special needs of a helpless child. Moreover, the family may feel very guilty at having produced a handicapped child, over-anxious about the child's future, worried about their feelings towards the child or the effect on other children in the family. In both these areas a social worker can help. They can ensure that the family receives all the practical help available from statutory and voluntary bodies – perhaps the use of a day nursery, better housing and so on – and they can help to reduce the parents' guilt and anxiety and encourage them to be accepting and relaxed and neither reject nor over-protect their handicapped child. Of particular importance is the social worker's contribution in helping parents make full use of the facilities offered by the mental health services. Parents may feel suspicious of these, or resentful, and will need help in using them to best advantage. Similarly, the families of the mentally ill need help in sudden emergencies when they cannot cope with a very disturbed relative, general help in understanding and accepting the nature of the disorder and support if they have to make difficult decisions such as agreeing to the compulsory admission of a severely disturbed relative to hospital. The strain of caring for a disturbed relative can be considerable and the need for an understanding and reliable friend to talk to and share the anxieties with is often very great.

Social workers can also help the mentally disordered themselves. For example, they can help handicapped youngsters in the difficult school-leaving period, encourage them to find work, keep an eye on their activities if they are trying to take on too much or are getting into bad company, help them to cope with family relationships and to become as independent and content as possible. They can help the mentally ill, encouraging them to seek treatment when necessary, supporting them in the trying period after hospitalization, and encouraging their efforts to find work, lodgings and companionship despite their disabilities.

Day care facilities for the mentally handicapped include what used to be known as adult training centres. These vary considerably in the facilities provided for the handicapped adults. Some are purpose-built and others are in makeshift premises. Some are glorified minding places while others attempt to develop social skills, encouraging handicapped people to learn about such things as public transport and the handling of money. Some concentrate on occupation and are run as industrial units. In some cases the day centres genuinely act as training centres, preparing those who attend for eventual independence, while in others the aim is simply to offer a daily change of environment and relief to their families for those too handicapped ever to lead independent lives. Day centres for the mentally ill are a more recent innovation. They exhibit similar variations in aims and activities. Despite variations, however, the day care facilities are enormously important and can make a tremendous difference to the lives of the mentally disordered. Provision is still far from adequate in this field.

Domiciliary services can help the handicapped and their families, especially when the mental disability is accompanied by physical handicap. In the area of social help and rehabilitation a variety of clubs can also help both the mentally handicapped and the mentally ill to make social contacts and gain the confidence to reintegrate themselves into society.

Residential provision is extremely important and at present totally inadequate in terms of the extent of the need. Local authorities have been providing hostels since 1959 but only in very small numbers. Although they were envisaged as an alternative to full institutional care, they tended to be used by those within the community who had hitherto remained dependent on family or friends. For the mentally handicapped especially, many hostels were welcomed by relatives who, often at great cost to their freedom and independence, had struggled to keep a close relative out of a stigmatized hospital, but were prepared to see them safely cared for in a local purpose-built home. So new provision uncovered new need and the numbers actually in hospital did not diminish, particularly among the mentally handicapped. The 1971 White Paper promised expansion here, but the building programme needed is huge and economy cuts repeatedly reduce it.

Hostels for the mentally ill are needed no less desperately than those for the handicapped. They have an important part to play in providing care to those discharged after long stays in hospital and also in providing temporary homes and rehabilitation to those trying to re-establish themselves in the community. There has been much confusion over their exact role for many years, but clearly there is room for a variety of provision: some rehabilitative, some permanent, some intense therapeutic communities, some experimental homes for disturbed adolescents. It is good that the demanding job of running hostels for the mentally ill and the mentally handicapped, together with other provision of residential care, should now be recognized as an important aspect of social work, for much needs to be done in this field and many able people need to be recruited for the work.

Day care, residential care and social work support essentially provide care *in* the community, rather than in large institutions. But they do not add up to or replace care *by* the community. The phrase 'community care' has been used since the 1960s, but it has never been too narrowly defined and a variety of activities can be numbered as belonging to a community approach to the care of the mentally disordered. Ultimately, however, the family (often though not invariably the women of the family) and sometimes the neighbours, friends and relatives of the mentally ill or handicapped person will be there to care and cope, either alone, or with some help from the health service and local authority. The local 'community' as such does not, on the whole, provide a caring response to the mentally disordered – in fact it can often provide a decidedly hostile response to the opening of new hostels or day centres, for example. The contribution of the informal care sector, particularly the family, is now being acknowledged and some attempts are being made to interweave the informal care and the formal provision more closely together.

The need for constructive partnerships between health authorities and the social services was increasingly recognized in a variety of reports throughout the 1970s and 1980s. Joint finance has been provided since 1976 to enable local authorities and health authorities, as well as voluntary organizations, to work together to provide facilities for care in the community for different groups, including both the mentally ill and the mentally handicapped. Whilst the overall sums have been low, and there has also been criticism that the time period for these grants has been too short for the more innovative projects, some success in the movement of mentally handicapped and ill people into the community has been achieved. The voluntary sector has become increasingly involved in projects designed to help mentally ill and handicapped people live independent lives, and the latest report on community care, the Griffiths Report in 1988, took the view that local authorities should stimulate a mixed economy of care in the community. Thus a range of groups, including both the voluntary sector and the private sector, should be encouraged to provide wide-ranging forms of care for different groups, including the mentally ill and mentally handicapped, with the local authority carrying overall responsibility for provision.

One of the signs of the extent to which community care for both of these groups has become reality is the decline in beds in long-stay hospitals over the past decade. However, in many instances hospital beds are being lost whilst the corresponding level of support outside the hospital is not being provided. Many mentally ill and handicapped adults are forced to live in hostels for the homeless, and many more are simply sleeping rough. Whilst the situation has not reached the endemic proportions of mentally ill people who are homeless in America, the situation of these groups in Britain is serious enough to warrant consideration and a commitment to funding of decent support in the community. Sadly, at a time of financial constraint in both health authority and local authority spending, such a commitment seems unlikely to be forthcoming. It is to be hoped that the long-awaited implementation of the Griffiths Report, by the 1990s, will improve provision. Meanwhile, however, the lack of adequate community care facilities has led to a campaign to save the old mental hospitals. The National Schizophrenia Fellowship has become so concerned that the severely mentally ill are being neglected that they are arguing against hospital closures.

OTHER SERVICES FOR THE MENTALLY ILL AND HANDICAPPED

Education also has an important role in the mental health field. It provides special education, as noted in Chapter 4, for educationally subnormal children and for those previously described as ineducable. In some instances it provides child guidance clinics, which offer psychiatric and social work help to children who have behaviour problems or manifest symptoms of mental disorder, and to their parents. It offers special education facilities for children who are maladjusted, usually those referred by the child guidance clinics.

The Department of Employment is responsible for the provision of services under the Disabled Persons (Employment) Acts. These include keeping registers of the employable disabled, the provision of disablement resettlement officers and the running of Employment Rehabilitation Centres and government training or skill centres. Most of these services were designed primarily to help the physically disabled, especially those who had been in work but who were unable to continue as a result of a crippling accident or disease. Since the 1959 Mental Health Act the services have increasingly extended their help to the mentally disabled, where this seems suitable. Both handicapped and mentally ill persons can be helped in finding and keeping suitable employment in open industry, and given courses of rehabilitation.

Finally, the DSS takes responsibility for meeting the financial needs of the mentally disordered, mainly through the National Insurance and income support schemes. However, there is still not enough help available at the moment to the *families* of the mentally disordered despite the costs to them of caring for severely handicapped or disturbed relatives.

THE VOLUNTARY CONTRIBUTION

Mention must be made, albeit briefly, of the voluntary effort in the field of mental welfare. The National Association for Mental Health (MIND), founded in 1946 as a result of the amalgamation of several older bodies concerned with the welfare of the mentally ill, is an important coordinating body for research and propaganda. It aims to disseminate information on the principles of mental health, promote research and aid experimental projects in the field. It also promotes local associations, and runs training courses and various homes, schools and publications. MIND has been of enormous importance in widening understanding of the social aspects of the problem of mental disorder and stimulating progressive work in this field.

The National Society for Mentally Handicapped Children (MENCAP), likewise aims to publicize the needs of the handicapped and encourage better provision for them. Where statutory provision is inadequate, the society aims to supply aid directly through its local branches. The Campaign for Mentally Handicapped is another important body that works for better provision and understanding.

Many other bodies are concerned with the mentally ill and handicapped. The Richmond Fellowship, for example, provides hostels, run as small communities, which offer a secure environment and an opportunity to regain confidence in social relationships and an enthusiasm for living to a limited number of mentally disturbed adults and young people. The Rudolf Steiner schools are renowned for their fine educational work with the mentally handicapped. Various colonies exist under voluntary foundation where the mentally handicapped can live useful and happy lives, to some extent sheltered from the outside world but permitted a considerable degree of independence and self-determination. The National Schizophrenia Fellowship is active in defence of the interests of the group of patients suffering from the baffling disorder of schizophrenia.

Voluntary effort is especially prominent in work with special problem groups – alcoholics and drug addicts, for example – where it both innovates and complements statutory provision. Disillusionment with traditional psychiatry has led to much interesting experimentation with small communities using new forms of therapy and espousing new philosophies and explanations of mental illness. Local projects to work with women or members of ethnic minority groups, for example, have adopted new approaches to depression or other illnesses, many involving a self-help element. Many new and fascinating approaches can be worked out in the voluntary setting and provide a base for constructive criticism of statutory provision and a fund of enthusiasm for change. In this as in so many fields of social service the voluntary contribution can be great both in a pioneering sense and in the steady provision of research, public education and good facilities.

The problem of mental disorder is a considerable one, both numerically and in the range of needs that it gives rise to. Partly because the public has been forced into awareness of the grave social problem the mentally disordered can present, the services are relatively well developed. But much still needs to be done to recruit staff at every level (consultant psychiatrists, mental nurses, social workers, teachers, etc.), to up-grade the hospital and residential facilities, particularly for the chronic cases, and to make available a more flexible range of community services to those individuals or families who are coping with mental illness or handicap without resort to hospital care.

Last, but by no means least, much still needs to be done to improve public attitudes and understanding, both to aid prevention of mental disorder, and to help the mentally handicapped overcome their disabilities and find a tolerable place in society. Only then could we hope to have both a community mental health programme and meaningful community care.

SUGGESTIONS FOR FURTHER READING

Barton, Russell, *Institutional Neurosis* (John Wright, 1960).

Bayley, Michael, *Mental Handicap and Community Care* (RKP, 1973).

Bluglass, R., *A Guide to the Mental Health Act 1983* (Churchill Livingstone, 1983).

Clarke, A. M. and Clarke, A. D. B., *Mental Deficiency: The Changing Outlook* (Methuen, 1974).

Cochrane, R., *The Social Creation of Mental Illness* (Longman, 1983).

Hays, Peter, *New Horizons in Psychiatry* (Penguin, 1964).

Jones, Kathleen, *A History of the Mental Health Services* (RKP, 1972).

Jones, K. *et al.*, *Opening the Door* (RKP, 1975).

Jones, Maxwell, *Social Psychiatry* (RKP, 1952).

Jones, Maxwell, *Social Psychiatry in Practice* (Penguin, 1968).

Martin, Dennis, *Adventure in Psychiatry* (Cassirer, 1962).

Miles, A., *Women and Mental Illness: The Social Context of Female Neurosis* (Wheatsheaf, 1988).

Morris, Pauline, *Put Away* (RKP, 1969).

Rehin, G. F. and Martin, F. M., *Patterns of Performance in Community Care* (Oxford, 1968).

Tizard, J., *Community Services for the Mentally Handicapped* (Oxford University Press, 1964).

Part Three

Some general issues

12

Financial and administrative issues

Clearly the social services that exist to cope with social problems of various kinds are large organizations. It follows that they absorb a large part of the national resources in terms of money and man- and womanpower, and that the financing, staffing and administration of them is very complex. This chapter will draw attention to some of the more obvious financial and administrative implications of the social services.

FINANCIAL ISSUES AND SOCIAL POLICY

Public expenditure on the social services is considerable: the money spent in recent years has been 40 per cent of Britain's gross domestic product (GDP). Government expenditure on actual goods and services, excluding cash transfers, is around one-quarter of the GDP. Social services costs account for over 70 per cent of the amount spent in the public sector. In 1987/8 total public expenditure for the United Kingdom was over £140,000 million and expenditure on social services, including housing and environmental services, amounted to around £98,000 million. Collectively the social services are by far the largest item on the analysis of public spending and single services such as social security dominate the list. Table 12.1 shows a more detailed breakdown of expenditure.

Table 12.1 Public expenditure summary by programme, 1987/8 (United Kingdom)

	£ billion
Social security	45.9
Health and personal social services	23.3
Education, libraries, museums, the arts and science	21.1
Housing	3.5
Environmental services	5.0
Law, order and protective services	7.5
Roads and transport	5.6
Defence, overseas aid and other overseas services	21.4
Other expenditure on programmes	8.0
Total public expenditure on programmes	141.3

Source: Social Trends, no. 19 (HMSO, 1989).

Public expenditure generally, and expenditure on social services in particular, have been growing rapidly in this century. At the turn of the century an amount equal to only approximately 2.5 per cent of the GDP was spent on social services; by the outbreak of the Second World War the percentage had risen to 11–12 per cent, and since the war it has risen to around 40 per cent. This trend is sometimes viewed with alarm, but then at the turn of the century social services were virtually non-existent and the social problems of poverty, sickness, squalor, ignorance, child neglect and so on were barely recognized, let alone tackled in any effective manner. Once the problems are recognized and society accepts some degree of commitment in the battle against social evils then, naturally, public expenditure is bound to rise. There is nothing inherently wrong in this situation; if we want to build a better society we have to be prepared, collectively, to pay for it.

Nevertheless, a high level of public spending does raise problems, especially when the general economic situation is bad. The money has to be raised by the government and this means high taxation levels, which are always unpopular. Moreover, it means a greater proportion of national income is in the hands of public officials, and care has to be taken to ensure that it is used well. A demand for a reduction in public expenditure can mean that the weaker services suffer because they lack powerful support groups.

It is argued that the country 'cannot afford' such a high level of social service expenditure. But social services are not a luxury: any complex industrial society must expect to spend a lot on social services. Although their output cannot be easily measured like the productivity of a factory, nevertheless they are vital to the nation's economy as well as to its stability and happiness.

Education, which is a major item of social service expenditure, is clearly a necessary investment if the nation is to have the trained people who are as necessary to production as raw materials. Where the services cannot be seen as making an economic contribution, they are clearly improving the quality of life for members of the community, which is presumably the ultimate goal of raising productivity and standards of living anyway.

Where does the money for the social services come from? Excluding the voluntary contribution element, the public money is raised by taxation and by contributions for specific services, by local rates and by charges for some services. The bulk of the money is raised by taxation – by taxes on income or taxes on expenditure – and the remainder by rent and interests, etc., or public borrowing. In 1987, total central government income amounted to £155,308 million, and local authorities, in addition to receiving £23,297 million in grants from central government, raised a further £24,727 million in rates, rent and borrowing. So total general government income amounted to about £180,000 million.

Of total central government income, only 26 per cent was raised by taxes on personal income. That proportion has fallen since the mid-1960s. Taxes on income by corporations, including profits tax, amount to nearly 10 per cent of the total. Taxes on expenditure, including VAT, amount to 33 per cent of the total, and National Insurance contributions (employers' and employees') amount to 18 per cent of the total. The borrowing requirement increased rapidly in the period from the 1960s to the early 1980s, but in 1987, as a result of tight expenditure control, it was down to 2.6 per cent of the total.

Local authority money is made up of around 48 per cent in grants from the government, 35 per cent from rates and 6 per cent from rents, the remainder being from interest, dividends and borrowing.

As we have seen, over two-thirds of public spending goes on the provision of the social services discussed in this book; the rest goes on defence, roads, employment, law and order, and so on. So the level and type of taxation and the direction of social policy are clearly interconnected. If the policy is to develop statutory services that are organized and paid for collectively, then public expenditure is likely to rise. If services are reduced in scope and operate on a more selective basis – that is, serve only certain categories and income groups within the population – then public expenditure could be reduced. Whether it rises or falls will naturally affect taxation.

Some social economists argue that, while social services such as health and education are clearly necessary, and a sound investment, they need not be financed entirely or even largely by public expenditure. If more were financed privately then taxation could be reduced and incentives increased accordingly. Some of the arguments and assumptions used to support this line of thinking are misleading. It is, for example, often assumed that one sector of the community finances social services, while other sectors benefit from it; that, in effect, social policies contribute to a massive redistribution from rich to poor. Apart from the arguments for or against such a redistribution, it is clear from the breakdown of taxation given above that this is greatly over-simplified. Taxes are not raised only or largely from any particular section of the community: everyone is subject to the expenditure taxes (on consumer goods, entertainment and so on), and all the working population pay National Insurance contributions. Indeed, studies of who pays what and who benefits from the overall redistribution of income involved in the social services have revealed remarkably little difference between the percentages of income left to family units of different income levels after they have paid taxes and received benefits in cash and kind. Where there is some redistribution of income, as a result of social policy, it is between families with children and the single and childless. Families of virtually all income levels get more out of the social services than they pay towards them and towards other public expenditure, although in recent years this advantage has been eroded. A prior, and misleading, assumption that the levels of direct taxation in Britain were very high has been eroded as levels of direct taxation have progressively been reduced in the 1980s, whilst the rates of indirect taxation – which are paid on goods and services and are therefore not levied according to income but according to expenditure – have increased. At the same time, the tax threshold - that is, the level at which people begin to pay tax on their income – has decreased, bringing a greater proportion of those on low incomes, into the tax bracket.

Nevertheless, it should be clear from these few facts that the financing of the social services is likely to cause political controversy. The social services are a large item of expenditure, and the financing of them affects everybody. They are, accordingly, the object of much heated discussion by economists and politicians as well as by social scientists. Decisions about them – their expansion, scope, and so on have such important economic implications that they cannot be, and are not, taken simply in the light of our knowledge of social needs. Social services set out to meet needs, and to solve problems, but they can also be used to bring about changes in the social and economic structure of society. For example, the social security system exists primarily to prevent poverty. But it could be used as an instrument to achieve greater equality in the distribution of the nation's resources. If it becomes a major instrument for redistribution of income then it is involved in the political arguments over equality and social justice as well as in meeting basic need. So the economic implications of social services can go far beyond the immediate practical ones of financing the current provision. Social policy is ultimately economic policy and cannot be viewed satisfactorily in isolation.

The economic implications of social policy have now become a central issue in British politics. There has always been some concern over levels of public spending and taxation, and this has played a part in the arguments about the scope and direction of social policy that are described in Chapter 13. However, this concern became a paramount consideration during the 1970s. The main reason for this was the overall economic situation. The rate of economic growth in Britain slowed down and for a period was in absolute decline. Thereafter a continued slow rate of growth was accompanied by high rates of inflation and growing industrial recession and unemployment. Public expenditure has, as indicated, grown rapidly over the years, largely alongside steady growth in the economy generally. When the rate of economic growth slowed, that of public expenditure did not. Accordingly, efforts have been made by successive governments to halt the growth in public spending. Since costs tend to rise inexorably, attempts to stabilize public spending have essentially meant cuts in actual services. The discussion of social policy has been increasingly dominated, therefore, by talk of cuts. The government's annual White Papers on public expenditure, which announce the detailed plans for spending and for expanding or cutting the various services, have become essential reading for students of social policy.

The first dramatic cuts in the rise in public expenditure were announced in 1976. As the social services account for a substantial part of public spending, cuts affected a wide range of services. Social security cannot easily be cut, as expenditure there is determined in part by demographic trends, such as rising numbers of old people, and economic trends, such as rising unemployment. So the main cuts were expected to fall on services such as housing, education, health and personal social services. In the education field, cuts were justified on the grounds that falling numbers of school-age children could lead to reductions in spending without reductions in standards. But most cuts have been justified on the slender base that services could be operated more efficiently and economically, and any fall in standards could be averted by careful management and avoidance of waste. In the personal social services field there has been reference to the need to encourage self-help and voluntary action to keep down the cost of providing professional social care.

Cuts are announced, and enforced, by the central government, but it is most often the local authorities that have to implement them. And local authorities have felt understandably confused by demands to improve services and to reduce costs. As we have seen from the chapters on health, education and other services, there are still many unsolved social problems and unmet needs for residential care, for housing, for better education facilities for children with special needs, for trained staff, etc. Not surprisingly, bitter campaigns have been mounted against the cuts and closures they have resulted in, by those who work in the services and those whose needs they seek to serve.

In addition to campaigns *against* cuts, however, there have been vociferous demands for even greater cuts in public expenditure generally and in social services in particular. The whole question of public spending has become a lively political issue at central and local levels.

The full debate over the relationship of the economy to public spending is complex, and the issues are not easily understood or proven either way. The debate is characterized by a fair amount of confusion and exaggeration, and there is some attempt to make the welfare state the scapegoat for all the political and economic ills of the nation. There is only room here to outline the bare facts about cuts and the main lines of argument that surround them.

The background to cuts was set out in the 1976 White Paper on Public Expenditure (Cmnd 6393): 'Popular expectations for improved public services and welfare programmes have not been matched by growth in output or by willingness to forgo improvements in private living standards in favour of these programmes.' Priority, it was argued, should be given to improving industrial investment and increasing productivity and export levels to ensure economic recovery. Basically that argument was simply that the country could not afford to go on expanding non-productive sectors such as social services. Since then the argument has hardened into one that actually blames the social services for the economic failure itself. The argument now is that, in order to finance welfare provision, governments have imposed unjustifiably high levels of taxation, which have hindered investment and reduced productivity, encouraged the brain drain and increased inflation. The very security of the welfare state, it is claimed, has destroyed initiative and crippled the entrepreneurial activity on which Britain's former prosperity was based. By the Public Expenditure White Paper for 1980/1 (Cmnd 7746) the message was plain: 'Public expenditure is at the heart of Britain's present economic difficulties.' The undisputed deterioration of the performance of the British economy was largely attributed to increases in taxation, high government borrowing and inflation. The central objectives of economic policy were, therefore, to reduce inflation by control of the money supply, to restore incentives by reductions in direct taxation, and to stabilize public spending.

These views have not gone unchallenged. It has been pointed out that high levels of welfare accompany prosperity as cause as well as effect. In comparative terms, Britain does not have particularly high levels of social spending. If demographic facts on numbers of old people, school-age children, etc., are taken into account, the resources devoted to services such as health or education do not seem to have increased immoderately. The validity of some of the figures used can be challenged and different methods of accounting can demonstrate different relationships between growth and spending. There is no evidence that reductions in public spending, as opposed to private consumption, would lead to increases in investment. If less money was taken by the public sector it is doubtful whether people would invest in British industry or continue to spend more on foreign consumer goods. Moreover, the undoubted problems of the British economy need to be explained by other factors ranging from obsolete management and union practices within British industry to the complex influences of patterns of world trade and rising oil prices. Finally, it is pointed out that if times are indeed bad then, in the name of justice and humanity, more rather than less should be spent on those services in cash and kind that cater for the welfare of those in need. This would make economic sense in times of unemployment and recession, and would reduce the hardship of those most vulnerable to the impact of inflation.

In practice it has not proved easy to achieve the drastic cuts in spending that are wanted. Reductions in spending on labour-intensive services increase unemployment and hence social security costs. Nevertheless the drive to achieve cuts even at the expense of standards has intensified. By the 1990s the threat to social services is greater than ever. To achieve the hoped-for reductions in public spending, the government appears prepared to see dramatic reductions in standards and in scope of provision. Sadly it is the most vulnerable people who are hurt most by indiscriminate cuts in services, and often the most imaginative and sensitive developments that are axed. For example, in education it is again pre-school nursery education that has been reduced; community work projects are being axed by hard-pressed social services departments, and pioneering psychiatric rehabilitation services are being closed down.

The government, through a rigorous cash limits approach, is forcing local authorities to carry out most of the unpopular cuts in actual services. Housing programmes are reduced to dismal levels. In 1987, the number of new houses added to the total stock was only 212,000, and of this number only 34,000 were in the public sector. Recent housing legislation has reduced the number of council houses for rent through the sale of local authority housing to both tenants and new landlords, whilst local authorities do not have the finance to provide more housing through new building works. The accommodation local authorities have left on their lists is poorer-quality stock, and the finance to maintain repairs is limited. The numbers of those on the waiting lists for housing has grown rapidly, as have the numbers of homeless in Britain. A report by the Schools' HM Inspectorate early in 1981 indicated that the effect of cuts in education budgets was severe despite falling pupil rolls. Special education was badly affected, many schools were unable to keep a wide curriculum open and others reported shortages of basic equipment, including textbooks. Social services departments have been very badly hit as the growing problems of poverty and unemployment add to the pressure of their work, and yet they have had to abandon services and cut back on staffing. Inevitably it is the preventive services that are most vulnerable to cuts – the playgroups and child-minder schemes, for example.

The financing of social services has now become a major issue of electoral concern. Inevitably this has meant some over-simplifying, stereotyping and exaggeration in the claims and counter-claims of the different schools of thought. It is likely that the arguments about public spending, taxation and economic prosperity will continue throughout the 1990s, and it is important that the facts about the real costs and benefits of welfare are as widely known as possible. Moreover, the bare facts about costs, cuts and cash limits need to be seen in the context of the larger ideological debate on the role of welfare which will be discussed in the final chapter on problems of policy in the social services.

ADMINISTRATIVE ISSUES AND THE MAKING OF SOCIAL POLICY

Like finance, the administration of the social services is a vast topic, which can only be touched on here. Something of the administrative framework of the social services will have been gleaned from the preceding chapters on particular social problems and the services created in response to them. Both central and local government are involved in the provision of services. Central government administers some services directly, such as social security, while others are a local responsibility, exercised under varying degrees of central government control.

We have looked at social problems and services mainly as they exist at the present. Most studies of social services, however, tend to look at them from the historical or development view. This is certainly extremely illuminating. Apart from being a fascinating story, a study of the development of social policy explains much of the present confusion of services, particularly of their administration. Few things are consistent in the social services: each service tends to be financed differently; the statutory basis, the context of the central/local government relationship and distribution of control, and the underlying social principles all tend to vary from service to service. The history of social action accounts for this to a considerable extent and all students of social administration must turn to some reading of the development of social policy.

The historical view is noted here because it is particularly relevant to the current administration. Central administration has been continually adapting itself to the new demands made upon it by the creation of services. Local administration, as we know it today, was itself the product of social action to a considerable extent. Local government had to be devised in order to operate local health, welfare and housing policies, and local government today is still very strongly involved in the social service area.

Central government is primarily concerned in the working out of policies, and only partially in the direct administration of services. The formal expression of a social policy is the legislation that creates services to tackle social problems. So the National Health Service Act, the Children Act, the National Assistance Act, etc., are statements of policy. They are passed by Parliament and are subject to debate and discussion, and reflect party political views on the nature of social problems. They are drafted by permanent government officials who are concerned to seek out expert opinion on the issues in question. Moreover, in many instances major Acts follow the recommendations of the reports of Royal Commissions or interdepartmental working parties and so forth, which try to discover the facts about a particular problem and seek advice and opinion from all the people concerned.

For example, the 1959 Mental Health Act consolidated prior policy of informality of treatment and community care for the mentally disordered, following the report of the Royal Commission on Mental Illness and Mental Deficiency in 1957. The Commission was made up of a wide range of eminent people involved in the existing mental health services, and it took evidence from a variety of those involved in the care of this group.

However, in the past few years such a model of enacting legislation after a wide-ranging commission that hears evidence from professionals in the field has not been followed. Thus the 1986 Social Security Act followed the so-called Fowler Reviews, which had a restricted membership, took only limited evidence (which was not reproduced in the final report) and resulted in a Green Paper that largely became the 1986 Act. In 1989 the White Paper on health, *Working for Patients*, was produced by a review team, the exact membership of which was never made public. No evidence was called for from the professionals working in the health services, yet this review and White Paper have introduced some of the most radical suggestions for running the health services since the original 1946 Act. This move towards legislation in the field of social policy that does not proceed from evidence or research by those professionals engaged in the field, but proceeds from the ideology of the political party in power, has doubtless significantly changed not only the structure of the social services but also the role of the legislative process.

The passing of an Act, though, is not the end of policy making. The actual administration of services authorized by Acts is a process that itself contributes to the making of social policy. On the whole, Acts, despite their legal precision, are fairly loose guides when it comes actually to setting up the services they authorize, and the decisions made by the administrators of services at central or local level are of great importance in shaping the provision.

It is not always clear who actually makes important decisions. At both central and local level of government there are elected representatives and professional administrators and other staff. The balance of power between the Houses of Parliament and the civil service and between the local council and the town hall officials is never clearly defined, and can vary enormously in different areas and functions. Similarly, it is not easy to generalize about the balance between central and local government when services are administered locally, and that between administrators and professionals within a particular service is equally obscure and variable.

The context of central/local government relationships is of particular interest to the student of social administration, as many of the social services are a local responsibility. The statutes of Parliament legally determine the shape of local government and the scope of its action. They impose certain duties – to provide education or residential accommodation, for example – and give local authorities certain powers – to provide other services, such as day nurseries or family planning. In many areas of social policy, local authorities have been given permission to provide a service, then, when the need for the service has been clearly demonstrated and resources for it are more widely available, the provision has become mandatory. For example, local authorities had power to provide a service promoting the welfare of the general classes of the physically handicapped from 1951, and in 1960 the provision of this service became a duty.

Through the statutes, central government can ensure some uniformity and minimum provision in certain areas of social need and encourage flexibility of provision, within certain limits, in others. In some areas Acts lay down clear central powers of control – the 1944 Education Act, for example – but in others the main statutes merely indicate by a variable form of words that the Ministry or Secretary of State of the central department is in the position of ultimate authority and will provide a general overall guidance. Some Acts require the local authorities to submit schemes and plans for approval by the central department in order to carry out their powers and duties. Subsequently the central department can influence events by issuing circulars, guiding, instructing or exhorting the local authorities, and it can carry out inspections, exercise confirmatory and adjudicatory powers and so forth. But the major instrument of central control is probably finance. The central government raises much of the money used by local authorities for education, welfare, housing, etc. Clearly the departments intend to keep a check on how it is spent, and they can even check the local authorities' own financial manoeuvres by the powerful instrument of loan sanction.

Central government, then, exercises considerable power, not only over the services it administers directly, such as social security, but also over those that are the local authorities' own concern, such as education or personal social services. There has been much anxiety about the role of local government in the last twenty years. Some critics have considered it to be too weak and idiosyncratic to carry responsibility for major public and social services. Local responsibility has meant variations in standards, which some regard as scandalous, especially since the bulk of local authority finance comes from central revenue. Other critics have felt that local government was a crucial democratic check on central bureaucratic control that needed to be strengthened and given more autonomy and independence and greater say in determining local affairs. Ironically, public interest in local government in terms of voting levels at local elections and knowledge of local provisions does not indicate a very healthy democratic base. Nevertheless, local government does have a powerful democratic role as well as an important executive one, and much thought and effort need to be given to the improvement and up-dating of the system to improve its performance.

In the past, major criticisms of local government were directed towards: its financial weakness; the relatively poor calibre of staff for the demanding professional work of modern services; public apathy and lack of interest; the inexcusable variations in local standards of basic provision; and the anomalous division of the country into authorities based on old historical boundaries rather than demographic and economic realities which resulted in a population range of from fewer than 50,000 to over 1 million. Response to this criticism was a spate of reports and committees culminating in radical reform and reorganization of the system. The Maud Report on the *Management of Local Government* published in 1967, and the Mallaby Report on *The Staffing of Local Government* published in the same year, were both concerned with internal organization. The Maud Report considered there was urgent need for reform and change within local government. It recommended, in brief, that council members confine themselves to debating broad issues of social policy, leaving the professionals responsible for the detailed execution; that there should be fewer committees and a management board of about seven council members supported by a corresponding group of chief officers to make most policy decisions on a corporate basis. Officials should be clearly headed by a chief executive, the chief officer to the management board and head of the small team of officers who should work closely together. Regarding central/local relations the report urged that local authorities should have greater powers to determine their own structure, organization and policy and should be put in a stronger financial position. Finally, the Maud Report made some interesting suggestions for improving the image of local government and its relations with the public. The Mallaby Report commented in detail on staffing problems and examined ways of improving the quality of staff in local government.

The more fundamental issue of the size and nature of local government was investigated by a Royal Commission which issued its report in 1969. The Redcliffe–Maud Report proposed radical changes to create a reduced number of unitary authorities, responsible for the provision of all services, to replace the existing pattern of 172 first-tier counties and county boroughs and over 1,200 second-tier district authorities. These recommendations were not accepted in total, and alternative proposals were put forward in a series of White Papers that involved a more complex change. These proposals became law in 1972 and new councils were elected in 1973, becoming fully operative in England and Wales from April 1974. Similar proposals were made for Scotland, and implemented at a later stage.

The position in England and Wales is now that in all areas there are two levels of administration, the county and district authority. There are forty-seven county councils in England and Wales, and these are responsible for the provision of education, personal social services, roads and planning. The smaller district authorities, of which there are over 400, have responsibility for housing and environmental services, and some developmental control. In London there are thirty-two London Boroughs, with responsibility for all the major services. Between 1974 and 1986 there were also metropolitan counties, but these were abolished and their powers passed to metropolitan district authorities. In London there was the Greater London Council, but this too was abolished in 1986. The powers of the GLC were passed to the London Boroughs, except in the cases of services that crossed boundaries, such as the fire services, which are managed under joint boards.

Some critics of the inequitable distribution of services and resources and of the poor quality of much local provision have argued that the fault lies not only with local government but with antiquated central government organization. Some argue for much greater administrative decentralization, to remove the 'Whitehall bottleneck', and urge that central government gives more thought to the formulation of clearly defined policies so that local authorities can be safely left to get on with the job within a clear policy framework.

At present, as indicated, central policy is often very vague and control over detail too meticulous. So local authorities make their own policies, which sometimes leads to conflict with central government and always to diversity of provision. Up to a point diversity is good; local government would be useless if it did not permit some variety and flexibility in provision. Needs vary locally and what suits one area might not be right for another. The advantages of diversity, however, cannot ever outweigh the need for a uniform minimum standard, which is not the same as rigid uniformity. At present, diversity all too often means that some areas are simply deficient in provision, particularly for minority groups such as the disabled. So it is not easy to strike the right balance between over-control by central government and the consequent stifling of local initiative, and too little check on local action resulting in serious neglect of some social needs.

We noted that the major instrument of central control over local activity was financial: local authorities depend on central government for nearly half their income, with most of the rest coming from rates.

The question of local government finance has been the subject of debate for some years. In 1976 the Layfield Report considered alternative ways of financing local authorities, and concluded that local income tax would be preferable to rates raised on property as a source of income. At the time, no action was taken, but the 1990s will see a major change in the way in which local finance is collected. The community charge was introduced by the Local Government Finance Bill of 1988. It is a universal charge, levied at a flat rate for all individuals over the age of 18 living in the local authority area. Claimants in receipt of income support, students and others on a low income may claim a rebate (up to 80 per cent of the community charge), but must pay at least 20 per cent themselves. The community charge was introduced first in Scotland, and was brought in in England and Wales in

1990. It has been widely criticized as inequitable, because all those who are not exempt pay the same rate, regardless of income. In addition, it is feared that methods of collecting the community charge by establishing a register of all residents over the age of 18 may result in those who cannot afford the tax not completing their electoral registration forms, as this may alert the authorities to their liability for the community charge (or Poll Tax as it has become known).

Central government money comes in the form of the rate support grant. This used to work on a complex formula based on the relative wealth of the areas, the structure of their populations, and various indicators of social needs. In practice, the formula worked roughly along the lines that the more the local authority spent on services, the more it would get. Such a formula was incompatible in the 1980s with a government determined to limit public expenditure, and a new approach was announced in 1981. Under new arrangements, local authorities are penalized by loss of grant if they spend too much – that is, more than the government thinks they ought to spend. The new formula is very complicated, but is based on a notional income figure for each authority – the grant-related poundage (GRP) – which it is assumed will be raised by rates or community charge. The block grant from central government is calculated as the difference between the GRP and what the authority plans to spend, so long as this expenditure is below a government assessment of what the local authority should spend. This, the grant-related expenditure (GRE), is calculated on similar levels of service to be provided by all local authorities. If the authority plans to spend more than this, the block grant is reduced and the extra costs of the expenditure have to be met from other service cuts or higher rates. With such determined central government measures to control local authority spending, the debate on the proper balance of local autonomy and central direction becomes, sadly, rather academic.

In addition, changes in the delivery and structure of services previously provided by local authorities have done much to further reduce local authority budgets and some of their autonomy over how these services are delivered. In particular, the moves in education to allow schools to become self-governing has shifted finance normally allocated and controlled by local authorities back to central government, whilst the selling of council houses has reduced both the size of the public housing sector controlled by local authorities and the level of financial control that accompanied this.

In practice, these attempts to control local government expenditure have become a major political issue in the past decade, with some authorities resisting central government controls. As a result, more extreme measures – rate limitation, or rate capping, as it has become known – have been introduced to curb those authorities that have been determined to provide a high level of public services despite the cost. Introduced in the Rates Bill 1983, this measure allows the Secretary of State to control permitted expenditure levels in authorities that are seen as having overspent in the past. Issues of efficiency, of expenditure control on ideological grounds, of the role of local authorities and of their degree of autonomy have been important in the debate.

Rate capping is clearly a political move to limit local authority independence, as was the abolition of the Greater London Council and the six other metropolitan county councils in 1986. The abolition was widely resisted, and was seen as having more to do with the government's dislike of local policies, particularly those of the GLC, than with questions of how best to manage public administration. The sheer political motivation of the abolition shocked many people from all sides of the political spectrum, and raised grave doubts about the balance of local/central government relations.

More recent measures to control local government include the Local Government Act, 1988, which, among other things, outlawed what was described as political propaganda on the rates, and prevented councils from including political conditions such as minimum wages in their agreements with private contractors used to provide services. This Act also included the notorious Clause 28, which prevented councils from supporting the activities of gay rights (including in many instances AIDs hotlines and counselling services) by outlawing any financial support for activities that were defined by the Act as promoting homosexuality. Again, despite wide-spread opposition from many sections of the community, the clause became part of the final legislation. This demonstrates not only a worrying return to the homophobia of earlier years, but an increasing desire on the part of central government to control the activities of locally elected government.

However inept or inefficient local government must inevitably appear at times, it does represent a vital element of Britain's constitution and a defence, albeit imperfect perhaps, of democracy and freedom. The Conservative government of the 1980s has aroused profound anxiety by its policies of centralization and executive control. It remains to be seen whether the traditional liberties in Britain, including a degree of local autonomy, can be rescued from arbitrary destruction in the name of the economic ideology of monetarism and the operation of the free market.

The protection of the rights of the citizen in the face of such ever-widening government powers must always be considered, whatever the balance of central/local relations may be. Two points are noted here very briefly. First, the existence of administrative tribunals operating in the areas of National Insurance, income support, rent assessment and mental health. These listen to appeals against official decisions by people who dispute the official interpretation of their rights. Tribunals are an essential check on the powers of officialdom but at the moment they do not work as well as they should to ensure justice in welfare provision. Too often their proceedings are confusing to the ordinary person and the quality of judgement at such tribunals is reportedly inconsistent. Their procedures should be made more intelligible and appellants need more support and help in putting their cases.

The other important check on bureaucratic dominance is the provision of a high-level complaints procedure through ombudsmen. In 1967, a parliamentary commissioner was established to investigate complaints passed on by Members of Parliament about maladministration in government departments. This was extended later to cover the National Health Service, and as part of local government reform a commission for local administration was established in 1974.

Local commissioners can now accept any complaint from members of the public about maladministration in local government. These measures are an important extension of consumers' rights and some safeguard of individual liberty.

It can be seen that many issues on the administrative side affect the social services. Relatively clear ones arise from the structure of central and local government, their internal problems and their relations with one another. The issues that stem from the nature of administration itself are more complex. It is becoming increasingly clear that this whole process, defined in one recent study as 'a set of procedures for uniting those who control the resources necessary for certain tasks (the members of a municipal council or the shareholders in a company for example) with those who use the goods or services produced from these resources (pupils, patients, tenants, customers, etc.)'[1] is itself part of policy making. More attention is therefore being given to it. In short, it is not enough to discover needs and legislate to meet them; the actual means by which the legislative intentions are put into practice are of equal importance.

In previous centuries needs were recognized reluctantly, if at all, when social problems were of such proportions they could no longer be ignored. Measures to deal with problems did not always meet the underlying needs: sometimes they ignored them, sometimes they reflected total ignorance of them. The classic example of this is the Victorian Poor Law which tried to deal with the very obvious social problems of poverty. It led to high costs and corruption in the administration of relief and social unrest. But it did not deal with the reasons why people were poor; it did not get down to the underlying needs of the sick, the disabled, the fatherless, and so on. Today, however, we make a conscious attempt to identify and measure social needs and to evaluate the services that try to meet them. The attempt is conscious, but it is still imprecise and unsure. Social administration itself is, as Chapter 1 explained, the academic study of social needs and problems and of social policies and services. However, both social needs and the range of social policies designed to meet these are constantly changing, whilst social policy itself is not divorced from the economic and political climate in which it is developed. It is this complexity that the study of social policy must somehow take account of.

Some formal, institutionalized ways of identifying need have been already indicated. The government can initiate inquiries by means of Royal Commissions, interdepartmental committees and so on. It can also carry out research through the Central Statistical Office and the Government Social Survey into a variety of topics. The government also finances research bodies and institutions, such as the Medical Research Council and the Economic and Social Research Council, which themselves initiate, approve and finance research topics into particular problems.

In addition to this research and inquiry, the government collects, through the various central departments, statistics and information relevant to the social services and attempts some forward planning on this basis. Collection of statistics, such as the housing returns, has always been part of the central department's work, but the more specific information currently requested that can form part of long-term planning is a relatively recent development.

Outside the governmental research activities major work is carried out by the universities, through departments of social administration and social policy, sociology, applied social science, social medicine and so on. Research bodies such as the Institute of Community Studies and the Policy Studies Institute also conduct inquiries into both social needs and the working of social policies. Large numbers of voluntary agencies also have a research function, sponsoring or undertaking research into needs. The big research foundations such as the Rowntree or Carnegie Trusts are of vital importance in financing much of the work carried out by universities or other organizations.

Finally, a good deal of inquiry is made at a local level by local authorities or local voluntary bodies attempting to assess a particular problem in the immediate area. Muuch of this small-scale inquiry is the result of the curiosity and the anxiety of the people currently working in the social services, whether statutory or voluntary. Part of the agitation for reform of local government concerned ways of improving this research function. Most local authorities now have a research and intelligence unit to collect and analyse information on their areas. Social services departments have a particular concern to research into needs on a more systematic basis. Following the establishment of statutory links between the reorganized health authorities and local authorities through the joint consultative committees, there have been some experimental attempts to establish joint social information units so that health and local government can share data collection and analysis.

Research is increasingly concerned with evaluation of services as well as assessment of need. Elementary evaluation involves collecting data on service provision, but examining the effectiveness and efficiency of services is a more demanding task. Evaluation is still rudimentary but it is increasingly accepted that with services as massive and costly as those described we must develop techniques for measuring their impact and comparing the success and failure of different approaches.

STAFFING

The growth of the social services to cope with existing social problems has necessitated the development of whole new professions to cope with the work. The more sophisticated and specialized health care is, the more people, and the more different kinds of people, we need to provide it. So the medical profession has developed, not only in numbers, but into increasingly numerous specializations. It is backed by research chemists, biologists, etc., and teams of professional and general ancillary staff such as radiotherapists, as well as by nursing staff. This growth and specialization mean that more and more people must be found to staff the hospitals, clinics and rehabilitation units, and that they have to be trained. Training schemes, recognized qualifications, professional institutes, salary negotiating machinery and so on have to be developed. This is so in every field of social service: we need teachers, social workers, housing managers and town planners, etc., to fill all the posts, and training establishments and programmes to produce the trained people. At the same time we need increasing numbers of civil servants and local government officials to administer the services and social science research workers continually to investigate needs and assess the provision.

Staffing becomes ever more complex. Any change of policy has enormous repercussions on the staffing situation. For example, the 1959 Mental Health Act indicated the need for much greater expansion of the community care services for the mentally ill and mentally handicapped. But workers for these services cannot just be recruited from the general population, because they should be trained to do the specialized work with which they are faced. So, ideally, we need to forecast changes in demand for personnel, particularly highly trained professional personnel, in order to have time to develop and staff more training institutions – medical schools, professional social work departments and so on – and then to recruit suitable trainees and give them the necessary education and training before we try to implement a major change in policy. In the social work field this was strikingly acknowledged by the Curtis Committee on the care of children, which recommended the setting up of a Central Training Council on Child Care before it published its final report recommending radical changes in the organization of the care of deprived children. Courses for training both residential and casework staff were organized rapidly so that when the 1948 Children Act came into force some influx of trained staff was anticipated to staff the new children's departments. But such instances are, unfortunately, rare: usually the need for staff is allowed to reach alarming proportions before steps are taken to boost the recruitment and training programmes. The need to plan for the staffing as well as the financing of the social services does not apply only to the professionals: we cannot decide to double our output of houses in order to deal with housing shortages and obsolescence without regard to the manpower resources of the building industry as well as to the availability of suitable architects.

Many factors affect the supply of workers to various aspects of the social services. The numbers involved are large – nearly 1 million people are employed by the National Health Service alone – and the social services have to compete with industry, trade, other public services and, significant especially with doctors at the moment, the attractions of work abroad. It is impossible to give a meaningful figure of the total personnel employed in social services, as definitions vary too much, but the social services are now an important sector of employment, and many of the personnel involved require training. Developments within the social services often mean that more training is needed at the same time as more staff and it is difficult to decide on priorities. If one wants to increase the output of trained social workers or teachers one can reduce the length of their training and dilute its standard, but this will conflict with the need for more specialized staff for the more specialized needs and problems that better services reveal.

Broad demographic factors can affect particular services sharply. For example, the change in the sex ratio of recent years has resulted in fewer women remaining single, but single women were heavily relied on in certain social fields, as teachers, social workers, nurses and residential staff; a shortage could have a marked effect on the staffing position in these fields. Clearly it is vital to recruit more men or take account of the problems facing the married woman who wants to return to work. However, because salaries are low in many social services as compared to work in industry, many men are put off, and the employment of married women creates problems that society is not yet willing to face – the need for day nursery accommodation, for example (which itself creates a further demand for staff), and for a more relaxed public attitude towards the working mother.

The overall employment situation is, of course, a key factor. Many social service jobs tend to be filled when unemployment in manufacturing industry increases the attractiveness of the relatively secure job that local government, for example, affords. But the motives that attract people to work within a social service are as variable as the jobs themselves and gen- eralization is not very useful. Instead, particular professions try to improve their individual staffing position. The Mallaby Report on the staffing of local government has already been mentioned. Other committees have considered the staffing of different services, and the recruitment and training of, for example, social workers, health visitors, residential care workers, nurses and teachers. These reports assess the situation for a particular service or type of trained staff and usually make recommendations for improving quality and supply.

The overall position on staffing tends, therefore, to defy much generalization beyond that the social services need a very large number of trained people, and that by and large they fail to get them. Shortages vary somewhat over the country. London and the South East tend to have more psychiatrists, teachers, medical social workers, etc., than other regions but shortages of lower-paid staff such as nurses and prison officers, largely because of inflated housing costs. Some areas, particularly in the North, are very short of staff at all levels and make do with less well-trained people. Inner-city areas are also often short staffed as a result of difficulties in recruiting staff to work in areas of heavy demand and high workloads where the work is particularly stressful. Throughout the social services there is a need for more and better training and better distribution and deployment of staff. The rate at which people can be absorbed into the public social service sector, or are willing and able to enter it, does not depend on the social planners alone, and there is much scope for improvement in our whole approach to manpower and womanpower problems.

NOTE

1 D. V. Donnison, V. Chapman *et al.* in *Social Policy and Administration Revisited* (Allen & Unwin, 1975).

SUGGESTIONS FOR FURTHER READING

Aves Report, *The Voluntary Worker in the Social Services* (Allen & Unwin, 1969).
Bell, Kathleen, *Tribunals in the Social Services* (RKP, 1969).
Brown, C. U. and Dawson, D. A., *Personal Taxation, Incentives and Reform* (PEP, 1969).
Brown, R. G. S., *The Administrative Process in Britain* (Methuen, 1970).

Buxton, R., *Local Government* (Penguin, 1973).

Community Work and Social Change, report of a study group on training set up by the Calouste Gulbenkian Foundation (Longman, 1968).

Culyer, A. J., *The Economics of Social Policy* (Martin Robertson, 1973).

Donnison, D. V. and Chapman, V., *Social Policy and Administration Revisited* (Allen & Unwin, 1975).

Forder, A., *Concepts in Social Administration* (RKP, 1974).

Glennerster, H., *Social Service Budgets and Social Policy* (Allen & Unwin, 1975).

Griffiths, J. A. G., *Central Departments and Local Authorities* (Allen & Unwin, 1966).

Maud Report, *Management of Local Government* (HMSO, 1967).

Prest, A. R. (ed.), *Public Finance in Theory and Practice* (Weidenfeld & Nicolson, 1974).

Redcliffe-Maud Report, *Report of the Royal Commission on Local Government in England*, Cmnd 4040 (HMSO, 1969).

Sandford, C., *Social Economics* (Heinemann, 1977).

Sandford, C., Pond, C. and Walker, R., *Taxation and Social Policy* (Heinemann, 1981).

Social Trends (HMSO, 1970–84).

Walker, A. (ed.), *Public Expenditure and Social Policy* (Heinemann, 1982).

Webb, A. L. and Sieve, J. E. B., *Income Redistribution and the Welfare State* (Bell, 1971).

Young, K. (ed.), *National Interests and Local Government* (Heinemann, 1983).

Younghusband Report, report of a working party on *Social Workers in the Local Authority Health and Welfare Services* (HMSO, 1959).

13

Problems of policy in the social services

In the first chapter we looked at some definitions of social administration and saw how the subject had gone beyond a straightforward description of the social services. Social administration is now the study both of social problems and of the social action that arises in response to the problems. Next, we examined some of the main problem areas and some of the major social services that are the outcome of society's response to these problems. We have not, however, looked closely at some of the main areas of conflict in social policy. We have, in fact, tended to assume that the recognition of social needs and problems means that some positive action will be taken to deal with them, and that the main area of action with which we are concerned is the action of the state, the collective response of society, expressed through the growth of statutory social services. Mention has been made of the voluntary contribution, which has been and still is of enormous importance in meeting need, and is likewise a collective response to social problems albeit on a much smaller scale than the major statutory provision. Little mention, however, has been made of the private enterprise activities that are also concerned with social needs – the private schools, the insurance companies and so on – or of the growing sector of occupational welfare, that is health schemes, pension funds and the like provided by firms and employers for those who work for them. The balance, however, between public, statutory provision and private and occupational provision for the income maintenance, health, education and housing needs of individuals is a highly controversial one. There are those who argue that, having recognized needs, the state should provide for them universally, and those who argue that the state should provide only for people who, for various reasons, are unable to provide for themselves. This argument affects several major areas of social policy, and is currently of some importance, as we have noted in the discussion on financing social services.

The debate about universal or selective provision of services mainly affects the basic social services. There is general agreement, on the whole, that groups with special needs should receive attention and welfare services provided collectively by society, although there is growing argument even in this sphere. The main argument concerns social security, health and education, but the debate is one that concerns all the aims of social policy and the assumptions behind the concept of a 'welfare state' – the unofficial title given to the collection of social services described in this book.

The term 'welfare state' implies that the state has assumed responsibility for the welfare of its individual members and for the removal of, or at least the tackling of, the major problems of society. The state does indeed concern itself with most of the major aspects of life and of human need. It does try to see that people work, are educated, live in pleasant houses and environments, have medical attention when they require it and receive care and help if they have special handicaps. To that extent it is a welfare state. But at no one time did society adopt a blueprint for a welfare state or suddenly decide to deal with social problems. The historical development of social policy shows that different problems aroused concern at different times and were acted upon in different ways, and only gradually did the scope of state concern for welfare become reasonably comprehensive, and almost consistent in its approach.

The origins of the present social services go back well into the nineteenth century. They are inextricably bound up with the social and economic effects of the industrial revolution. But the phrase 'the welfare state' has only been used since the Second World War – a result of the remarkable spate of post-war social legislation creating some new social services and involving the wholesale reorganization of others. One of the more significant features of this reorganization was that, in some of the major areas of social policy, the principle of universal provision was firmly adopted. That is, that services should be available to all, provided by the community as a whole for the benefit not just of certain needy sections of society but for all its members.

The principle of universality was not, of course, applied in every sphere of social action. It was never, for example, assumed that the state should actually provide houses directly for everyone, although the public housing sector grew considerably in the years after the war. The principle was adopted, however, on a wide enough scale for it to mark a new era in social policy, and to occasion the widespread use of the term 'welfare state'. It is seen most clearly in the National Insurance Scheme of 1946, which brought basic income maintenance services to all members of the community irrespective of income levels or occupation; in the National Health Service Act which in 1948 made free comprehensive health care available to everyone; and in the 1944 Education Act. None of these Acts initiated new social services, but they were all a significant point in the development of social policy because of the universal scope of their coverage.

Since the war the universal principle has been attacked, and a strong body of opinion has argued for a reduction in the role of statutory provision and financing of social services. This is not to say that people argue that the social problems of poverty, sickness, education and so on should not be tackled; simply that there are different ways of tackling them from those adopted in Britain. There is a considerable consensus of opinion that problems should be eradicated, but considerable diversity of opinion regarding the best way to do this. It is always easier to agree on negative goals than on positive ones. This is primarily because, as the previous chapter indicated, social services are sufficiently important in financial and administrative terms and in the ways in which they affect the social and economic structure of society that they can themselves bring about radical change in social organization. It is hardly surprising that there is considerable argument over what form this change should take, and how far it should be allowed to go.

Take the example, already raised in this book, of social security provision: we may agree that poverty should be eradicated from a civilized, relatively affluent society – but some people feel that the state should go further and use social policy as a means of effecting greater equality, while others accept the existing unequal distribution of resources as natural and necessary for a thriving society.

Those who currently attack the present provision of relatively universal social services do so on several grounds. One is that it is too costly. To find the money for universal services means very high taxation levels, which reduce incentives and slow down economic expansion and productivity generally. Furthermore, universal provision means that some people receive benefits, in cash or kind, that they do not need, which is wasteful, while others cannot receive adequate services because the provision is too thinly spread. Too much state provision, it is claimed, undermines the stability of the family: a man does not have to feel so responsible for his family if he knows that the state will help him with the costs of their keep, education and medical care, etc. Moreover, it undermines the individual's independence and freedom if they are not able to choose how they spend their money or what kind of service they get. If the state takes their money by taxes and provides free medical care, they have no choice over how much of their income they want to spend on medical care, rather than on holidays, for example, and they have no say in the type of care offered. On the other hand, if they buy the services they require in a free market, they exercise choice and can influence the provision by taking their custom to the most satisfactory service. How much more important, it is argued, that an individual should exercise choice in welfare, which is so fundamentally important to the quality of life, than merely in consumer goods.

The arguments range from practical ones of cost to ideological ones about freedom. One outcome of such arguments is a demand for more selective provision. That is, state services should be available only to those who cannot afford to buy their own security, health care, education and so forth. But defenders of universal state provision argue that selectivity would mean a double standard of service in areas that they agree are of fundamental importance. The wealthy would buy a better standard of say, medical care, than the poor could obtain from the statutory service. This is partly because the relatively wealthy would be financing the state provision as well as their own private provision and they would not want to see it on an equal standard, otherwise there would be no incentive to people to improve their position and buy better care. Better-quality resources would tend to accumulate in the private sector: private education, for example, would command better facilities and attract better teachers than a state system that was merely provided for a minority. Furthermore, two services, public and private, would tend to exacerbate the divisions of society and perpetuate inequalities. There are enormous practical difficulties in distinguishing the recipients of state care from those who look after themselves. For example, it is necessary to have some kind of means test to determine eligibility for free, state provision, and it has not yet been proved that a means test can operate without stigma and humiliation for those who have to admit their relative poverty. Means tests are clearly a disincentive to some people, who find that if they earn more they lose their entitlement to free provision and so are hardly better off. Arguments about the effect of state welfare on family responsibility are dismissed on the grounds of both historical evidence and current sociological investigations.

The essence of the argument of those who oppose selectivity of provision according to income is that it implies some basic justice in the initial distribution of resources. Within a free enterprise, capitalist society resources are very unevenly distributed. If social services accept this by providing only for the poor, this implies that the poor in some way are poor because they are of less value in society; they earn less because they contribute less. Many people feel passionately, however, that the inequalities do not reflect worth in any way, but are the consequence of a complicated economic system that tends towards social injustice, and that social policy should attempt to cancel out this injustice and provide greater equality for all members of society.

So the basic ideological conflict tends to be between 'freedom' and 'equality'. Universalists argue that freedom is illusory for it is the freedom only of the better off – the poor cannot choose. Selectivists argue that inequality is natural and desirable, and the state should intervene only to the extent of preventing gross exploitation and suffering, but must not interfere with individuals' natural inclination to better themselves.

In practice, of course, there are different arguments appropriate to particular services. For example, it is pointed out that education should be a state service because it is provided largely for children who cannot themselves exercise choice. Health care is regarded by many as a commodity that cannot be equated with consumer goods and left to the market, as demand is too unpredictable. There are many variations of the basic universality/selectivity conflict: in some cases one can argue for state provision but private finance, or state finance but private provision; services provided and financed by the state versus services provided and financed by the private sector are only one possible model.

These arguments are currently prominent for several reasons. The main one is probably the economic situation, which has already been discussed. In times of financial stringency it is clear that public expenditure has to be closely scrutinized, and as social service expenditure accounts for over two-thirds of total public expenditure, there is a ready demand for a cutback on spending on the social services. At the same time, those working in the services, or doing research into social problems, have revealed startling deficiencies in the existing provision: poverty exists despite the social security system; the conditions in some primary schools and hospitals are appalling; community services are inadequate and wildly understaffed. We are therefore plainly in a dilemma: more money should be spent to improve the provision, yet we feel we must cut back on public spending. It is hardly surprising that many people have seen the answer to this dilemma in greater selectivity: provide more for the minorities in greatest need, and let the rest take care of themselves. This line certainly has an appealing simplicity. But, as we have seen, it ignores the practical and ideological problems that selectivity gives rise to. On the other hand, it could be argued that if more needs to be spent in total on, let us say, health care, it would not make much difference if less came from the public sector and more from private spending. So one could argue for greater public expenditure on essentials such as medical care and reductions in the private sector generally, in the interests of national economy. But this is always a politically awkward solution and therefore rarely canvassed.

Different political parties quite rightly reflect different views of social organization and social justice. The Conservatives are traditionally concerned with upholding individual rights in a free market system, while Labour advocates a socialist conception of collective action for the common good. Thus, trends towards greater selectivity or universality in social policy are primarily determined at a political level.

Selective measures proliferated after the change of government in 1971 – family income supplement and rent allowances are two examples of selective measures introduced thereafter – and much official emphasis was placed on finding ways of maximizing the take-up of means tested benefits. When the government changed again in 1974 the trend towards selectivity slowed down but was not really reversed. There was still a lack of commitment to a truly universalist approach and a tendency to cloud the ideological argument with economic distractions.

From 1979, with a decisive victory for a Conservative government openly committed to a monetarist stance and the control of public expenditure, the attack on universal social services was intensified. Support for independent education was reaffirmed with the introduction of the assisted places scheme. The Housing Act 1980 gave council tenants a right to buy their houses, thereby accelerating the residualization of the public housing sector, and proposals for alternative systems of financing health care and sickness benefits were seriously advanced. Most importantly, the strict implementation of policies to cut back the growth of public expenditure damaged the scope and quality of a wide range of services: social security benefits, the provision of health care, education, housing and personal social services were all badly affected.

The pace of change in the provision of welfare intensified, however, in the late 1980s, as the Conservative government entered its third term of office. Increasingly, services such as housing have become marginalized, whilst legislation on education has had the effect of introducing more elements of consumer choice into the public sector. In the health services, proposals include both a greater move towards a form of market system within the health service, and greater incentives for individuals to switch to private health care as an alternative to the NHS. Thus the third term of office for the government reinforced the concept of selective measures in welfare services and the use of the private sector wherever possible.

In part, the Conservative government has been able to use a growing disillusionment with the welfare state – amongst politicians, academics and society in general – as support for this increasing marginalization of the services provided. Systematic study of the scope and effect of social provision has developed over the past forty years since the inception of the welfare state to reveal the inequities that exist within the system. Thus, access to education has proved to be far from equal, poverty persists despite the introduction of income support and a contributory system of benefits, and inequalities in health between the social classes remain despite the introduction of a national health service. In addition, there has been growing discontent with the ways in which services are delivered. The income maintenance system and the health services have both been criticized for being too impersonal, too remote from the needs of those they serve, too intimidating, and too bureaucratic. Consumers have voiced discontent with a variety of services – the officialdom of the housing authorities or social services, for example – whilst those on the left have been critical of the elements of social control within the delivery of welfare services.

The Conservative government's commitment to restricting state services to those who show genuine need, measured by means tests, and to increasing private provision as an alternative to state services, together with their ability to win electoral support, must be seen within this context of existing concern over the ability of social policy to provide for the needs of all. However, the period of government from 1979 onwards also marks a shift in the ideological background to the delivery of social policy. The present emphasis is on targeting benefits which are paid at minimum levels, whilst the policing of benefits has required claimants to prove not only need but worthiness – that they have sought alternative employment, if they are unemployed, for example.

In terms of the ideology of the New Right, individuals are seen as responsible for providing for themselves and their families, whilst the role of the welfare state is seen as residual – to provide a minimum of support only in the last resort. It is believed that to provide welfare at a level greater than this bare minimum discourages self-reliance and fosters a dependency culture in which all would willingly allow the state to provide. Within this model, the market is seen as the best provider of all forms of welfare other than the residual minimum, and individuals are encouraged to provide for themselves by buying private insurance, for example. The state should intervene in the market only as a last resort, for the market is seen as most efficient when left to its own devices. Short term imbalances in supply or costing will rapidly settle, given this non-intervention. Whilst it is clear that the current welfare state survives to a greater extent than this model would predict, the moves towards greater marginalization of state welfare, and the encouragement given to the private market in welfare, must be seen within this ideological context.

Alternative models see the welfare state and the role of government very differently. Directly opposite the thinking of the New Right, Marxist analysts see the welfare state as either irrelevent or as a palliative for the worst effects of the economic system. It is argued that the dominant force of capitalism prevents any true collective welfare system from operating, although, to an extent, it is argued that the current welfare state must be seen as a positive gain of the organized working class, won from capitalism. However, in this model, welfare will always be secondary to the economic system, and thus there must always be failure to provide adequately for the welfare needs of society.

Yet another theory suggests that the goal of the welfare state, within a society in which economic competition under capitalism dominates, must be to effect gradual reform. This Fabian approach argues for the redistributive merits of the welfare state in shifting resources from the rich to the poor. The welfare state is seen to be blatantly compensatory in an unfair society. However, critics of this model argue that vertical redistribution – *between* socio-economic classes – has not resulted from the welfare state, and that in fact the little redistribution that has occurred has largely been horizontal – that is, *within* the classes. In many ways, basic inqualities have indeed increased within society, and the persistence of poverty despite the welfare state supports this view. The difficulty arises in determining the answer within the existing system. The rediscovery of poverty in the 1960s demonstrated that gradual reformist approaches using the tools of social policy did not eliminate this most basic inequality. Thus even before the advent of cuts in welfare services and a radical change in the way the welfare state is viewed, there was fierce debate over the role of social policy and the use of universal or selective measures as redistributive mechanisms or simply as the means to meet immediate social needs.

The principle of universality has been seen as central to any system of social policy that aims to eradicate both poverty and ignorance and also humiliation and discrimination from our society. Universality not only removes the stigma, and take-up problems, of selective benefits, it also establishes values and ideas about welfare and the collective meeting of social needs that are fundamental. However, the failure of universality, in an unequal society, to work well for everyone is a grave problem that must be tackled. Universal benefits, most importantly, are poor tools of redistribution and, where inequalities already exist in society, these will largely remain.

This problem gives rise to the argument for positive discrimination, the direction of additional resources to areas or categories of special need on top of a basic universal provision. Richard Titmuss put the case for positive discrimination most clearly and forcefully in *Commitment to Welfare* (1968), in which he argued that universal services should form the bases around which could grow socially acceptable selective services, aiming to discriminate positively and without stigma in favour of those whose needs are greatest. Of course, the dilemma over how to develop measures that combine selectivity with high take-up and no stigma remains unresolved, and is unlikely to be resolved in a climate such as the current one when selective measures predominate.

Moving on from ideology to practice, some efforts have been made over time to shift social policies in this direction of positive discrimination. The establishment of educational priority areas (EPAs) as advocated by the Plowden Report was a pioneering example. Extra resources were channelled to areas or institutions with special needs. EPA schools received higher equipment grants and teacher quotas, priority capital allocations and staff salaries. In 1969 the Local Government Grants (Social Need) Act was passed,, which created the Urban Programme. Urban aid was administered by central government and it was designed to target additional resources to urban areas of special social need. Resources were directed towards local projects with a wide range of objectives run by local statutory or voluntary bodies with particular emphasis on multiple projects. Initially aid went to the improvement of nursery facilities, children's homes and community centres. Priority in selecting projects was then given to those that catered for newly perceived community needs or utilized new methods of meeting needs rather than those that added to existing facilities. Urban aid was not a large programme in financial terms but it encouraged an imaginative and flexible approach to dealing with old problems and directed more resources to areas of extreme urban deprivation.

Further development of positive discrimination included the action research Community Development Project, Housing Action Areas and the Inner Cities Programme. The Community Development Project (CDP) operated in a few selected areas of high social need from 1969 to 1978. The project set out to 'find ways of meeting more effectively the needs of individuals, families and communities, whether native or immigrant, suffering from many forms of social deprivation'. It tried to do this by a mixture of methods that, on the one hand, helped the people concerned to achieve greater involvement and self-determination, and, on the other hand, aimed to improve the local delivery of services. The basic assumptions underlying the CDP were that social problems were concentrated in certain areas and could be solved by a combination of self-help and service coordination.

The results of the action research projects were soon very clear to the teams concerned: the symptoms of disadvantage that the projects were trying to tackle were caused not by concentrations of problem families but by structural constraints. The project workers emphasized that industrial change and decline had created a general depression of certain localities and vulnerable groups had been left behind as the skilled and mobile moved on in search of better opportunities. But the real problems of the deprived areas were not poor families, or even poor social service facilities and low take-up of benefits, but unemployment, neglected housing and low income. The projects demonstrated that much could be done by community work and development to improve service facilities, stimulate involvement and improve neighbourly feeling. However, the key issues were beyond the scope of the local project teams: the basic need was to create work opportunities and improve national income maintenance programmes.

The uncomfortable message from the Community Development Project was that in a very real sense the poverty of certain urban areas is related to the prosperity of others. It is all part of a pattern of inequality, of differential life chances, that affects the whole country. It cannot just be tackled by well-meaning local experiments. A massive shift of resources in the direction of decaying and declining areas to revitalize their industry and refurbish their environment is urgently required. In other words, what is needed is positive discrimination in the distribution of basic resources as well as of marginal social services, and positive discrimination on a really large scale.

The CDP message was pessimistic and politically unpopular. But it rested on an important reassertion of the essential connection between the overall economic and social structure and the experience of deprivation. This message was underlined by the Inner Area Studies, which were carried out in the early 1970s under the Department of the Environment's initiative in Lambeth, Liverpool and Birmingham. Although these studies noted differences in the causes of decline and patterns of deprivation in their different areas, they all stressed that a combination of poverty, physical decay and economic decline characterized the inner city.

Following on from these studies, and the various reports and analyses of the CDP, the government produced a White Paper called *Policy for the Inner Cities* (Cmnd 6845) in 1977. This discussed ways of intervening in the inner cities to arrest decline and improve the physical fabric of the areas as well as to alleviate the pressing problems of poverty and isolation among their more vulnerable members. The approach was to combine positive discrimination in the main service areas with priority in industrial and manpower policies. The practical outcome of this set of policy proposals has so far included the establishment of some partnership areas in larger cities, where central and local government cooperate to stimulate development. In working to improve economic and social conditions and deal with physical decay, the help of the private sector and of the community is being sought alongside the central–local government partnership to create a truly unified approach.

The positive discrimination programmes described so far have all looked at areas and sought to tackle deprivation on an area base. This has been much criticized as a clumsy approach, but it does have the merit of fostering some new work to tackle old problems, even if the scale is too small. Another approach is to extend positive discrimination to a group. This has to some extent been developed towards the disabled. While no explicit programme has been set up, a good deal of legislation has been passed that benefits the disabled, and extra resources have been channelled to meet their needs through local services, access schemes, the mobility allowance and so forth, though these are in no way commensurate to the need. In contrast, relatively little action followed the suggestions for positive discrimination towards single-parent families. Problems of equity and value confusion clouded the issue of helping them as a group. Similarly, there has been great reluctance to extend a positive discrimination approach to disadvantaged ethnic minorities.

In the last decade, the problem of racial discrimination and disadvantage has become depressingly apparent. Britain now has a substantial black minority (that is, primarily people of West Indian, Pakistani and Indian origins), albeit one very unevenly concentrated in certain cities and areas. As a group, blacks are clearly disadvantaged in terms of income levels, housing standards, employment opportunities and educational facilities. This is, to a considerable extent, the result of racial prejudice and discrimination rather than of clear differences in levels of skill and qualification between groups.

The statutory response to the problem has been as ambivalent as the popular one: legislation has been passed, first to control immigration, in an attempt to contain the size of the group, and then to outlaw discrimination. Race Relations Acts were passed in 1968 and 1976. These statutes have progressively strengthened the law against discrimination on the grounds of race, making it illegal to discriminate in housing, employment and social services, etc. The Commission for Racial Equality has a duty to work towards the elimination of discrimination and the promotion of equality of opportunity and good race relations. But, although local authorities now have various powers (to help overcome linguistic barriers, for example), they do not really pursue affirmative action – that is, positive measures to combat disadvantage as well as discrimination. Presumably this can best be explained in the light of hostility and racial tension. There has been a definite reluctance on the part of local authorities to appear to be favouring racial minorities in the provision of housing or education services for fear of arousing a politically threatening backlash. As a result the disadvantaged position of black people has not been much alleviated and racial discontent and tension have increased despite the Race Relations legislation.

The problem of racial disadvantage in Britain is a complex and emotional one that has been no more than touched on here. It is likely to demand greater thought and action during the 1990s. As the recession deepens, and more people generally suffer from unemployment and redundancy, the relatively disadvantaged groups suffer even more. So, for example, black youngsters suffer disproportionately high levels of unemployment and their frustration turns increasingly to protest. This situation demands action of a positive kind but sadly it too often provokes a repressive response.

Positive discrimination has not been operated on a large scale to date, but it remains an important step forward, out of the universal/selective dilemma, and a practical tool of great potential for evening up standards of provision and directing extra resources to some of the most deprived, without undue stigma. Critics of the various programmes have said that deprivation would be better tackled by creating job opportunities, increasing benefit rates and mounting an all-out attack on bad housing. This is undoubtedly true, but in a sense irrelevant. There is in reality scant agreement on how best to create jobs, and current policies are effectively cutting benefit rates and bringing housing programmes to a standstill. At such times it is important to keep some initiatives in social policy even if, like the inner-city scheme, they are on a small scale. And from such tentative practical measures as have been taken so far much has been learnt for future policies on a large scale when the political and economic climate is more favourable.

Positive discrimination has been one low-cost compromise to tackle area deprivation. Another essentially practical response to the problems of the social services has been to seek solutions in organizational changes. The argument here is that services would work well if they were better managed, if they were planned ahead, if priorities were allocated on an informed and rational basis, if different services coordinated their activities better. To improve service delivery we have recently seen the total reorganization of personal social services, the National Health Service and local government. There has also been considerable interest in many services in better management and in social planning.

While administrative reform alone cannot make amends for inadequate resources or inequitable provision, it should help to provide more efficient organizations for the operation and delivery of social services. In particular, the greater emphasis now placed on research into need and the monitoring and evaluation of provision should provide at least the information base on which to act more decisively in future. Moreover, although reorganization has moved us towards even larger public bodies, with their inherent problems of impersonal, bureaucratic control, we are increasingly seeking to understand the operation of such organizations. The hope is that if the behaviour of organizations and the people in them is understood, the ability to control them to our own advantage and direct them more effectively to fulfil our social aims will eventually be found.

Centrally the government sought means of improving service efficiency by considering ways in which services could work together to achieve agreed policy ends. The Central Policy Review Staff – a select body often referred to as the government's social policy 'think tank' – published a report entitled *A Joint Framework for Social Policies* in 1975. This was the result of extensive discussions with officials of the main government departments responsible for social policies. Its authors set out to find ways of improving coordination between services. They emphasized the need for a better analysis of complex social problems and the importance of agreeing priorities as between different programmes, problems and groups. They proposed: regular meetings between the ministers and senior civil servants most concerned; periodic forward looks at likely developments in the social field; improvements to the data base, including more provision for sharing data; systematic monitoring of service developments; and depth studies of specific topics that cut across departmental boundaries. The developments in social policy outlined here and in other chapters reflect an increased awareness of the need for social planning, although in the past few years this has increasingly had to take a back seat to the demands of efficiency and cost control.

To an extent the move towards greater planning led to a wider recognition of the importance of involving the recipients of the services in planning their development and future need. This was encouraged by the Skeffington Report as long ago as 1969, and the introduction of Community Health Councils in the health services was one example of how this might be achieved, although CHCs in effect have little power over the decision-making of regional or district health authorities. Participation in the planning of services, even at this low level, has been threatened and reduced by recent government policy. Whilst the CHCs survived the 1989 White Paper on health services, changes introduced include the removal of local authority representatives from health authority boards. The decline in the participation of those working in a service in the reviews of social policy has been remarked upon earlier – clearly public participation at different levels of social policy planning is unlikely to increase over the next few years.

A further concept in social policy is the encouragement of private provision of services in a wide range of areas of social policy. The boost to private providers of residential care by allowing residents' fees to be paid by the DSS, and tax incentives to some groups taking out private health insurance, are two illustrations of what has been a comprehensive shift towards the private sector as a leading contender in the provision of welfare. As we have seen, such a move towards a privatized welfare state is commensurate with both practical goals of cost control in the public sector and ideological aims of restricting public welfare to a safety net level of minimum services.

Positive discrimination, social planning, participation and privatization are just some of the issues that have been drawn into the contemporary analysis of social policy. In addition, there are other areas of debate – both the detailed question of the organization of specific services in the light of new needs, and wider debates stemming from new perspectives in the study of social policy. The issue of gender has been used to analyse social policy, and has revealed important differential impacts of social policies on men and women. Although the Equal Pay Act and Sex Discrimination Act became law in the 1970s, and the Equal Opportunities Commission was established to work towards the elimination of sex discrimination, such inequalities persist. These inequalities are marked in the area of employment and pay, but social policy also has a profound impact on the lives of women, and can be seen to hold implicit assumptions about the lives of men and women that operate ultimately to discriminate against women. In some instances, this discrimination has been challenged through recourse to the law of the European Economic Community, most notably in the case of payment of social security benefits to women. However, it remains true that an examination of social policies from a gender-conscious angle reveals and challenges powerful traditional assumptions about priorities and the lives of men and women.

Similarly, as has been indicated in previous pages, analysis of social policy from the perspective of race highlights important and disturbing inequities in the welfare system suffered by black people in Britain. Such an analysis increasingly reveals not only the failure of social policy to reduce the inequality that results from discrimination, but also discrimination within the structure and delivery of social services themselves.

In addition, the use off comparative studies in the analysis of social policy can be a useful exercise. An examination of the social policy and welfare systems of both Europe and America, as well as wider afield, demonstrates how very insular much analysis of social policy is. In recent years, as social policy makers have turned to American examples of private welfare, and as Britain moves into the European market, such comparative study is a necessity rather than an interesting diversion, and this seems unlikely to decline as the discipline of social policy itself takes on a more internationalist perspective.

Finally, as social policy has once more entered a new phase in the past decade, with a shift in emphasis towards private markets, minimal state services and the role of the economy, the importance of other disciplines in the study of social policy becomes ever more apparent. Whilst unemployment in terms of official numbers may now be decreasing, the importance of the operation of the labour market and employment policies has been clearly demonstrated.

There is now clear evidence of the relationship between the basic economic structure, and the pattern of rewards and opportunities that flow from it, and the problems with which social administration or social policy is traditionally concerned – problems such as poverty, urban squalor, ill-health and difficulties in old age. Social policy studies must move radically into the economic field. The debate over the resolution of shortcomings in social provision – in terms both of ideology and actual practical solutions – is bound up with an understanding of the economic system, and the student of social policy must develop this understanding.

In the Preface it was claimed that our intention was to keep this introduction to the subject of social administration simple. If readers who have persevered this far have found it has become progressively more difficult to follow, this is partly the consequence of the shortcomings of this book, but also very largely the consequence of the inherent difficulty of the subject. It is, as the first chapter indicated, a dynamic subject and the precise area of study keeps changing. So at the end of this book readers should not be too surprised to be told that they have hardly begun! The original edition concluded with a quotation from Richard Titmuss's *Commitment to Welfare*: 'The more I try to understand the role of welfare and the human condition, the more untidy it all becomes.' It is still apposite. Readers who feel some degree of confusion at this stage should not be deterred from further study. Richard Titmuss was both an eminent scholar and an original thinker in the field of social administration, and a strikingly humane and compassionate man. If he could be so honest about his confusion, no reader of this introduction should feel ashamed to admit a similar bewilderment and carry on the study regardless.

SUGGESTIONS FOR FURTHER READING

Brown, M. (ed.), *The Structure of Disadvantage* (Heinemann, 1983).
Brown, M. and Madge, N., *Despite the Welfare State* (Heinemann, 1982).
Fabian Society:
  Socialism and Affluence (1967)
  Social Services for All (1968)
  Labour and Inequality: A Review of Social Policy 1964–70 (1971)
  Positive Discrimination and Inequality (1974)
  Towards Participation in Local Services (1973).
George, V. and Wilding, P., *Ideology and Social Welfare* (RKP, 1976).
Glennerster, H. (ed.), *The Future of the Welfare State* (Heinemann, 1983).

Gough, I., *The Political Economy of the Welfare State* (Macmillan, 1979).

Hadley, R. and Hatch, S., *Social Welfare and the Failure of the State* (Allen & Unwin, 1981).

Institute of Economic Affairs:
  Towards a Welfare Society (1967)
  Universal or Selective Social Services? (1970).

Jones, K., Brown, J. and Bradshaw, J., *Issues in Social Policy* (RKP, 1983).

Loney, M., *Community Against Government* (Heinemann, 1983).

Loney, M., *The Politics of Greed: The New Right and the Welfare State.* (Pluto, 1986).

Loney, M. and Allen, M., *The Crisis of the Inner City* (Macmillan, 1979).

Marshall, T. H., *The Right to Welfare* (Heinemann, 1981).

Mishra, R., *Society and Social Policy* (Macmillan, 1981).

Mishra, R., *The Welfare State in Crisis* (Harvester, 1984).

National Community Development Project:
  Inter Project Report (1974)
  Forward Plan (1975).

Pascall, G., *Social Policy: A Feminist Analysis.* (Tavistock, 1986).

Pinker, R., *Social Theory and Social Policy* (Heinemann, 1971).

Pinker, R., *The Idea of Welfare* (Heinemann, 1975).

Robson, W. A., *Welfare State and Welfare Society* (Allen & Unwin, 1976).

Smith, D. J., *Racial Disadvantage in Britain* (Penguin Books, 1977).

Tawney, R. H., *Equality* (1931).

Taylor Gooby, P. and Dale, J., *Social Theory and Social Welfare* (Arnold, 1981).

Titmuss, R. M., *Essays on the Welfare State* (Allen & Unwin, 1958).

Titmuss, R. M., *Commitment to Welfare* (Allen & Unwin, 1968).

Titmuss, R. M., *The Gift Relationship* (Allen & Unwin, 1971).

Weale, A., *Political Theory and Social Policy* (Macmillan, 1983).

Index